DIABETIC
COOKBOOK FOR BEGINNERS

*1000 Easy, Delicious and Healthy Recipes
for The Newly Diagnosed to Manage Type 2 Diabetes
and Prediabetes | 28 Day Meal Plan Included*

Jeanette Jones

Table Of Contents

Introduction

D o you know how to cook for a diabetic? Do you need to know? Well, chances are, if someone in your family is diabetic or you're just looking to be more conscious of what they're eating (or maybe you have diabetes yourself!), then the answer to both questions is yes!

There are several kinds of diabetes, each with its own set of peculiarities and limitations.

Type II Diabetes is caused by a problem with the body's production of insulin. The blood sugar level is regulated by the hormone insulin, w/c can lead to diabetes when it is too low. This means that to properly care for a diabetic, you need to make sure they get plenty of high-quality protein and fiber with every meal as well as controlling their blood sugar always levels.

High protein foods are extremely important because they give us the building blocks for everything else in our bodies. Protein is also thought to slow down digestion and thereby slow down the rate at which glucose enters the bloodstream - this is called The Glycemic Index (GI). Foods with a low GI are ideal for any diabetic.

The Glycemic Index can be roughly broken down into three groups: low, medium, and high. Low GI foods (55 or less) include foods like nuts, seeds, fish, vegetables, and fruit. Medium GI foods (56-69) include things like whole-grain bread, and anything made from white flour or enriched grains. High GI foods (70 or greater) include anything that contains refined sugar or high-fructose corn syrup. That's a lot of food! Foods that measure between are also important to check out, though.

You may be disappointed to find that many of our meals are "bad" for us, but taken moderately, may be very healthful. For example, an apple or orange can have a GI score of around 40 and still be considered low in carbohydrates. The same thing goes for other fruit, vegetables, and even certain types of meat like chicken breast or turkey. This is because the GI ratings are not very accurate for these kinds of foods - it's by weight rather than specifically by carbohydrate content or fiber content (which isn't included).

Fibers are the key to controlling blood sugar levels. Fibers are carbohydrates that we can't digest, and they help with a variety of other things like cholesterol levels and keeping us fuller for longer. Vegetables and fruits contain varying amounts of fiber, as do whole grains.

You can also determine how much fiber a food has in it by keeping track of the number of carbohydrates it contains. Fiber is present if the carbohydrate content is less than 5 grams.

So, what do you do with all this data? You need to make sure that your diabetic eats foods containing 5 grams or more of carbohydrate per portion. You may achieve this by selecting foods that are compatible with the information you've acquired. While the amount of carbohydrate in a serving may be 5 grams, serving sizes will vary between different food sources (e.g., one medium apple contains around 15 grams of carbohydrate while a half cup of raisins contains around 12 grams). When it comes to providing your diabetic with the proper nourishment, nutrition facts supplied by the US government (and other trustworthy sources) are the best way to go.

All You Need to Know About Diabetes

What Is Diabetes?

In modern society there is a huge increment of non-communicable diseases. The poor living standards and improper food consumption has led society towards this issue. There are several common diseases we can hear of nowadays. Out of them diabetes is one of the most common diseases we can experience. The number of instances is increasing every day all across the world.

Most people tend to think that diabetes is a blood born disease. That is a common myth. Actually, diabetes is a disease that has a relationship with a hormone called insulin. Insulin is an important hormone that is produced in our pancreas. The main duty of insulin is to help glucose (which comes from our food) to pass through our bloodstream to the cells in our body. Inside the cells the glucose is broken down into energy. Overall, we can say without insulin it is not possible for glucose to get into our cells.

"Important point: Sometimes the pancreas won't be able to produce insulin anymore. And in some people's bodies can't make good use of the insulin which is produced in their pancreas. As a result of that, the glucose level in the blood will be increased. If someone is experiencing one or both of these instances, we can diagnose him or her as a diabetic patient."

Types of Diabetes

When it comes to diabetes mainly, we can identify 3 types. They are as follows.

1. Type 1 Diabetes
2. Type 2 Diabetes
3. Gestational Diabetes

Type 1 Diabetes

This type of diabetes can develop at the age stage. But most of the time cases are being reported among children and young adults. Actually, it is caused by an autoimmune reaction of their bodies. Their own immune system begins to attack their insulin-producing cells in the pancreas. As a result of that, there won't be any insulin to work with glucose. So, the blood glucose result will climb sky-high within a short amount of time. Type 1 diabetes patients have only one last option for survival. That is to inject insulin every day for the rest of their lives. Still scientist is working on various researches to find the actual reason and cure for type 1 diabetes.

Type 2 Diabetes

This is the most common diabetes type. This type can be developed at any age as well. But it is mostly found in adult people. This is not an autoimmune-related issue like Type 1 diabetes. Most of the time patient's body is not making proper use of the insulin which is made by the pancreas. Sometimes with time the insulin production functionality of the pancreas may get reduced as well. Luckily this diabetes type is manageable. In extreme but rare instances insulin injections may require. Most of the time proper medications, physical activities and good eating habits will help you to manage Type 2 diabetes-like pro.

Gestational Diabetes

This is a special type of diabetes. Pregnant women who haven't had diabetes in their lifetime are the targeted category in this type. Most of the time this could happen as a result of irresponsible eating habits. This is a serious situation. Because the mother and the baby are at risk. The mother could develop Type 2 diabetes later in life. Also, the baby could become obese later in life, plus could develop Type 1 or Type 2 diabetes as well.

What Is Healthy Eating?

It is more about discipline than any other thing. Because most of the time people know what is good to eat and what is not good to eat. Most of the time they don't think twice to break a rule. The most common excuse they make is "I don't eat like this all the time". I do this only on special occasions. Well, a number of small occasions make a whole picture. So that is a weak argument. Always be honest to yourself. Your success is depending on the amount of discipline you carry.

With discipline you have to try these things.

1. Having meals on time
2. Keep the focus on a balanced diet
3. Carry on calorie and carb count
4. Staying hydrated throughout the day
5. Quit junk foods
6. Quit smoking
7. Avoid alcohol

I mentioned discipline. That is because if you have that, none of the above tips will be difficult for you to follow.

Foods That Are Good for Diabetes

1. Whole wheat bread
2. Brown rice
3. Lentils (Dhal)
4. Spinach
5. Almonds
6. Peanuts
7. Avocado
8. Onion
9. Cinnamon
10. Garlic
11. Oats
12. Tuna
13. Eggs
14. Zucchini
15. Carrots
16. Tofu
17. Pumpkin
18. Dark chocolate
19. Chickpeas
20. Cauliflower

Foods Which Are Bad for Diabetes

1. Sugar added drinks
2. Fruit juices with sweet flavor
3. Snacks with added preservatives
4. Honey
5. Sugar flavored cereals
6. White rice
7. White wheat products
8. Process Foods

Essential Things about Sugar and Nutrients

Should I Eliminate Sugar from My Diet?

So many people tend to believe that sugar consumption has a link with diabetes. It is not actually true. Especially for type 1 diabetes. It is not caused by sugar. It is caused by an autoimmune condition of the body. In type 2 diabetes the situation is not the same. There are few factors that could cause type 2 diabetes. High-calorie diet and obesity have a direct connection. If someone eliminates sugar and still consumes a high-calorie diet with proper exercises, there is a huge chance of increasing weight. In later life that could lead to developing diabetes. So having diabetes doesn't mean you should eliminate sugar completely from your diet. Make sure they are not artificial or processed sugars. I would highly recommend brown sugar as a healthy sugar source. You must cut off sugary drinks. Because liquids get absorbed by the body quicker than solid foods. Which can lead to a sudden increment of blood sugar levels. The other main point is that it is not practical to cut off sugar completely from your diet. When it comes to sugar there are two main ways we can identify. Direct sugars and indirect sugars.

Direct sugars can be considered as desserts, sugary drinks and some snacks. Indirect sugars can be considered as sugars from fruits and vegetables. Therefore, we cannot live without consuming sugar. We may cover our macronutrients from other sources. But most of our micronutrients come from fruits and vegetables. The main point is to manage high levels of calories. Then we can live a happy life while enjoying the foods we like.

Daily Calorie Consumption

For an adult person with diabetes the recommended calorie amount is 1400 to 1700 per day. Make sure that you cover that amount mainly from complex carbohydrates. As previously mentioned, you have to focus on 44% of total calories from carbohydrates. The rest of it should be covered with proteins and healthy fats. Consuming this many calories will help you to maintain a healthy weight and good blood sugar content. Please note that I have given the average measures. You may have to change the figures if you are on a weight loss journey or weight gaining journey. If you are following a certain task like that, please seek the advice of health professionals.

How Much of Sugar Is Too Much?

The standard sugar intake for an average man is 36g or 9 teaspoons per day. For average women it is 24g or 6 teaspoons per day. Children should not use more than 6 teaspoons of sugar per day. You have to focus well on hidden sugars. Because most of the time people do not pay attention to this area. So many brands use some shroud marketing strategies in order to hide the sugar quantity in the food. They use names like fructose, maltose and syrup. Consumers won't think twice about purchasing such an item.

Sometimes they might think that product is healthier than other products. The reality is those products do more harm than honest products which shows the sugar presence. Most of the time we tend to think that hidden sugars are present in drinks, cereals and jams. But sadly no. There are hidden sugars in foods that are famous for being healthier. Protein bars, Salad dressings, Chili sauces, Peanut butter and Soy milk are some of them. Those items may have almost the same or else more sugar levels than traditional sugary items. The main point I want to make is that never trust any food label saying low sugar. All most every brand is following some trick behind the scenes. I would prefer to use sugar-free versions of those foods.

Foods with High Sugar Content

In general, we know sweets, cookies, cakes, ice cream and soft drinks contain more sugar. So, it is easy for us to avoid them. But in the present market there are various types of food items that you don't even assume to contain huge amounts of sugars. It is always better to avoid other than taking a risk. By understanding the foods which are high in sugar, you can eliminate them or manage the consumption and move on towards a healthy lifestyle.

I have identified a list of special foods. The specialty of these foods is that they have other main priorities such as flavoring, color effect, enriched with vitamins, essential sauces, energy drinks, artificial sweeteners, iced teas & coffees, premade foods (soup) and canned food items can be identified under that category. Most of the time people focus only on the primary outcome of that certain product. That is not a good thing to do always you have to think outside the box and discover new things.

Chapter 3

Breakfast

Coconut and Berry Smoothie

Preparation time: 5 minutes
Cooking time: 0 minutes
Servings 2
Ingredients:

- ½ cup mixed berries (blueberries, strawberries, blackberries)
- 1 tablespoon ground flaxseed
- 2 tablespoons unsweetened coconut flakes
- ½ cup unsweetened plain coconut milk
- ½ cup leafy greens (kale, spinach)
- ¼ cup unsweetened vanilla nonfat yogurt
- ½ cup ice

Directions:

1. In a blender jar, combine the berries, flaxseed, coconut flakes, coconut milk, greens, yogurt, and ice.
2. Process until smooth. Serve.

Walnut and Oat Granola

Preparation time: 10 minutes
Cooking time: 30 minutes
Servings 16
Ingredients:

- 4 cups rolled oats
- 1 cup walnut pieces
- ½ cup pepitas
- ¼ teaspoon salt
- 1 teaspoon ground cinnamon
- 1 teaspoon ground ginger
- ½ cup coconut oil, melted
- ½ cup unsweetened applesauce
- 1 teaspoon vanilla extract
- ½ cup dried cherries

Directions:

1. Preheat the oven to 350°F (180°C). Line a baking sheet with parchment paper.
2. In a large bowl, toss the oats, walnuts, pepitas, salt, cinnamon, and ginger.
3. In a large measuring cup, combine the coconut oil, applesauce, and vanilla. Pour over the dry mixture and mix well.
4. Transfer the mixture to the prepared baking sheet. Cook for 30 minutes, stirring about halfway through. Remove from the oven and let the granola sit

undisturbed until completely cool. Break the granola into pieces, and stir in the dried cherries.
5. Transfer to an airtight container, and store at room temperature for up to 2 weeks.

Crispy Pita with Canadian bacon

Preparation time: 5 minutes
Cooking time: 15 minutes
Servings 2
Ingredients:

- 1 (6-inch) whole-grain pita bread
- 3 teaspoons extra-virgin olive oil, divided
- 2 eggs
- 2 Canadian bacon slices
- Juice of ½ lemon
- 1 cup microgreens
- 2 tablespoons crumbled goat cheese
- Freshly ground black pepper, to taste

Directions:

1. Heat a large skillet over medium heat. Cut the pita bread in half and brush each side of both halves with ¼ teaspoon of olive oil (using a total of 1 teaspoon oil). Cook for 2 to 3 minutes on each side, then remove from the skillet.
2. In the same skillet, heat 1 teaspoon of oil over medium heat. Crack the eggs into the skillet and cook until the eggs are set, 2 to 3 minutes. Remove from the skillet.
3. In the same skillet, cook the Canadian bacon for 3 to 5 minutes, flipping once.
4. In a large bowl, whisk together the remaining 1 teaspoon of oil and the lemon juice. Add the microgreens and toss to combine.
5. Top each pita half with half of the microgreens, 1 piece of bacon, 1 egg, and 1 tablespoon of goat cheese. Season with pepper and serve.

Coconut-Berry Sunrise Smoothie

Preparation time: 5 minutes
Cooking time: 0 minute
Servings: 2
Ingredients:

- ½ cup mixed berries (blueberries, strawberries, blackberries)
- 1 tablespoon ground flaxseed
- 2 tablespoons unsweetened coconut flakes
- ½ cup unsweetened plain coconut milk

- ½ cup leafy greens (kale, spinach)
- ¼ cup unsweetened vanilla nonfat yogurt
- ½ cup ice

Directions:
1. In a blender jar, combine the berries, flaxseed, coconut flakes, coconut milk, greens, yogurt, and ice.
2. Process until smooth. Serve.

Avocado and Goat Cheese Toast

Preparation time: 5 minutes
Cooking time: 5 minutes
Servings: 2 (1 slice each)
Ingredients:
- 2 slices whole-wheat thin-sliced bread (I love Ezekiel sprouted bread and Dave's Killer Bread)
- ½ avocado
- 2 tablespoons crumbled goat cheese
- Salt

Directions:
1. In a toaster or broiler, toast the bread until browned.
2. Remove the flesh from the avocado. In a medium bowl, use a fork to mash the avocado flesh. Spread it onto the toast.
3. Sprinkle with the goat cheese and season lightly with salt.
4. Add any toppings and serve.

Oat and Walnut Granola

Preparation time: 10 minutes
Cooking time: 30 minutes
Servings: 16
Ingredients:
- 4 cups rolled oats
- 1 cup walnut pieces
- ½ cup pepitas
- ¼ teaspoon salt
- 1 teaspoon ground cinnamon
- 1 teaspoon ground ginger
- ½ cup coconut oil, melted
- ½ cup unsweetened applesauce
- 1 teaspoon vanilla extract
- ½ cup dried cherries

Directions:
1. Preheat the oven to 350°F. Line a baking sheet with parchment paper.
2. In a large bowl, toss the oats, walnuts, pepitas, salt, cinnamon, and ginger.
3. In a large measuring cup, combine the coconut oil, applesauce, and vanilla. Pour over the dry mixture and mix well.
4. Transfer the mixture to the prepared baking sheet. Cook for 30 minutes, stirring about halfway through. Remove from the oven and let the granola sit undisturbed until completely cool. Break the granola into pieces, and stir in the dried cherries.
5. Transfer to an airtight container, and store at room temperature for up to 2 weeks.

Zucchini Noodles with Creamy Avocado Pesto

Preparation Time: 10 minutes
Cooking Time: 20 minutes

Servings: 4
Ingredients:
- 6 c of spiralized zucchini
- 1 Tablespoon olive oil
- 6 oz. of avocado
- 1 basil leaf
- 3 garlic cloves
- 1/3 oz. pine nuts
- 2 Tablespoon lemon juice
- 1/2 teaspoon salt
- 1/4 teaspoon black pepper

Directions:
Spiralize the courgettis and set them aside on paper towels to absorb the surplus water.
In a kitchen appliance, put avocados, juice basil leaves, garlic, pine nuts, and sea salt and pulse until chopped. Then put vegetable oil in a slow stream till emulsified and creamy.
Drizzle vegetable oil in a skillet over medium-high heat and add zucchini noodles, cooking for about 2 minutes till tender.
Put zucchini noodles into a large bowl and toss with avocado pesto. Season with cracked pepper and a little Parmesan and serve.

Avocado Chicken Salad

Preparation Time: 5 minutes
Cooking Time: 10 minutes
Servings: 2
Ingredients:
- 10 oz. diced cooked chicken
- 1/2 cup 2% Plain Greek yogurt
- 3 oz. chopped avocado
- 12 teaspoon garlic powder
- 1/4 teaspoon salt
- 1/8 teaspoon pepper
- 1 tablespoon + 1 teaspoon lime juice
- 1/4 cup fresh cilantro, chopped

Directions:
Combine all Ingredients: in a medium-sized bowl. Refrigerate until able to serve.
Cut the salad in half and serve it together with your favorite greens.

Pancakes with Berries

Preparation Time: 5 minutes
Cooking Time: 20 minutes
Servings: 2
Ingredients:
Pancake:
- 1 egg
- 50 g spelled flour
- 50 g almond flour
- 15 g coconut flour 150 ml of water salt

Directions:
1. Put the flour, egg, and a few salts in a blender jar.
2. Add 150 ml of water.
3. Mix everything with a whisk.
4. Mix everything into a batter.
5. Heat a coated pan.
6. Put in half the batter.

7. Once the pancake is firm, turn it over.
8. Remove the pancake, add the last half of the batter to the pan, and repeat.
9. Melt chocolate over a water bath.
10. Let the pancakes cool.
11. Brush the pancakes with the yogurt.
12. Wash the berry and let it drain.
13. Put berries on the yogurt.
14. Roll up the pancakes.
15. Sprinkle them with granulated sugar.
16. Decorate the entire thing with the melted chocolate.

Omelette à la Margherita

Preparation Time: 10 minutes
Cooking Time: 20 minutes
Servings: 2
Ingredients:

- 3 eggs
- 50 g parmesan cheese
- 2 tablespoon heavy cream
- 1 tablespoon olive oil
- 1 teaspoon oregano
- Nutmeg
- Salt
- Pepper

For covering:

- 3 - 4 stalks of basil
- 1 tomato
- 100 g grated mozzarella

Directions:

1. Mix the cream and eggs in a medium bowl.
2. Add the grated parmesan, nutmeg, oregano, pepper, and salt and stir everything.
3. Heat the oil in a pan.
4. Add 1/2 of the egg and cream to the pan.
5. Let the omelet set over medium heat, turn it, then remove it.
6. Repeat with the last half of the egg mixture.
7. Cut the tomatoes into slices and place them on top of the omelets.
8. Scatter the mozzarella over the tomatoes.
9. Place the omelets on a baking sheet.
10. Cook at 180°C for five to 10 minutes.
11. Then, take the omelets out and decorate them with the basil leaves.

Spanakopita Frittata

Preparation time: 10 minutes
Cooking time: 15 minutes
Servings: 4
Ingredients:

- 2 tablespoons extra-virgin olive oil
- ½ sweet onion, chopped
- 1 red bell pepper, seeded and chopped
- ½ teaspoon minced garlic
- ¼ teaspoon sea salt
- ½ teaspoon freshly ground black pepper
- 8 egg whites
- 2 cups shredded spinach
- ½ cup crumbled low-sodium feta cheese
- 1 teaspoon chopped fresh parsley, for garnish

Directions:

1. Preheat the oven to 375°F (190°C). Place a heavy ovenproof skillet over medium-high heat and add the olive oil. Sauté the onion, bell pepper, and garlic until softened, about 5 minutes. Season with salt and pepper. Whisk together the egg whites in a medium bowl, then pour them into the skillet and lightly shake the pan to disburse.
2. Cook the vegetables and eggs for 3 minutes, without stirring. Scatter the spinach over the eggs and sprinkle the feta cheese evenly over the spinach.
3. Put the skillet in the oven and bake, uncovered, until cooked through and firm, about 10 minutes.
4. Loosen the edges of the frittata with a rubber spatula, then invert it onto a plate.
5. Garnish with the chopped parsley and serve.

Ratatouille Egg Bake

Preparation time: 20 minutes
Cooking time: 50 minutes
Servings: 4
Ingredients:

- 2 teaspoons extra-virgin olive oil
- ½ sweet onion, finely chopped
- 2 teaspoons minced garlic
- ½ small eggplant, peeled and diced
- 1 green zucchini, diced
- 1 yellow zucchini, diced
- 1 red bell pepper, seeded and diced
- 3 tomatoes, seeded and chopped
- 1 tablespoon chopped fresh oregano
- 1 tablespoon chopped fresh basil
- Pinch red pepper flakes
- Sea salt and freshly ground black pepper, to taste
- 4 large eggs

Directions:

1. Preheat the oven to 350°F (180°C). Place a large ovenproof skillet over medium heat and add the olive oil.
2. Sauté the onion and garlic until softened and translucent, about 3 minutes. Stir in the eggplant and sauté for about 10 minutes, stirring occasionally. Stir in the zucchini and pepper and sauté for 5 minutes.
3. Reduce the heat to low and cover. Cook until the vegetables are soft, about 15 minutes.
4. Stir in the tomatoes, oregano, basil, and red pepper flakes, and cook 10 minutes more. Season the ratatouille with salt and pepper. Use a spoon to create four wells in the mixture. Crack an egg into each well. Place the skillet in the oven and bake until the eggs are firm, about 5 minutes.
5. Remove from the oven. Serve the eggs with a generous scoop of vegetables.

Cottage Pancakes

Preparation time: 10 minutes
Cooking time: 20 minutes

Servings: 4
Ingredients:
- 2 cups low-fat cottage cheese
- 4 egg whites
- 2 eggs
- 1 tablespoon pure vanilla extract
- 1½ cups almond flour
- Nonstick cooking spray

Directions:
1. Place the cottage cheese, egg whites, eggs, and vanilla in a blender and pulse to combine.
2. Add the almond flour to the blender and blend until smooth.
3. Place a large nonstick skillet over medium heat and lightly coat it with cooking spray.
4. Spoon ¼ cup of batter per pancake, 4 at a time, into the skillet. Cook the pancakes until the bottoms are firm and golden, about 4 minutes.
5. Flip the pancakes over and cook the other side until they are cooked through, about 3 minutes.
6. Remove the pancakes to a plate and repeat with the remaining batter.
7. Serve with fresh fruit.

Greek Yogurt and Oat Pancakes

Preparation time: 5 minutes
Cooking time: 20 minutes
Servings: 4
Ingredients:
- 1 cup 2 percent plain Greek yogurt
- 3 eggs
- 1½ teaspoons pure vanilla extract
- 1 cup rolled oats
- 1 tablespoon granulated sweetener
- 1 teaspoon baking powder
- 1 teaspoon ground cinnamon
- Pinch ground cloves
- Nonstick cooking spray

Directions:
1. Place the yogurt, eggs, and vanilla in a blender and pulse to combine.
2. Add the oats, sweetener, baking powder, cinnamon, and cloves to the blender and blend until the batter is smooth.
3. Place a large nonstick skillet over medium heat and lightly coat it with cooking spray.
4. Spoon ¼ cup of batter per pancake, 4 at a time, into the skillet. Cook the pancakes until the bottoms are firm and golden, about 4 minutes.
5. Flip the pancakes over and cook the other side until they are cooked through, about 3 minutes.
6. Remove the pancakes to a plate and repeat with the remaining batter.
7. Serve with fresh fruit.

Savory Breakfast Egg Bites

Preparation Time: 10 minutes
Cooking Time: 20 to 25 minutes
Servings: 8

Ingredients:
- 6 eggs, beaten
- 1/4 cup unsweetened plain almond milk
- 1/4 cup crumbled goat cheese
- 1/2 cup sliced brown mushrooms
- 1 cup chopped spinach
- 1/4 cup sliced sun-dried tomatoes
- 1 red bell pepper, diced
- Salt and freshly ground black pepper, to taste
- Nonstick cooking spray
- Special Equipment:
- An 8-cup muffin tin

Directions:
1. Preheat the oven to 350°F (180°C). Grease an 8-cup muffin tin with nonstick cooking spray.
2. Make the egg bites: Mix the beaten eggs, almond milk, cheese, mushroom, spinach, tomatoes, bell pepper, salt, and pepper in a large bowl, and whisk to combine.
3. Spoon the mixture into the prepared muffin cups, filling each about three-quarters full.
4. Bake in the preheated oven for 20 to 25 minutes, or until the top is golden brown and a fork comes out clean.
5. Let the egg bites sit for 5 minutes until slightly cooled. Remove from the muffin tin and serve warm.
6. Tip: If you want to make a quick and easy breakfast, you can make these egg bites in single servings in the microwave.

Simple Grain-Free Biscuits

Preparation Time: 10 minutes
Cooking Time: 15 minutes
Servings: 4
Ingredients:
- 2 tablespoons unsalted butter
- 1/4 cup plain low-fat Greek yogurt
- Pinch salt
- 11/2 cups finely ground almond flour

Directions:
1. Preheat the oven to 375°F (190°C). Line a baking sheet with parchment paper and set aside.
2. Place the butter in a microwave-safe bowl and microwave for 15 to 20 seconds, or until it is just enough to soften.
3. Add the yogurt and salt to the bowl of butter and blend well.
4. Slowly pour in the almond flour and keep stirring until the mixture just comes together into a slightly sticky, shaggy dough.
5. Use a 1/4-cup measuring cup to mound balls of dough onto the parchment-lined baking sheet and flatten each into a rounded biscuit shape, about 1 inch thick.
6. Bake in the preheated oven for 13 to 15 minutes, or until the biscuits are lightly golden brown.
7. Let the biscuits cool for 5 minutes before serving.

Brussels Sprout with Fried Eggs

Preparation Time: 10 minutes

Cooking Time: 15 minutes
Servings: 4
Ingredients:

- 3 teaspoons extra-virgin olive oil, divided
- 1 pound (454 g) Brussels sprouts, sliced
- 2 garlic cloves, thinly sliced
- 1/4 teaspoon salt
- Juice of 1 lemon
- 4 eggs

Directions:

1. Heat 1 1/2 teaspoons of olive oil in a large skillet over medium heat.
2. Add the Brussels sprouts and sauté for 6 to 8 minutes until crispy and tender, stirring frequently.
3. Stir in the garlic and cook for about 1 minute until fragrant. Sprinkle with the salt and lemon juice.
4. Remove from the skillet to a plate and set aside.
5. Heat the remaining oil in the skillet over medium-high heat. Crack the eggs one at a time into the skillet and fry for about 3 minutes. Flip the eggs and continue cooking, or until the egg whites are set and the yolks are cooked to your liking.
6. Serve the fried eggs over the crispy Brussels sprouts.

Vanilla Coconut Pancakes

Preparation Time: 5 minutes
Cooking Time: 15 minutes
Servings: 4
Ingredients:

- 1/2 cup coconut flour
- 1 teaspoon baking powder
- 1/2 teaspoon ground cinnamon
- 1/8 teaspoon salt
- 8 large eggs
- 1/3 cup unsweetened almond milk
- 2 tablespoons avocado or coconut oil
- 1 teaspoon vanilla extract

Directions:

1. Stir together the flour, baking powder, cinnamon, and salt in a large bowl. Set aside.
2. Beat the eggs with the almond milk, oil, and vanilla in a medium bowl until fully mixed.
3. Heat a large nonstick skillet over medium-low heat.
4. Make the pancakes: Pour 1/3 cup of batter into the hot skillet, tilting the pan to spread it evenly. Cook for 3 to 4 minutes until bubbles form on the surface. Flip the pancake with a spatula and cook for about 3 minutes, or until the pancake is browned around the edges and cooked through. Repeat with the remaining batter.
5. Serve the pancakes on a plate while warm.

Cheesy Spinach and Egg Casserole

Preparation Time: 10 minutes
Cooking Time: 35 minutes
Servings: 8
Ingredients:

- 1 (10-ounce / 284-g) package frozen spinach, thawed and drained
- 1 (14-ounce / 397-g) can artichoke hearts, drained
- 1/4 cup finely chopped red bell pepper
- 8 eggs, lightly beaten
- 1/4 cup unsweetened plain almond milk
- 2 garlic cloves, minced
- 1/2 teaspoon salt
- 1/2 teaspoons freshly ground black pepper
- 1/2 cup crumbled goat cheese
- Nonstick cooking spray

Directions:

1. Preheat the oven to 375°F (190°C). Spray a baking dish with nonstick cooking spray and set aside.
2. Mix the spinach, artichoke hearts, bell peppers, beaten eggs, almond milk, garlic, salt, and pepper in a large bowl, and stir to incorporate.
3. Pour the mixture into the greased baking dish and scatter the goat cheese on top.
4. Bake in the preheated oven for 35 minutes, or until the top is lightly golden around the edges and eggs are set.
5. Remove from the oven and serve warm.

Chocolate-Zucchini Muffins

Preparation time: 15 minutes
Cooking time: 20 minutes
Servings: 12 (1 muffin each)
Ingredients:

- 1 1/2 cups grated zucchini
- 1 1/2 cups rolled oats
- 1 teaspoon ground cinnamon
- 2 teaspoons baking powder
- 1/4 teaspoon salt
- 1 large egg
- 1 teaspoon vanilla extract
- 1/4 cup coconut oil, melted
- 1/2 cup unsweetened applesauce
- 1/4 cup honey
- 1/4 cup dark chocolate chips

Directions:

1. Preheat the oven to 350°F. Grease the cups of a 12-cup muffin tin or line with paper baking liners. Set aside.
2. Place the zucchini in a colander over the sink to drain.
3. In a blender jar, process the oats until they resemble flour. Transfer to a medium mixing bowl and add the cinnamon, baking powder, and salt. Mix well.
4. In another large mixing bowl, combine the egg, vanilla, coconut oil, applesauce, and honey. Stir to combine.
5. Press the zucchini into the colander, draining any liquids, and add to the wet mixture.
6. Stir the dry mixture into the wet mixture and mix until no dry spots remain. Fold in the chocolate chips.
7. Transfer the batter to the muffin tin, filling each cup a little over halfway. Cook for 16 to 18 minutes until the muffins are lightly browned and a toothpick inserted in the center comes out clean.
8. Store in an airtight container, refrigerated, for up to 5 days.

Gluten-Free Carrot and Oat Pancakes

Preparation time: 10 minutes
Cooking time: 20 minutes
Servings: 4 (3 pancakes each)
Ingredients:

- 1 cup rolled oats
- 1 cup shredded carrots
- 1 cup low-fat cottage cheese
- 2 eggs
- ½ cup unsweetened plain almond milk
- 1 teaspoon baking powder
- ½ teaspoon ground cinnamon
- 2 tablespoons ground flaxseed
- ¼ cup plain nonfat Greek yogurt
- 1 tablespoon pure maple syrup
- 2 teaspoons canola oil, divided

Directions:
1. In a blender jar, process the oats until they resemble flour. Add the carrots, cottage cheese, eggs, almond milk, baking powder, cinnamon, and flaxseed to the jar. Process until smooth.
2. In a small bowl, combine the yogurt and maple syrup and stir well. Set aside.
3. In a large skillet, heat 1 teaspoon of oil over medium heat. Using a measuring cup, add ¼ cup of batter per pancake to the skillet. Cook for 1 to 2 minutes until bubbles form on the surface and flip the pancakes. Cook for another minute until the pancakes are browned and cooked through. Repeat with the remaining 1 teaspoon of oil and remaining batter.
4. Serve warm topped with the maple yogurt.

Breakfast Egg Bites

Preparation time: 10 minutes
Cooking time: 25 minutes
Servings: 8 (1 egg bite each)
Ingredients:

- Nonstick cooking spray
- 6 eggs, beaten
- ¼ cup unsweetened plain almond milk
- 1 red bell pepper, diced
- 1 cup chopped spinach
- ¼ cup crumbled goat cheese
- ½ cup sliced brown mushrooms
- ¼ cup sliced sun-dried tomatoes
- Salt
- Freshly ground black pepper

Directions:
1. Preheat the oven to 350°F. Spray 8 muffin cups of a 12-cup muffin tin with nonstick cooking spray. Set aside.
2. In a large mixing bowl, combine the eggs, almond milk, bell pepper, spinach, goat cheese, mushrooms, and tomatoes. Season with salt and pepper.
3. Fill the prepared muffin cups three-fourths full of the egg mixture. Bake for 20 to 25 minutes until the eggs are set. Let cool slightly and remove the egg bites from the muffin tin.

4. Serve warm, or store in an airtight container in the refrigerator for up to 5 days or in the freezer for up to 1 month.

Tacos with Pico De Gallo

Preparation time: 5 minutes
Cooking time: 10 minutes
Servings: 4
Ingredients:
For the Taco Filling:

- Avocado oil cooking spray
- 1 medium green bell pepper, chopped
- 8 large eggs
- ¼ cup shredded sharp Cheddar cheese
- 4 (6-inch) whole-wheat tortillas
- 1 cup fresh spinach leaves
- ½ cup Pico de Gallo
- Scallions, chopped, for garnish (optional)
- Avocado slices, for garnish (optional)

For the Pico De Gallo:

- 1 tomato, diced
- ½ large white onion, diced
- 2 tablespoons chopped fresh cilantro
- ½ jalapeño pepper, stemmed, seeded, and diced
- 1 tablespoon freshly squeezed lime juice
- 1/8 teaspoon salt

Directions:
To Make the Taco Filling
1. Heat a medium skillet over medium-low heat. When hot, coat the cooking surface with cooking spray and put the pepper in the skillet. Cook for 4 minutes.
2. Meanwhile, whisk the eggs in a medium bowl, then add the cheese and whisk to combine. Pour the eggs and cheese into the skillet with the green peppers and scramble until the eggs are fully cooked, about 5 minutes.
3. Microwave the tortillas very briefly, about 8 seconds.
4. For each serving, top a tortilla with one-quarter of the spinach, eggs, and Pico de gallo. Garnish with scallions and avocado slices (if using).

To Make the Pico De Gallo
1. In a medium bowl, combine the tomato, onion, cilantro, pepper, lime juice, and salt. Mix well and serve.

Coconut and Chia Pudding

Preparation time: 5 minutes
Cooking time: 0 minutes
Servings: 2
Ingredients:

- 7 ounces (198 g) light coconut milk
- ¼ cup chia seeds
- 3 to 4 drops liquid stevia
- 1 clementine
- 1 kiwi
- Shredded coconut (unsweetened)

Directions:
1. Start by taking a mixing bowl and adding in the light coconut milk. Add in the liquid stevia to sweeten the milk. Mix well.

2. Add the chia seeds to the milk and whisk until well-combined. Set aside.
3. Peel the clementine and carefully remove the skin from the wedges. Set aside.
4. Also, peel the kiwi and dice it into small pieces.
5. Take a glass jar and assemble the pudding. For this, place the fruits at the bottom of the jar; then add a dollop of chia pudding. Now spread the fruits and then add another layer of chia pudding.
6. Finish by garnishing with the remaining fruits and shredded coconut.

Tomato Waffles

Preparation Time: 15 minutes
Cooking Time: 40 minutes
Servings: 8
Ingredients:

- 2 cups low-fat buttermilk
- 1/2 cup crushed tomato
- 1 medium egg
- 2 medium egg whites
- 1 cup gluten-free all-purpose flour
- 1/2 cup almond flour
- 1/2 cup coconut flour
- 2 teaspoons baking powder
- 1/2 teaspoon baking soda
- 1/2 teaspoon dried chives
- Nonstick cooking spray

Directions:
1. Heat a waffle iron.
2. In a medium bowl, whisk the buttermilk, tomato, egg, and egg whites together.
3. In another bowl, whisk the all-purpose flour, almond flour, coconut flour, baking powder, baking soda, and chives together.
4. Add the wet Ingredients: to the dry ingredients.
5. Lightly spray the waffle iron with cooking spray.
6. Gently pour 1/4- to 1/2-cup portions of batter into the waffle iron. Cooking Time for waffles will vary depending on the kind of waffle iron you use, but it is usually 5 minutes per waffle. (Note: Once the waffle iron is hot, the cooking process is a bit faster.) Repeat until no batter remains.
7. Enjoy the waffles warm with Dandelion Greens with Sweet Onion.

Breakfast Homemade Poultry Sausage

Preparation Time: 15 minutes
Cooking Time: 15 minutes
Servings: 10
Ingredients:

- 1/2 red bell pepper, minced
- 1/2 orange bell pepper, minced
- 1/2 jalapeño pepper, minced
- 1 cup chopped tomatoes
- 1 garlic clove, minced
- 1 pound (454 g) ground chicken

- 1 pound (454 g) ground turkey
- 1/4 teaspoon smoked paprika
- 1/4 teaspoon ground cumin
- 1 tablespoon Worcestershire sauce

Directions:
1. Preheat the oven to 350°F (180°C).
2. In a large bowl, combine the red bell pepper, orange bell pepper, jalapeño pepper, tomatoes, garlic, chicken, turkey, paprika, cumin, and Worcestershire sauce. Gently fold together until well mixed.
3. With clean hands, take about 1/3-cup portions, and shape into balls about the size of a golf ball.
4. Gently press the balls into flat disks, and place on a rimmed baking sheet in a single layer at least 1 inch apart. Repeat with the remaining meat. You should have 10 patties.
5. Transfer the baking sheet to the oven and cook for 5 to 7 minutes.
6. Flip the patties and cook for 5 to 7 minutes, or until the juices run clear.
7. Serve with Not-So-Traditional Gravy and Veggie Hash.

Sausage and Pepper Burrito

Preparation Time: 10 minutes
Cooking Time: 15 minutes
Servings: 4
Ingredients:

- 8 ounces (227 g) bulk pork breakfast sausage
- 1/2 onion, chopped
- 1 green bell pepper, seeded and chopped
- 8 large eggs, beaten
- 4 (6-inch) low-carb tortillas
- 1 cup shredded pepper Jack cheese
- 1/2 cup sour cream (optional, for serving)
- 1/2 cup prepared salsa (optional, for serving)

Directions:
1. In a large nonstick skillet on medium-high heat, cook the sausage, crumbling it with a spoon, until browned, about 5 minutes. Add the onion and bell pepper. Cook, stirring, until the veggies are soft, about 3 minutes. Add the eggs and cook, stirring, until eggs are set, about 3 minutes more.
2. Spoon the egg mixture onto the 4 tortillas. Top each with the cheese and fold into a burrito shape.
3. Serve with sour cream and salsa, if desired.

Gouda Egg Casserole

Preparation Time: 12 minutes
Cooking Time: 20 minutes
Servings: 4
Ingredients:

- Nonstick cooking spray
- 1 slice whole grain bread, toasted
- 1/2 cup shredded smoked Gouda cheese
- 3 slices Canadian bacon, chopped
- 6 large eggs
- 1/4 cup half-and-half
- 1/4 teaspoon kosher salt

- 1/4 teaspoon freshly ground black pepper
- 1/4 teaspoon dry mustard

Directions:

1. Spray a cake pan with cooking spray, or if the pan is nonstick, skip this step. If you don't have a 6-inch cake pan, any bowl or pan that fits inside your pressure cooker should work.
2. Crumble the toast into the bottom of the pan. Sprinkle with the cheese and Canadian bacon.
3. In a medium bowl, whisk together the eggs, half-and-half, salt, pepper, and dry mustard.
4. Pour the egg mixture into the pan. Loosely cover the pan with aluminum foil.
5. Pour 11/2 cups water into the electric pressure cooker and insert a wire rack or trivet. Place the covered pan on top of the rack.
6. Close and lock the lid of the pressure cooker. Set the valve to sealing.
7. Cook on high pressure for 20 minutes.
8. When the cooking is complete, hit Cancel and quick release the pressure.
9. Once the pin drops, unlock and remove the lid.
10. Carefully transfer the pan from the pressure cooker to a cooling rack and let it sit for 5 minutes.
11. Cut into 4 wedges and serve.

Breakfast Diabetic Pancakes

Preparation Time: 5 minutes
Cooking Time: 5 minutes
Servings: 6
Ingredients:

- 1 cup Almond flour (blanched)
- 1/4 cup Coconut flour
- 2 3 tablespoons Erythritol
- 1 teaspoon baking powder (gluten-free)
- 5 large Eggs
- 1/3 cup Almond milk (unsweetened)
- 1/4 cup Avocado oil
- 1 1/2 teaspoons Vanilla extract
- 1/4 teaspoon Sea salt

Directions:

1. Begin by taking a mixing bowl and add in the blanched almond flour, coconut flour, erythritol, baking powder, eggs, almond milk, avocado oil, vanilla extract, and sea salt.
2. Use a whisk to mix all the ingredients: until smooth.
3. Take a nonstick pan and place it on a medium-low flame. Grease the pan with a cooking spray.
4. Once the pan is hot enough, drop 1/4 cup batter onto the pan and cook for about 2 minutes. Flip over and cook for another 2 minutes. Repeat the process with the remaining batter.
5. Transfer the cooked pancakes onto a serving platter and stack one over the other. Serve hot!

Blueberry Muffins

Preparation time: 10 minutes
Cooking time: 25 minutes
Servings: 18 muffins
Ingredients:

- 2 cups whole-wheat pastry flour
- 1 cup almond flour
- ½ cup granulated sweetener
- 1 tablespoon baking powder
- 2 teaspoons freshly grated lemon zest
- ¾ teaspoon baking soda
- ¾ teaspoon ground nutmeg
- Pinch sea salt
- 2 eggs
- 1 cup skim milk, at room temperature
- ¾ cup 2 percent plain Greek yogurt
- ½ cup melted coconut oil
- 1 tablespoon freshly squeezed lemon juice
- 1 teaspoon pure vanilla extract
- 1 cup fresh blueberries

Directions:

1. Preheat the oven to 350°F (180°C).
2. Line 18 muffin cups with paper liners and set the tray aside.
3. In a large bowl, stir together the flour, almond flour, sweetener, baking powder, lemon zest, baking soda, nutmeg, and salt.
4. In a small bowl, whisk together the eggs, milk, yogurt, coconut oil, lemon juice, and vanilla.
5. Add the wet Ingredients: to the dry Ingredients: and stir until just combined.
6. Fold in the blueberries without crushing them. Spoon the batter evenly into the muffin cups. Bake the muffins until a toothpick inserted in the middle comes out clean, about 25 minutes.
7. Cool the muffins completely and serve.
8. Store leftover muffins in a sealed container in the refrigerator for up to 3 days or in the freezer for up to 1 month.

Apple and Bran Muffins

Preparation time: 10 minutes
Cooking time: 20 minutes
Servings: 18
Ingredients:

- 2 cups whole-wheat flour
- 1 cup wheat bran
- 1/3 cup granulated sweetener
- 1 tablespoon baking powder
- 2 teaspoons ground cinnamon
- ½ teaspoon ground ginger
- ¼ teaspoon ground nutmeg
- Pinch sea salt
- 2 eggs
- 1½ cups skim milk, at room temperature
- ½ cup melted coconut oil
- 2 teaspoons pure vanilla extract
- 2 apples, peeled, cored, and diced

Directions:

1. Preheat the oven to 350°F (180°C). Line 18 muffin cups with paper liners and set the tray aside.
2. In a large bowl, stir together the flour, bran, sweetener, baking powder, cinnamon, ginger, nutmeg,

and salt. In a small bowl, whisk the eggs, milk, coconut oil, and vanilla until blended.

3. Add the wet Ingredients: to the dry Ingredients, stirring until just blended. Stir in the apples and spoon equal amounts of batter into each muffin cup. Bake the muffins until a toothpick inserted in the center of a muffin comes out clean, about 20 minutes. Cool the muffins completely and serve.

4. Store leftover muffins in a sealed container in the refrigerator for up to 3 days or in the freezer for up to 1 month.

Coconut and Berry Oatmeal

Preparation time: 10 minutes
Cooking time: 35 minutes
Servings: 6
Ingredients:

- 2 cups rolled oats
- ¼ cup shredded unsweetened coconut
- 1 teaspoon baking powder
- ½ teaspoon ground cinnamon
- ¼ teaspoon sea salt
- 2 cups skim milk
- ¼ cup melted coconut oil, plus extra for greasing the baking dish
- 1 egg
- 1 teaspoon pure vanilla extract
- 2 cups fresh blueberries
- 1/8 cup chopped pecans, for garnish
- 1 teaspoon chopped fresh mint leaves, for garnish

Directions:

1. Preheat the oven to 350°F (180°C). Lightly oil a baking dish and set it aside.
2. In a medium bowl, stir together the oats, coconut, baking powder, cinnamon, and salt.
3. In a small bowl, whisk together the milk, oil, egg, and vanilla until well blended.
4. Layer half the dry Ingredients: in the baking dish, top with half the berries, then spoon the remaining half of the dry Ingredients: and the rest of the berries on top. Pour the wet Ingredients: evenly into the baking dish. Tap it lightly on the counter to disperse the wet Ingredients: throughout.
5. Bake the casserole, uncovered, until the oats are tender, about 35 minutes. Serve immediately, topped with the pecans and mint.

Crispy Breakfast Pita with Egg and Canadian bacon

Preparation time: 5 minutes
Cooking time: 15 minutes
Servings: 2
Ingredients:

- 1 (6-inch) whole-grain pita bread
- 3 teaspoons extra-virgin olive oil, divided
- 2 eggs
- 2 Canadian bacon slices
- Juice of ½ lemon

- 1 cup microgreens
- 2 tablespoons crumbled goat cheese
- Freshly ground black pepper

Directions:

1. Heat a large skillet over medium heat. Cut the pita bread in half and brush each side of both halves with ¼ teaspoon of olive oil (using a total of 1 teaspoon oil). Cook for 2 to 3 minutes on each side, then remove from the skillet.

2. In the same skillet, heat 1 teaspoon of oil over medium heat. Crack the eggs into the skillet and cook until the eggs are set, 2 to 3 minutes. Remove from the skillet.

3. In the same skillet, cook the Canadian bacon for 3 to 5 minutes, flipping once.

4. In a large bowl, whisk together the remaining 1 teaspoon of oil and the lemon juice. Add the microgreens and toss to combine.

5. Top each pita half with half of the microgreens, 1 piece of bacon, 1 egg, and 1 tablespoon of goat cheese. Season with pepper and serve.

Apple and Pumpkin Waffles

Preparation time: 10 minutes
Cooking time: 20 minutes
Servings: 6
Ingredients:

- 2¼ cups whole-wheat pastry flour
- 2 tablespoons granulated sweetener
- 1 tablespoon baking powder
- 1 teaspoon ground cinnamon
- 1 teaspoon ground nutmeg
- 4 eggs
- 1¼ cups pure pumpkin purée
- 1 apple, peeled, cored, and finely chopped
- Melted coconut oil, for cooking

Directions:

1. In a large bowl, stir together the flour, sweetener, baking powder, cinnamon, and nutmeg. In a small bowl, whisk together the eggs and pumpkin. Add the wet Ingredients: to the dry and whisk until smooth.
2. Stir the apple into the batter.
3. Cook the waffles according to the waffle maker manufacturer's directions, brushing your waffle iron with melted coconut oil, until all the batter is gone. Serve immediately.

Lavender Blueberry Chia Seed Pudding

Preparation Time: 1 hour 10 minutes
Cooking Time: 0 minutes
Servings: 4
Ingredients:

- 100 g blueberries
- 70 g organic quark
- 50 g soy yogurt
- 30 g hazelnuts
- 200 ml almond milk
- 2 tablespoon chia seeds
- 2 teaspoons agave syrup

- 2 teaspoons of lavender

Directions:
1. Bring the almond milk to a boil alongside the lavender.
2. Let the mixture simmer for 10 minutes at a reduced temperature.
3. Allow them to calm down afterward.
4. If the milk is cold, add the blueberries and puree everything.
5. Mix the entire thing with the chia seeds and agave syrup.
6. Let everything soak in the refrigerator for an hour.
7. Mix the yogurt and curd cheese.
8. Add both to the crowd.
9. Divide the pudding into glasses.
10. Finely chop the hazelnuts and sprinkle them on top.

Yogurt with Granola and Persimmon

Preparation Time: 5 minutes
Cooking Time: 5 minutes
Servings: 1
Ingredients:
- 150g Greek-style yogurt
- 20g oatmeal
- 60g fresh persimmons
- 30 ml of tap water

Directions:
1. Put the nonfat oatmeal in the pan.
2. Toast them, continually stirring, until golden brown.
3. Then, put them on a plate and allow them to calm down briefly.
4. Peel the persimmons and put it in a bowl with the water. Mix the entire thing into a fine puree.
5. Put the yogurt, the toasted oatmeal, and then puree in layers in a glass and serve.

Smoothie Bowl with Spinach, Mango, and Muesli

Preparation Time: 10 minutes
Cooking Time: 0 minutes
Servings: 1
Ingredients:
- 150g yogurt
- 30g apple
- 30g mango
- 30g low carb muesli
- 10g spinach
- 10g chia seeds

Directions:
1. Soak the spinach leaves and allow them to drain.
2. Peel the mango and cut it into strips.
3. Remove apple core and cut it into pieces.
4. Put everything except the mango alongside the yogurt in a blender and make a fine puree out of it.
5. Put the spinach smoothie in a bowl.
6. Add the muesli, chia seeds, and mango.
7. Serve the entire thing

Fried Egg with Bacon

Preparation Time: 5 minutes
Cooking Time: 10 minutes
Servings: 1
Ingredients:
- 2 eggs
- 30 grams of bacon
- 2 tablespoon olive oil
- Salt
- Pepper

Directions:
1. Heat oil in the pan and fry the bacon.
2. Reduce the heat and beat the eggs in the pan.
3. Cook the eggs and season with salt and pepper.
4. Serve the fried eggs hot with the bacon.

Buckwheat Crêpes

Preparation time: 20 minutes
Cooking time: 20 minutes
Servings: 5
Ingredients:
- 1½ cups skim milk
- 3 eggs
- 1 teaspoon extra-virgin olive oil, plus more for the skillet
- 1 cup buckwheat flour
- ½ cup whole-wheat flour
- ½ cup 2 percent plain Greek yogurt
- 1 cup sliced strawberries
- 1 cup blueberries

Directions:
1. In a large bowl, whisk together the milk, eggs, and 1 teaspoon of oil until well combined.
2. Into a medium bowl, sift together the buckwheat and whole-wheat flours. Add the dry Ingredients: to the wet Ingredients: and whisk until well combined and very smooth.
3. Allow the batter to rest for at least 2 hours before cooking.
4. Place a large skillet or crêpe pan over medium-high heat and lightly coat the bottom with oil.
5. Pour about ¼ cup of batter into the skillet. Swirl the pan until the batter completely coats the bottom.
6. Cook the crêpe for about 1 minute, then flip it over. Cook the other side of the crêpe for another minute, until lightly browned. Transfer the cooked crêpe to a plate and cover with a clean dish towel to keep warm. Repeat until the batter is used up; you should have about 10 crêpes.
7. Spoon 1 tablespoon of yogurt onto each crêpe and place two crêpes on each plate. Top with berries and serve.

Ham and Cheese Breakfast Biscuits

Preparation Time: 5 minutes
Cooking Time: 15 minutes
Servings: 4

Ingredients:
- 1 cup ham, diced
- 2 eggs
- 3/4 cup Mozzarella cheese, grated
- 1/2 cup low fat Cheddar cheese, grated
- 1/2 cup reduced fat grated Parmesan, grated

Directions:
1. Heat oven to 375ºF (190ºC). Line a baking sheet with parchment paper.
2. In a large bowl, combine the cheeses and eggs until fully combined. Stir in the ham.
3. Divide the mixture evenly into 8 parts and form into round rolls. Bake for 15 to 20 minutes or until cheese is completely melted and the rolls are nicely browned.

Ham and Jicama Hash

Preparation Time: 10 minutes
Cooking Time: 15 minutes
Servings: 4
Ingredients:
- 6 eggs, beaten
- 2 cups jicama, grated
- 1 cup low fat Cheddar cheese, grated
- 1 cup ham, diced
- From the Cupboard:
- Salt and ground black pepper, to taste
- Nonstick cooking spray

Directions:
1. Spray a large nonstick skillet with cooking spray and place over medium-high heat. Add jicama and cook, stirring occasionally, until it starts to brown, about 5 minutes.
2. Add remaining Ingredients: and reduce heat to medium. Cook for about 3 minutes, then flip over and cook until eggs are set, about 3 to 5 minutes more. Season with salt and pepper and serve.

Greek Yogurt Sundae

Preparation Time: 5 minutes
Cooking Time: 0 minutes
Servings: 1
Ingredients:
- 3/4 cup plain nonfat Greek yogurt
- 1/4 cup mixed berries (blueberries, strawberries, blackberries)
- 2 tablespoons cashew, walnut, or almond pieces
- 1 tablespoon ground flaxseed
- 2 fresh mint leaves, shredded

Directions:
1. Spoon the yogurt into a small bowl. Top with the berries, nuts, and flaxseed.
2. Garnish with the mint and serve.
3. Substitution tip: Use fresh or frozen berries in this sundae, as available. If using frozen, take the berries out of the freezer about 10 or 15 minutes before you make the sundae, so they can thaw.

Mushroom Frittata

Preparation time: 10 minutes

Cooking time: 15 minutes
Servings: 4
Ingredients:
- 8 large eggs
- ½ cup skim milk
- ¼ teaspoon ground nutmeg
- Sea salt and freshly ground black pepper, to taste
- 2 teaspoons extra-virgin olive oil
- 2 cups sliced wild mushrooms (cremini, oyster, shiitake, portobello, etc.)
- ½ red onion, chopped
- 1 teaspoon minced garlic
- ½ cup goat cheese, crumbled

Directions:
1. Preheat the broiler. In a medium bowl, whisk together the eggs, milk, and nutmeg until well combined. Season the egg mixture lightly with salt and pepper and set it aside.
2. Place an ovenproof skillet over medium heat and add the oil, coating the bottom completely by tilting the pan. Sauté the mushrooms, onion, and garlic until translucent, about 7 minutes.
3. Pour the egg mixture into the skillet and cook until the bottom of the frittata is set, lifting the edges of the cooked egg to allow the uncooked egg to seep under.
4. Place the skillet under the broiler until the top is set, about 1 minute.
5. Sprinkle the goat cheese on the frittata and broil until the cheese is melted, about 1 minute more. Remove from the oven.
6. Cut into 4 wedges to serve.

Tropical Yogurt Kiwi Bowl

Preparation time: 5 minutes
Cooking time: 0 minutes
Servings: 2
Ingredients:
- 1½ cups plain low-fat Greek yogurt
- 2 kiwis, peeled and sliced
- 2 tablespoons shredded unsweetened coconut flakes
- 2 tablespoons halved walnuts
- 1 tablespoon chia seeds
- 2 teaspoons honey, divided (optional)

Directions:
1. Divide the yogurt between two small bowls.
2. Top each serving of yogurt with half of the kiwi slices, coconut flakes, walnuts, chia seeds, and honey (if using).

Banana Crêpe Cakes

Preparation time: 5 minutes
Cooking time: 20 minutes
Servings: 4
Ingredients:
- Avocado oil cooking spray
- 4 ounces (113 g) reduced-fat plain cream cheese, softened
- 2 medium bananas
- 4 large eggs

- 1/2 teaspoon vanilla extract
- 1/8 teaspoon salt

Directions:

1. Heat a large skillet over low heat. Coat the cooking surface with cooking spray, and allow the pan to heat for another 2 to 3 minutes.
2. Meanwhile, in a medium bowl, mash the cream cheese and bananas together with a fork until combined. The bananas can be a little chunky.
3. Add the eggs, vanilla, and salt, and mix well.
4. For each cake, drop 2 tablespoons of the batter onto the warmed skillet and use the bottom of a large spoon or ladle to spread it thin. Let it cook for 7 to 9 minutes.
5. Flip the cake over and cook briefly, about 1 minute.

Brussels Sprout Hash and Eggs

Preparation Time: 15 Minutes
Cooking Time: 15 Minutes
Servings: 4
Ingredients:

- 3 teaspoons extra-virgin olive oil, divided
- 1 pound Brussels sprouts, sliced
- 2 garlic cloves, thinly sliced
- ¼ teaspoon salt
- Juice of 1 lemon
- 4 eggs

Directions:

1. In a large skillet, heat 1½ teaspoons of oil over medium heat. Add the Brussels sprouts and toss. Cook, stirring regularly, for 6 to 8 minutes until browned and softened. Add the garlic and continue to cook until fragrant, about 1 minute. Season with the salt and lemon juice. Transfer to a serving dish.
2. In the same pan, heat the remaining 1½ teaspoons of oil over medium-high heat. Crack the eggs into the pan. Fry for 2 to 4 minutes, flip, and continue cooking to desired doneness. Serve over the bed of hash.

Spinach, Artichoke, and Goat Cheese Breakfast Bake

Preparation time: 10 minutes
Cooking time: 35 minutes
Servings: 8
Ingredients:

- Nonstick cooking spray
- 1 (10-ounce) package frozen spinach, thawed and drained
- 1 (14-ounce) can artichoke hearts, drained
- ¼ cup finely chopped red bell pepper
- 2 garlic cloves, minced
- 8 eggs, lightly beaten
- ¼ cup unsweetened plain almond milk
- ½ teaspoon salt
- ½ teaspoon freshly ground black pepper
- ½ cup crumbled goat cheese

Directions:

1. Preheat the oven to 375°F. Spray an 8-by-8-inch baking dish with nonstick cooking spray.
2. In a large mixing bowl, combine the spinach, artichoke hearts, bell pepper, garlic, eggs, almond milk, salt, and pepper. Stir well to combine.
3. Transfer the mixture to the baking dish. Sprinkle with the goat cheese.
4. Bake for 35 minutes until the eggs are set. Serve warm.

Homemade Turkey Breakfast Sausage

Preparation time: 10 minutes
Cooking time: 10 minutes
Servings: 8 (1 patty each)
Ingredients:

- 1-pound lean ground turkey
- ½ teaspoon salt
- ½ teaspoon dried sage
- ½ teaspoon dried thyme
- ½ teaspoon freshly ground black pepper
- ¼ teaspoon ground fennel seeds
- 1 teaspoon extra-virgin olive oil

Directions:

1. In a large mixing bowl, combine the ground turkey, salt, sage, thyme, pepper, and fennel. Mix well.
2. Shape the meat into 8 small, round patties.
3. Heat the olive oil in a skillet over medium-high heat. Cook the patties in the skillet for 3 to 4 minutes on each side until browned and cooked through.
4. Serve warm, or store in an airtight container in the refrigerator for up to 3 days or in the freezer for up to 1 month.

Sweet Potato, Onion, and Turkey Sausage Hash

Preparation time: 10 minutes
Cooking time: 25 minutes
Servings: 4
Ingredients:

- 1 tablespoon extra-virgin oil
- 2 medium sweet potatoes, cut into ½-inch dice
- ½ recipe Homemade Turkey Breakfast Sausage (here)
- 1 small onion, chopped
- ½ red bell pepper, seeded and chopped
- 2 garlic cloves, minced
- Chopped fresh parsley, for garnish

Directions:

1. In a large skillet, heat the oil over medium-high heat. Add the sweet potatoes and cook, stirring occasionally, for 12 to 15 minutes until they brown and begin to soften.
2. Add the turkey sausage in bulk, onion, bell pepper, and garlic. Cook for 5 to 6 minutes until the turkey sausage is cooked through and the vegetables soften.
3. Garnish with parsley and serve warm.

Chapter 4

Lunch

Warm Chicken and Spinach Salad

Preparation Time: 10 Minutes
Cooking Time: 16 - 20 Minutes
Servings: 4
Ingredients:
3 (5-ounce) low-sodium boneless, skinless chicken breasts, cut into 1-inch cubes

- 5 teaspoons olive oil
- 1/2 teaspoon dried thyme
- 1 medium red onion, sliced
- 1 red bell pepper, sliced
- 1 small zucchini, cut into strips
- 3 tablespoons freshly squeezed lemon juice
- 6 cups fresh baby spinach

Directions:
1. In a huge bowl, blend the chicken with the olive oil and thyme. Toss to coat. Transfer to a medium metal bowl and roast for 8 minutes in the air fryer.
2. Add the red onion, red bell pepper, and zucchini. Roast for 8 to 12 minutes more, stirring once during cooking, or until the chicken grasps an inner temperature of 165F on a meat thermometer.
3. Remove the bowl from the air fryer and stir in the lemon juice.
4. Lay the spinach in a serving bowl and top with the chicken mixture. Toss to combine and serve immediately.

Stuffed Chicken

Preparation Time: 15 Minutes
Cooking Time: 30 Minutes
Servings: 4
Ingredients:

- 2 chicken breasts
- 2 tomatoes
- 200 g basil
- 1 teaspoon black pepper
- 1 teaspoon cayenne pepper
- 100 g tomato juice
- 40 g goat's cheese

Directions:
1. Make a "pocket" from chicken breasts and rub it with black pepper and cayenne pepper.
2. Slice tomatoes and chop basil.
3. Chop the goat cheese.
4. Combine all the Ingredients:–it will be the filling for breasts.
5. Fill the chicken breasts with this mixture.
6. Take a needle and thread and sew "pockets".

7. Preheat the air fryer oven to 200 C. Put the chicken breasts in the tray and pour it with tomato juice.
8. Serve.

Chicken Sandwich

Preparation time: 40 minutes
Cooking time: 20 minutes
Servings: 6
Ingredients:

- 4 chicken breasts, pastured
- 1 cup almond flour
- ¾ teaspoon ground black pepper
- 1/2 teaspoon paprika
- 1 teaspoon salt
- 1/2 teaspoon celery seeds
- 1 teaspoon potato starch
- 1/4 cup milk, reduced-fat
- 4 cups dill pickle juice as needed
- 2 eggs, pastured
- 4 hamburger buns
- 1/8 teaspoon dry milk powder, nonfat
- ¼ teaspoon xanthan gum
- 1/8 teaspoon erythritol sweetener

Directions:
1. Place the chicken in a large plastic bag, seal the bag and then pound the chicken with a mallet until ½-inch thick.
2. Brine the chicken and for this, pour the dill pickle juice in the plastic bag containing chicken, then seal it and let the chicken soak for a minimum of 2 hours.
3. After 2 hours, remove the chicken from the brine, rinse it well, and pat dry with paper towels.
4. Place flour in a shallow dish, add black pepper, paprika, salt, celery, potato starch, milk powder, xanthan gum, and sweetener and stir until well mixed.
5. Crack eggs in another dish and then whisk until blended.
6. Switch on the air fryer, insert fryer basket, grease it with olive oil, then shut with its lid, set the fryer at 375 degrees F and preheat for 5 minutes.
7. Meanwhile, dip the chicken into the egg and then coat evenly with the flour mixture.
8. Open the fryer, add chicken breasts in it in a single layer, close with its lid, then cook for 10 minutes, flip the chickens and continue cooking for 5 minutes or until chicken is nicely golden and cooked.
9. When air fryer beeps, open its lid, transfer chicken into a plate and cook remaining chicken in the same manner.
10. Sandwich a chicken breast between toasted hamburger buns, top with favorite dressing and serve.

Buttermilk Fried Chicken

Preparation time: 20 minutes
Cooking time: 10 minutes
Servings: 4
Ingredients:

- 3 tablespoons cornmeal, ground
- 1-pound chicken breasts, pastured
- 6 tablespoons cornflakes
- 1 teaspoon garlic powder
- ¼ teaspoon ground black pepper
- 1 teaspoon paprika
- ¼ teaspoon salt
- ¼ teaspoon hot sauce
- 1/3 cup buttermilk, low-fat

Directions:
1. Pour milk in a bowl, add hot sauce and whisk until well mixed.
2. Cut the chicken in half lengthwise into four pieces, then add into buttermilk, toss well until well coated and let it sit for 15 minutes.
3. Place cornflakes in a blender or food processor, pulse until mixture resembles crumbs, then add remaining Ingredients, pulse until well mixed and then tip the mixture into a shallow dish.
4. After 15 minutes, remove chicken from the buttermilk, then coat with cornflakes mixture until evenly coated and place the chicken on a wire rack.
5. Switch on the air fryer, insert fryer basket, grease it with olive oil, then shut with its lid, set the fryer at 375 degrees F and preheat for 5 minutes.
6. Then open the fryer, add chicken in it in a single layer, spray with oil, close with its lid and cook for 10 minutes until nicely golden and cooked, turning the chicken halfway through the frying.
7. When air fryer beeps, open its lid, transfer chicken onto a serving plate and serve.

Zaatar Lamb Loin Chops

Preparation Time: 10 minutes
Cooking Time: 15-20 minutes
Servings: 4
Ingredients:

- 8: 3½-ounces bone-in lamb loin chops, trimmed
- 3 garlic cloves, crushed
- 1 tbsp. fresh lemon juice
- 1 tsp. olive oil
- 1 tbsp. Zaatar
- Salt and black pepper, to taste

Directions:
1. Preheat the Air fryer to 400°F and grease an Air fryer basket.
2. Mix the garlic, lemon juice, oil, Zaatar, salt, and black pepper in a large bowl.
3. Coat the chops generously with the herb mixture and arrange the chops in the air fryer basket.
4. Cook for about 15 minutes, flipping twice in between, and dish out the lamb chops to serve hot.

Vietnamese Grilled Pork

Preparation Time: 6 minutes

Cooking Time: 16 minutes
Servings: 6
Ingredients:

- 1-pound sliced pork shoulder, pastured, fat trimmed
- 2 tbsp. chopped parsley
- ¼ cup crushed roasted peanuts

For the Marinade:

- ¼ cup minced white onions
- 1 tbsp. minced garlic
- 1 tbsp. lemongrass paste
- 1 tbsp. erythritol sweetener
- ½ tsp. ground black pepper
- 1 tbsp. fish sauce
- 2 tsp. soy sauce
- 2 tbsp. olive oil

Directions:
1. Place all the Ingredients: for the marinade in a bowl, stir well until combined and add it into a large plastic bag.
2. Cut the pork into ½-inch slices, cut each slice into 1-inches pieces, then add them into the plastic bag containing marinade, seal the bag, turn it upside down to coat the pork pieces with the marinade, and marinate for a minimum of 1 hour.
3. Then switch on the air fryer, insert fryer basket, grease it with olive oil, then shut with its lid, set the fryer at 400°F, and preheat for 5 minutes.
4. Open the fryer, add marinated pork in it in a single layer, close with its lid and cook for 10 minutes until nicely golden and cooked, flipping the pork halfway through the frying.
5. When the air fryer beeps, open its lid, transfer pork onto a serving plate, and keep warm.
6. Air fryer the remaining pork pieces in the same manner and then serve.

Provencal Ribs

Preparation Time: 6 minutes
Cooking Time: 20-25 minutes
Servings: 4
Ingredients:

- 500 g pork ribs
- Provencal herbs
- Salt
- Ground pepper
- Oil

Directions:
1. Put the ribs in a bowl and add some oil, Provencal herbs, salt, and ground pepper.
2. Stir well and leave in the fridge for at least 1 hour.
3. Put the ribs in the basket of the air fryer and select 200°C for 20 minutes.
4. From time to time, shake the basket and remove the ribs.

Steak

Preparation Time: 6 minutes
Cooking Time: 18 minutes
Servings: 2
Ingredients:
2 steaks, grass-fed, each about 6 ounces and ¾ inch thick

- 1 tbsp. butter, unsalted
- ¾ tsp. ground black pepper

- ½ tsp. garlic powder
- ¾ tsp. salt
- 1 tsp. olive oil

Directions:

1. Switch on the air fryer, insert fryer basket, grease it with olive oil, then shut with its lid, set the fryer at 400°F, and preheat for 5 minutes.
2. Meanwhile, coat the steaks with oil and then season with black pepper, garlic, and salt.
3. Open the fryer, add steaks in it, close with its lid and cook 10 to 18 minutes at until nicely golden and steaks are cooked to desired doneness, flipping the steaks halfway through the frying.
4. When the air fryer beeps, open its lid and transfer steaks to a cutting board.
5. Take two large aluminum foil pieces, place a steak on each piece, top steak with ½ tbsp. butter, then cover with foil and let it rest for 5 minutes.
6. Serve straight away.

Marinated Loin Potatoes

Preparation Time: 8 minutes
Cooking Time: 40-50 minutes
Servings: 2
Ingredients:

- 2 medium potatoes
- 4 fillets marinated loin
- A little extra virgin olive oil
- Salt

Directions:

1. Peel the potatoes and cut. Cut with match-sized mandolin, potatoes with a cane but very thin.
2. Wash and immerse in water for 30 minutes.
3. Drain and dry well.
4. Add a little oil and stir so that the oil permeates well in all the potatoes.
5. Go to the basket of the air fryer and distribute well.
6. Cook at 160°C for 10 minutes.
7. Take out the basket, shake so that the potatoes take off. Let the potato tender. If it is not, leave 5 more minutes.
8. Place the steaks on top of the potatoes.
9. Select 10 minutes, and 180°C for 5 minutes again.

Beef with Mushrooms

Preparation Time: 8 minutes
Cooking Time: 41 minutes
Servings: 4
Ingredients:

- 300 g beef
- 150 g mushrooms
- 1 onion
- 1 tsp. olive oil
- 100 g vegetable broth
- 1 tsp. basil
- 1 tsp. chili
- 30 g tomato juice

Directions:

1. For this recipe, you should take a solid piece of beef. Take the beef and pierce the meat with a knife.

2. Rub it with olive oil, basil, chili, and lemon juice.
3. Chop the onion and mushrooms and pour it with vegetable broth.
4. Cook the vegetables for 5 minutes.
5. Take a big tray and put the meat in it. Add vegetable broth to the tray too. It will make the meat juicy.
6. Preheat the air fryer oven to 180°C and cook it for 35 minutes.

Cheesy and Crunchy Russian Steaks

Preparation Time: 6 minutes
Cooking Time: 22 minutes
Servings: 4
Ingredients:

- 800 g minced pork
- 200 g cream cheese
- 50g peeled walnuts
- 1 onion
- Salt
- Ground pepper
- 1 egg
- Breadcrumbs
- Extra virgin olive oil

Directions:

1. Put the onion cut into quarters in the Thermo mix glass and select 5 seconds speed 5.
2. Add the minced meat, cheese, egg, salt, and pepper.
3. Select 10 seconds, speed 5, turn left.
4. Add the chopped and peeled walnuts and select 4 seconds, turn left, speed 5.
5. Pass the dough to a bowl.
6. Make Russian steaks and go through breadcrumbs.
7. Paint the Russian fillets with extra virgin olive oil on both sides with a brush.
8. Put in the basket of the air fryer without stacking the Russian fillets.
9. Select 180°C for 15 minutes.

Chicken Nuggets

Preparation time: 10 minutes
Cooking time: 24 minutes
Servings: 4
Ingredients:

- 1-pound chicken breast, pastured
- 1/4 cup coconut flour
- 6 tablespoons toasted sesame seeds
- 1/2 teaspoon ginger powder
- 1/8 teaspoon sea salt
- 1 teaspoon sesame oil
- 4 egg whites, pastured

Directions:

1.   Switch on the air fryer, insert fryer basket, grease it with olive oil, then shut with its lid, set the fryer at 400 degrees F and preheat for 10 minutes.
2.   Meanwhile, cut the chicken breast into 1-inch pieces, pat them dry, place the chicken pieces in a bowl, sprinkle with salt and oil and toss until well coated.

3.   Place flour in a large plastic bag, add ginger and chicken, seal the bag and turn it upside down to coat the chicken with flour evenly.

4.   Place egg whites in a bowl, whisk well, then add coated chicken and toss until well coated.

5.   Place sesame seeds in a large plastic bag, add chicken pieces in it, seal the bag and turn it upside down to coat the chicken with sesame seeds evenly.

6.   Open the fryer, add chicken nuggets in it in a single layer, spray with oil, close with its lid and cook for 12 minutes until nicely golden and cooked, turning the chicken nuggets and spraying with oil halfway through.

7.   When air fryer beeps, open its lid, transfer chicken nuggets onto a serving plate and fry the remaining chicken nuggets in the same manner.

8.   Serve straight away.

Pork Chops

Preparation time: 5 minutes
Cooking time: 15 minutes
Servings: 5
Ingredients:

- 4 slices of almond bread
- 5 pork chops, bone-in, pastured
- 5 ounces coconut flour
- 1 teaspoon salt
- 3 tablespoons parsley
- ½ teaspoon ground black pepper
- 1 tablespoon pork seasoning
- 2 tablespoons olive oil
- 1/3 cup apple juice, unsweetened
- 1 egg, pastured

Directions:

1. Switch on the air fryer, insert fryer basket, grease it with olive oil, then shut with its lid, set the fryer at 350 degrees F and preheat for 5 minutes.

2. Meanwhile, place bread slices in a food processor and pulse until mixture resembles crumbs.

3. Tip the bread crumbs in a shallow dish, add parsley, ½ teaspoon salt, ¼ teaspoon ground black pepper and stir until mixed.

4. Place flour in another shallow dish, add remaining salt and black pepper, along with pork seasoning and stir until mixed.

5. Crack the egg in a bowl, pour in apple juice and whisk until combined.

6. Working on one pork chop at a time, first coat it into the flour mixture, then dip into egg and then evenly coat with breadcrumbs mixture.

7. Open the fryer, add coated pork chops in it in a single layer, close with its lid and cook for 10 minutes until nicely golden and cooked, flipping the pork chops halfway through the frying.

8. When air fryer beeps, open its lid, transfer pork chops onto a serving plate and serve.

Buffalo Chicken Hot Wings

Preparation time: 10 minutes
Cooking time: 45 minutes
Servings: 6
Ingredients:

- 16 chicken wings, pastured
- 1 teaspoon garlic powder
- 2 teaspoons chicken seasoning
- ¾ teaspoon ground black pepper
- 2 teaspoons soy sauce
- 1/4 cup buffalo sauce, reduced-fat

Directions:

1. Switch on the air fryer, insert fryer basket, grease it with olive oil, then shut with its lid, set the fryer at 400 degrees F and preheat for 5 minutes.

2. Meanwhile, place chicken wings in a bowl, drizzle with soy sauce, toss until well coated and then season with black pepper and garlic powder.

3. Open the fryer, stack chicken wings in it, then spray with oil and close with its lid.

4. Cook the chicken wings for 10 minutes, turning the wings halfway through, and then transfer them to a bowl, covering the bowl with a foil to keep the chicken wings warm.

5. Air fry the remaining chicken wings in the same manner, then transfer them to the bowl, add buffalo sauce and toss until well coated.

6. Return chicken wings into the fryer basket in a single layer and continue frying for 7 to 12 minutes or until chicken wings are glazed and crispy, shaking the chicken wings every 3 to 4 minutes. Serve straight away.

Herb Chicken Thighs

Preparation time: 6 hours and 25 minutes
Cooking time: 40 minutes
Servings: 6
Ingredients:

- 6 chicken thighs, skin-on, pastured
- 2 teaspoons garlic powder
- 1/2 teaspoon onion powder
- 1 teaspoon dried basil
- 1 teaspoon spike seasoning
- 1/2 teaspoon dried sage
- 1/4 teaspoon ground black pepper
- 1/2 teaspoon dried oregano
- 2 tablespoons lemon juice
- 1/4 cup olive oil

Directions:

1. Prepare the marinade and for this, place all the Ingredients: in a bowl, except for chicken, stir until well combined and then pour the marinade in a large plastic bag.

2. Add chicken thighs in the plastic bag, seal the bag, then turn in upside down until chicken thighs are coated with the marinade and let marinate in the refrigerator for minimum of 6 hours.

3. Then drain the chicken, arrange the chicken thighs on a wire rack and let them rest for 15 minutes at room temperature.

4. Meanwhile, switch on the air fryer, insert fryer basket, grease it with olive oil, then shut with its lid, set the fryer at 360 degrees F and preheat for 5 minutes.

5. Then open the fryer, add chicken thighs in it in a single layer top-side down, close with its lid, cook the chicken for 8 minutes, turn the chicken, and continue frying for 6 minutes.

6. Turn the chicken thighs and then continue cooking for another 6 minutes or until chicken is nicely browned and cooked.

7. When air fryer beeps, open its lid, transfer chicken onto a serving plate and cook the remaining chicken thighs in the same manner.

8. Serve straight away.

Air Fryer Beef Steak Kabobs with Vegetables

Preparation Time: 9 minutes
Cooking Time: 11 minutes
Servings: 4
Ingredients:

- Light soy sauce: 2 tbsp.
- Lean beef chuck ribs: 4 cups, cut into one-inch pieces
- Low-fat sour cream: 1/3 cup
- Half onion
- 8 skewers: 6 inches
- One bell pepper

Directions:

1. In a mixing bowl, add soy sauce and sour cream, mix well. Add the lean beef chunks, coat well, and let it marinate for half an hour or more.

2. Cut onion, bell pepper into one-inch pieces. In water, soak skewers for ten minutes.

3. Add onions, bell peppers, and beef on skewers; alternatively, sprinkle with black pepper.

4. Let it cook for 10 minutes in a preheated air fryer at 400°F, flip halfway through.

5. Serve with yogurt dipping sauce.

Pork Liver

Preparation Time: 9 minutes
Cooking Time: 16 minutes
Servings: 4
Ingredients:

- 500 g pork liver cut into steaks
- Breadcrumbs
- Salt
- Ground pepper
- 1 lemon
- Extra virgin olive oil

Directions:

1. Put the steaks on a plate or bowl.

2. Add the lemon juice, salt, and ground pepper.

3. Leave a few minutes to macerate the pork liver fillets.

4. Drain well and go through breadcrumbs; it is not necessary to pass the fillets through beaten egg because the liver is very moist, the breadcrumbs are perfectly glued.

5. Spray with extra virgin olive oil. If you don't have a sprayer, paint with a silicone brush.

6. Put the pork liver fillets in the air fryer basket.

7. Program 180°C, 10 minutes.

8. Take out if you see them golden to your liking and put another batch.

9. You should not pile the pork liver fillets, which are well extended so that the empanada is crispy on all sides.

Air Fried Meatloaf

Preparation Time: 6 minutes
Cooking Time: 25-30 minutes

Servings: 2
Ingredients:

- ½ lb. ground beef
- ½ lb. ground turkey
- 1 onion, chopped
- ¼ cup panko breadcrumbs
- 3 tbsp. ketchup
- ¼ cup brown sugar
- 1 egg, beaten
- Salt and pepper to taste

Directions:

1. Preheat the air fryer to 400°F.

2. Let the ground beef and ground turkey sit on the counter for 10 to 15 minutes, as it will be easier to hand mix without being chilled from the refrigerator.

3. Combine all the Ingredients.

4. Form into a loaf in a dish and place the dish in the frying basket. Spritz the top with a little olive oil.

5. Bake for 25 minutes, or until well browned. Let settle for about 10 minutes before serving.

Pork Bondiola Chop

Preparation Time: 8 minutes
Cooking Time: 22 minutes
Servings: 4
Ingredients:

- 1 kg bondiola in pieces
- Breadcrumbs
- 2 beaten eggs
- Seasoning to taste

Directions:

1. Cut the bondiola into small pieces.

2. Add seasonings to taste.

3. Pour the beaten eggs on the seasoned bondiola.

4. Add the breadcrumbs.

5. Cook in the air fryer for 20 minutes while turning the food halfway.

6. Serve

Air Fry Rib-Eye Steak

Preparation Time: 11 minutes
Cooking Time: 18 minutes
Servings: 2
Ingredients:

- Lean rib eye steaks: 2 medium-sized
- Salt and freshly ground black pepper, to taste

Directions:

1. Let the air fry preheat at 400°F. Pat dry steaks with paper towels.

2. Use any spice blend or just salt and pepper on steaks.

3. Generously on both sides of the steak.

4. Put steaks in the air fryer basket. Cook according to the rareness you want. Or cook for 14 minutes and flip after halftime.

5. Take out from the air fryer and let it rest for about 5 minutes.

6. Serve.

Lemon Pepper Chicken

Preparation time: 1 hour and 10 minutes

Cooking time: 28 minutes
Servings: 4
Ingredients:
4 chicken breasts, pastured
1/4 cup lemon juice
3 tablespoon lemon pepper seasoning
2 teaspoons Worcestershire sauce
1/4 cup olive oil
Directions:
1. Prepare the marinade and for this, place oil, Worcestershire sauce, salt and lemon juice in a bowl and whisk until combined.
2. Cut each chicken breast into four pieces, add the chicken pieces into the marinade, toss until well coated and marinate the chicken in the refrigerator for a minimum of 1 hour.
3. Then switch on the air fryer, insert fryer basket, grease it with olive oil, then shut with its lid, set the fryer at 350 degrees F, and preheat for 5 minutes.
4. Open the fryer, add chicken pieces in it in a single layer, spray with oil, close with its lid and cook for 14 minutes at the 350 degrees F until nicely golden and cooked, turning the chicken halfway through the frying.
5. When air fryer beeps, open its lid, transfer chicken onto a serving plate and cook the remaining chicken pieces in the same manner.
6. Serve straight away.

Caribbean Spiced Chicken

Preparation time: 45 minutes
Cooking time: 20 minutes
Servings: 4
Ingredients:
- 1.5-pound boneless chicken thigh fillets, skinless, pastured
- ½ tablespoon ground ginger
- ¾ teaspoon ground black pepper
- ½ tablespoon ground nutmeg
- 1 teaspoon salt
- ½ tablespoon cayenne pepper
- ½ tablespoon ground coriander
- ½ tablespoon ground cinnamon
- 1½ tablespoon olive oil

Directions:
1. Meanwhile, take a baking sheet, line it with paper towels, then place chicken on it, season the chicken with salt and black pepper on both sides and let it sit for 30 minutes.
2. Prepare the spice mix and for this, place remaining Ingredients: in a bowl, except for oil, and then stir well until mixed.
3. Pat dry the chicken, then season well with the spice mix and brush with oil.
4. Switch on the air fryer, insert fryer basket, grease it with olive oil, then shut with its lid, set the fryer at 390 degrees F, and preheat for 5 minutes.
5. Then open the fryer, add seasoned chicken in it in a single layer, close with its lid and cook for 10 minutes until nicely golden and cooked, turning the chicken halfway through the frying.

6. When air fryer beeps, open its lid, transfer chicken into a heatproof dish and then cover it with foil to keep the chicken warm. Cook remaining chicken in the same manner and serve.

Chicken in Tomato Juice

Preparation Time: 20 Minutes
Cooking Time: 15 Minutes
Servings: 3
Ingredients:
- 350 g chicken fillet
- 200 g tomato juice
- 100 g tomatoes
- 2 teaspoon basils
- 1 teaspoon chili
- 1 teaspoon oregano
- 1 teaspoon rosemary
- 1 teaspoon olive oil
- 1 teaspoon mint
- 1 teaspoon lemon juice

Directions:
1. Take a bowl and make the tomato sauce: combine basil, chili, oregano, rosemary, and olive oil, mint and lemon juice and stir the mixture carefully.
2. You can use a hand mixer to mix the mass. It will make the mixture smooth.
3. Take a chicken fillet and separate it into 3 pieces.
4. Put the meat to the tomato mixture and leave for 15 minutes.
5. Meanwhile, preheat the air fryer oven to 230 C.
6. Put the meat mixture on the tray and put it in the oven for at least 15 minutes.

Chicken Wings with Curry

Preparation Time: 15 Minutes
Cooking Time: 20 Minutes
Servings: 4
Ingredients:
- 400 g chicken wings
- 30 g curry
- 1 teaspoon chili
- 1 teaspoon cayenne pepper
- 1 teaspoon salt
- 1 lemon
- 1 teaspoon basil
- 1 teaspoon oregano
- 3 teaspoon mustards
- 1 teaspoon olive oil

Directions:
1. Rub the wings with chili, curry, cayenne pepper, salt, basil, and oregano.
2. Put it to the bowl and mix it carefully.
3. Leave the mixture at least for 10 minutes in the fridge.
4. Take away the mixture from the fridge and add mustard and sprinkle with chopped lemon. Stir the mixture gently again.
5. Sprig the pan with olive oil and put the wings in it.
6. Preheat the air fryer oven to 180 C and put wings there.
7. Cook it for 20 minutes.

Chapter 5

Meatless Mains

Crispy Parmesan Cups with White Beans and Veggies

Preparation time: 10 minutes
Cooking time: 5 minutes
Servings: 4 (2 cups each)
Ingredients:

- 1 cup grated Parmesan cheese, divided
- 1 (15-ounce) can low-sodium white beans, drained and rinsed
- 1 cucumber, peeled and finely diced
- ½ cup finely diced red onion
- ¼ cup thinly sliced fresh basil
- 1 garlic clove, minced
- ½ jalapeño pepper, diced
- 1 tablespoon extra-virgin olive oil
- 1 tablespoon balsamic vinegar
- ¼ teaspoon salt
- Freshly ground black pepper

Directions:
1. Heat a medium nonstick skillet over medium heat. Sprinkle 2 tablespoons of cheese in a thin circle in the center of the pan, flattening it with a spatula.
2. When the cheese melts, use a spatula to flip the cheese and lightly brown the other side.
3. Remove the cheese "pancake" from the pan and place into the cup of a muffin tin, bending it gently with your hands to fit in the muffin cup.
4. Repeat with the remaining cheese until you have 8 cups.
5. In a mixing bowl, combine the beans, cucumber, onion, basil, garlic, jalapeño, olive oil, and vinegar, and season with the salt and pepper.
6. Fill each cup with the bean mixture just before serving.

Lime Asparagus with Cashews

Preparation time: 10 minutes
Cooking Time: 15 To 20 minutes
Servings: 4
Ingredients:

- 2 pounds (907 g) asparagus, woody ends trimmed
- 1 tablespoon extra-virgin olive oil
- Sea salt and freshly ground black pepper, to taste
- ½ cup chopped cashews
- Zest and juice of 1 lime

Directions:
1. Preheat the oven to 400°F (205°C). Line a baking sheet with aluminum foil.
2. Toss the asparagus with the olive oil in a medium bowl. Sprinkle the salt and pepper to season.
3. Arrange the asparagus on the baking sheet and bake for 15 to 20 minutes, or until lightly browned and tender.
4. Remove the asparagus from the oven to a serving bowl. Add the cashews, lime zest and juice, and toss to coat well. Serve immediately.

Cabbage Wedges

Preparation time: 20 minutes
Cooking Time: 29 minutes
Servings: 6
Ingredients:

- 1 small head of green cabbage
- 6 strips of bacon, thick cut, pastured
- 1-teaspoon onion powder
- ½-teaspoon ground black pepper
- 1-teaspoon garlic powder
- ¾-teaspoon salt
- 1/4 teaspoon red chili flakes
- 1/2 teaspoon fennel seeds
- 3 tablespoons olive oil

Directions:
1. Switch on the air fryer, insert fryer basket, grease it with olive oil, then shut with its lid, set the fryer at 350 degrees F, and preheat for 5 minutes.
2. Open the fryer, add bacon strips in it, close with its lid and cook for 10 minutes until nicely golden and crispy, turning the bacon halfway through the frying.
3. Meanwhile, prepare the cabbage, for this, remove the outer leaves of the cabbage, and then cut it into eight wedges, keeping the core intact.
4. Prepare the spice mix and for this, place onion powder in a bowl, add black pepper, garlic powder, salt, red chili, and fennel and stir until mixed.
5. Drizzle cabbage wedges with oil and then sprinkle with spice mix until well coated.
6. When air fryer beeps, open its lid, transfer bacon strips to a cutting board and let it rest.
7. Add seasoned cabbage wedges into the fryer basket, close with its lid, then cook for 8 minutes at 400 degrees F, flip the cabbage, spray with oil, and continue air frying for 6 minutes until nicely golden and cooked.
8. When done, transfer cabbage wedges to a plate.
9. Chop the bacon, sprinkle it over cabbage and serve.

Black Pepper & Garlic Tofu

Preparation time: 20 minutes
Cooking Time: 40 minutes

Servings: 4
Ingredients:

- 14 oz. pkg. extra firm tofu
- 1 lb. asparagus, trim & cut in 1-inch pieces
- 8 oz. kale, remove stems & slice leaves
- 3 oz. Shiitake mushrooms, sliced
- 1 onion, halved & slice in thin wedges
- 1 green bell pepper, sliced
- What you'll need from store cupboard:
- ½ cup low sodium vegetable broth
- 8 cloves garlic, pressed, divided
- 2 ½ tbsp. light soy sauce, divided
- 2 -4 tbsp. water
- 2 tsp cornstarch
- 2 tsp black pepper, freshly ground, divided
- 1 tsp rice vinegar
- 1 tsp sriracha

Directions:
1. Heat oven to 400 degrees. Line a baking sheet with parchment paper.
2. Cut tofu in ½-inch slices and press between paper towels to remove excess moisture. Cut each slice into smaller rectangles.
3. In a Ziploc bag combine, 1 tablespoon soy sauce, water, 2 tablespoons garlic, rice vinegar, and 1 teaspoon pepper. Add tofu and turn to coat. Let marinate 15 minutes.
4. Place the tofu on the prepared pan and bake 15 minutes. Flip over and bake 15 minutes more. Remove from oven.
5. Place a large nonstick skillet over med-high heat. Add onion and cook until translucent, stirring frequently. Add bell pepper and cook 1 minute more.
6. Add garlic and mushrooms and cook 2 minutes, add a little water if the vegetables start to stick.
7. Stir in the kale and 2 tablespoons water and cover. Let cook 1 minutes, then stir and add more water if needed. Cover and cook another minute before adding asparagus and cook, stirring, until asparagus is tender crisp.
8. in a small bowl, stir together remaining soy sauce, broth, Sriracha, cornstarch, and pepper. Pour over vegetables and cook until heated through.
9. To serve plate the vegetables and place tofu on top.

Watermelon & Arugula Salad

Preparation time: 35 minutes
Cooking Time: 1 hour
Servings: 6
Ingredients:

- 4 cups watermelon, cut in 1-inch cubes
- 3 cup arugula
- 1 lemon, zested
- ½ cup feta cheese, crumbled
- ¼ cup fresh mint, chopped
- 1 tbsp. fresh lemon juice
- What you'll need from store cupboard:
- 3 tbsp. olive oil
- Fresh ground black pepper
- Salt to taste

Directions:

1. Combine oil, zest, juice, and mint in a large bowl. Stir together.
2. Add watermelon and gently toss to coat. Add remaining Ingredients: and toss to combine. Taste and adjust seasoning as desired.
3. Cover and chill at least 1 hour before serving.

Broccoli & Mushroom Salad

Preparation time: 10 minutes
Cooking Time: 10 minutes
Servings: 4
Ingredients:

- 4 sun-dried tomatoes, cut in half
- 3 cup torn leaf lettuce
- 1 ½ cup broccoli florets
- 1 cup mushrooms, sliced
- 1/3 cup radishes, sliced
- What you'll need from store cupboard:
- 2 tbsp. water
- 1 tbsp. balsamic vinegar
- 1 tsp vegetable oil
- ¼ tsp chicken bouillon granules
- ¼ tsp parsley - ¼ tsp dry mustard
- 1/8 tsp cayenne pepper

Directions:
1. Place tomatoes in a small bowl and pour boiling water over, just enough to cover. Let stand 5 minutes, drain.
2. Chop tomatoes and place in a large bowl. Add lettuce, broccoli, mushrooms, and radishes.
3. In a jar with a tight-fitting lid, add remaining Ingredients: and shake well. Pour over salad and toss to coat. Serve.

French toast

Preparation time: 10 minutes
Cooking Time: 15 minutes
Servings: 8
Ingredients:

- For the bread:
- 500g of flour
- 25g of oil - 300 g of water
- 25g of fresh bread yeast
- 12g of salt
- For French toast:
- Milk and cinnamon or milk and sweet wine
- Eggs - Honey

Directions:
1. The first thing is to make bread a day before. Put in the Master Chef Gourmet the Ingredients: of the bread and knead 1 minute at speed Let the dough rise 1 hour and knead 1 minute at speed 1 again. Remove the dough and divide into 4 portions. Make a ball and spread like a pizza. Roll up to make a small loaf of bread and let rise 1 hour or so.
2. Take to the oven and bake 40 minutes, 2000C. Let the bread cool on a rack and reserve for the next day. Cut the bread into slices and reserve.
3. Prepare the milk to wet the slices of bread.
4. To do so, put the milk to heat, like 500 ml or so with a cinnamon stick or the same milk with a glass of sweet wine, as you like.

5. When the milk has started to boil, remove from heat, and let cool.

6. Beat the eggs.

7. Place a rack on a plate and we dip the slices of bread in the cold milk, then in the beaten egg and pass to the rack with the plate underneath to release the excess liquid.

8. Put the slices of bread in the bucket of the air fryer, in batches, not piled up, and we take the air fryer, 180 degrees, 10 minutes each batch.

9. When you have all the slices passed through the air fryer, put the honey in a casserole, like 500g, next to 1 small glass of water and 4 tablespoons of sugar. When the honey starts to boil, lower the heat, and pass the bread slices through the honey.

10. Place in a fountain and the rest of the honey we put it on top, bathing again the French toast. Ready our French toast, when they cool, they can already be eaten.

Butter-orange Yams

Preparation time: 30 minutes
Cooking Time: 45 minutes
Servings: 8
Ingredients:

- 2 medium jewel yams, cut into 2-inch dices
- 2 tablespoons unsalted butter
- Juice of 1 large orange
- 1½ teaspoons ground cinnamon
- ¼ teaspoon ground ginger
- ¾ teaspoon ground nutmeg
- 1/8 teaspoon ground cloves

Directions:

1. Preheat the oven to 350°F (180°C).

2. Arrange the yam dices on a rimmed baking sheet in a single layer. Set aside.

3. Add the butter, orange juice, cinnamon, ginger, nutmeg, and garlic cloves to a medium saucepan over medium-low heat. Cook for 3 to 5 minutes, stirring continuously, or until the sauce begins to thicken and bubble.

4. Spoon the sauce over the yams and toss to coat well.

5. Bake in the preheated oven for 40 minutes until tender.

6. Let the yams cool for 8 minutes on the baking sheet before removing and serving.

Grilled Portobello & Zucchini Burger

Preparation time: 5 minutes
Cooking Time: 10 minutes
Servings: 2
Ingredients:

- 2 large portabella mushroom caps
- ½ small zucchini, sliced
- 2 slices low fat cheese
- Spinach
- What you'll need from store cupboard:
- 2 100% whole wheat sandwich thins
- 2 tsp roasted red bell peppers
- 2 tsp olive oil

Directions:

1. Heat grill, or charcoal, to med-high heat.

2. Lightly brush mushroom caps with olive oil. Grill mushroom caps and zucchini slices until tender, about 3-4 minutes per side.

3. Place on sandwich thin. Top with sliced cheese, roasted red bell pepper, and spinach. Serve.

Tarragon Spring Peas

Preparation time: 10 minutes
Cooking Time: 12 minutes
Servings: 6
Ingredients:
 1 tablespoon unsalted butter
 ½ Vidalia onion, thinly sliced
 1 cup low-sodium vegetable broth
 3 cups fresh shelled peas
 1 tablespoon minced fresh tarragon
Directions:

1. Melt the butter in a skillet over medium heat.

2. Sauté the onion in the melted butter for about 3 minutes until translucent, stirring occasionally.

3. Pour in the vegetable broth and whisk well. Add the peas and tarragon to the skillet and stir to combine.

4. Reduce the heat to low, cover, and cook for about 8 minutes more, or until the peas are tender.

5. Let the peas cool for 5 minutes and serve warm.

Crust Less Broccoli Quiche

Preparation time: 40 minutes
Cooking Time: 1 hour
Servings: 6
Ingredients:

- 3 large eggs
- 2 cups broccoli florets, chopped
- 1 small onion, diced
- 1 cup cheddar cheese, grated
- 2/3 cup unsweetened almond milk
- ½ cup feta cheese, crumbled
- What you'll need from store cupboard:
- 1 tbsp. extra virgin olive oil
- ½ tsp sea salt
- ¼ tsp black pepper
- Nonstick cooking spray

Directions:

1. Heat oven to 350 degrees. Spray a 9-inch baking dish with cooking spray.

2. Heat the oil in a large skillet over medium heat. Add onion and cook 4-5 minutes, until onions are translucent.

3. Add broccoli and stir to combine. Cook until broccoli turns a bright green, about 2 minutes. Transfer to a bowl.

4. In a small bowl, whisk together almond milk, egg, salt, and pepper. Pour over the broccoli. Add the cheddar cheese and stir the ingredients: together. Pour into the prepared baking dish.

5. Sprinkle the feta cheese over the top and bake 45 minutes to 1 hour, or until eggs are set in the middle and top is lightly browned. Serve.

Potatoes with Provencal Herbs with Cheese

Preparation time: 10 minutes

Cooking Time: 20 minutes
Servings: 4
Ingredients:

- 1kg of potatoes
- Provencal herbs
- Extra virgin olive oil
- Salt
- Grated cheese

Directions:
1. Peel the potatoes and cut the cane salt and sprinkle with Provencal herbs.
2. Put in the basket and add some strands of extra virgin olive oil.
3. Take the air fryer and select 1800C, 20 minutes.
4. Take out and move on to a large plate.
5. Cover cheese.
6. Gratin in the microwave or in the oven, a few minutes until the cheese is melted.

Spiced Potato Wedges

Preparation time: 20 minutes
Cooking Time: 40 minutes
Servings: 4
Ingredients:

- 8 medium potatoes
- Salt
- Ground pepper
- Garlic powder
- Aromatic herbs, the one we like the most
- 2 tbsp. extra virgin olive oil
- 4 tbsp. breadcrumbs or chickpea flour.

Directions:
1. Put the unpeeled potatoes in a pot with boiling water and a little salt.
2. Let cook 5 minutes. Drain and let cool. Cut into thick segments, without peeling.
3. Put the potatoes in a bowl and add salt, pepper, garlic powder, the aromatic herb that we have chosen oil and breadcrumbs or chickpea flour.
4. Stir well and leave 15 minutes. Pass to the basket of the air fryer and select 20 minutes, 1800C.
5. From time to time shake the basket so that the potatoes mix and change position. Check that they are tender.

Roasted Delicata Squash with Thyme

Preparation time: 10 minutes
Cooking Time: 20 Minutes
Servings: 4
Ingredients:

- 1 (1- to 1½-pound / 454- to 680-g) delicata squash, halved, seeded, and cut into ½-inch-thick strips
- 1 tablespoon extra-virgin olive oil
- ½ teaspoon dried thyme
- ¼ teaspoon salt
- ¼ teaspoon freshly ground black pepper

Directions:

1. Preheat the oven to 400ºF (205ºC). Line a baking sheet with parchment paper and set aside.
2. Add the squash strips, olive oil, thyme, salt, and pepper in a large bowl, and toss until the squash strips are fully coated.
3. Place the squash strips on the prepared baking sheet in a single layer. Roast for about 20 minutes until lightly browned, flipping the strips halfway through.
4. Remove from the oven and serve on plates.

Creamy Macaroni and Cheese

Preparation time: 15 minutes
Cooking Time: 25 minutes
Servings: 6
Ingredients:

- 1 cup fat-free evaporated milk
- ½ cup skim milk
- ½ cup low-fat Cheddar cheese
- ½ cup low-fat cottage cheese
- 1 teaspoon nutmeg
- Pinch cayenne pepper
- Sea salt and freshly ground black pepper, to taste
- 6 cups cooked whole-wheat elbow macaroni
- 2 tablespoons grated Parmesan cheese

Directions:
1. Preheat the oven to 350ºF (180ºC).
2. Heat the milk in a large saucepan over low heat until it steams.
3. Add the Cheddar cheese and cottage cheese to the milk, and keep whisking, or until the cheese is melted.
4. Add the nutmeg and cayenne pepper and stir well. Sprinkle the salt and pepper to season.
5. Remove from the heat. Add the cooked macaroni to the cheese mixture and stir until well combined. Transfer the macaroni and cheese to a large casserole dish and top with the grated Parmesan cheese.
6. Bake in the preheated oven for about 20 minutes, or until bubbly and lightly browned.
7. Divide the macaroni and cheese among six bowls and serve.

Creamy Pasta with Peas

Preparation time: 5 minutes
Cooking Time: 10 minutes
Servings: 4
Ingredients:

- 4 tomatoes, deseeded & diced
- 4 oz. fat free cream cheese, cut in cubes
- 1 cup peas, thawed
- ½ cup skim milk
- 4 tbsp. fresh parsley, diced
- What you'll need from store cupboard:
- ½ recipe Homemade Pasta, cook & drain
- 4 cloves garlic, diced fine
- 3 tbsp. olive oil
- 1 tsp oregano
- 1 tsp basil
- ½ tsp garlic salt

Directions:
1. Heat oil in a large skillet over medium heat. Add garlic and tomatoes, cook 3-4 minutes, stirring frequently.

2. Add peas, milk, cream cheese, and seasonings. Cook, stirring, 5 minutes, or until cream cheese has melted.

3. Add pasta and toss to coat. Serve garnished with parsley.

Sesame Bok Choy with Almonds

Preparation time: 5 minutes
Cooking Time: 7 minutes
Servings: 4
Ingredients:
2 teaspoons sesame oil
2 pounds (907 g) bok choy, cleaned and quartered
2 teaspoons low-sodium soy sauce
Pinch red pepper flakes
½ cup toasted sliced almonds
Directions:
1. Heat the sesame oil in a large skillet over medium heat until hot.
2. Sauté the bok choy in the hot oil for about 5 minutes, stirring occasionally, or until tender but still crisp.
3. Add the soy sauce and red pepper flakes and stir to combine. Continue sautéing for 2 minutes.
4. Transfer to a plate and serve topped with sliced almonds.

Roasted Cauliflower with Tomatoes

Preparation time: 30 minutes
Cooking Time: 45 Minutes
Servings: 4
Ingredients:
- 1 large head cauliflower, separated in florets
- 3 scallions, sliced
- 1 onion, diced fine
- What you'll need from store cupboard:
- 15 oz. can petite tomatoes, diced
- 4 cloves garlic, diced fine
- 4 tbsp. olive oil, divided
- 1 tbsp. red wine vinegar
- 1 tbsp. balsamic vinegar
- 3 tsp Splenda
- 1 tsp salt
- 1 tsp pepper
- ½ tsp chili powder

Directions:
1. Heat oven to 400 degrees.
2. Place cauliflower on a large baking sheet and drizzle with 2 tablespoons of oil. Sprinkle with salt and pepper, to taste. Use hands to rub oil and seasoning into florets then lay in single layer. Roast until fork tender.
3. Heat 1 tablespoon oil in a large skillet over med-low heat. Add onion and cook until soft.
4. Stir in tomatoes, with juice, Splenda, both vinegars, and the teaspoon of salt. Bring to a boil, reduce heat and simmer 20-25 minutes. For a smooth sauce, use an immersion blender to process until smooth, or leave it chunky.
5. In a separate skillet, heat remaining oil over med-low heat and sauté garlic 1-2 minutes. Stir in tomato sauce and increase heat to medium. Cook, stirring frequently, 5 minutes. Add chili powder and cauliflower and toss to coat. Serve garnished with scallions.

Fried Avocado

Preparation time: 5 minutes
Cooking Time: 10 minutes
Servings: 2
Ingredients:
- 2 avocados cut into wedges 25 mm thick
- 50g Pan crumbs bread
- 2g garlic powder
- 2g onion powder
- 1g smoked paprika
- 1g cayenne pepper
- Salt and pepper to taste
- 60g all-purpose flour
- 2 eggs, beaten
- Nonstick Spray Oil
- Tomato sauce or ranch sauce, to serve

Directions:
1. Cut the avocados into 25 mm thick pieces.
2. Combine the crumbs, garlic powder, onion powder, smoked paprika, cayenne pepper and salt in a bowl.
3. Separate each wedge of avocado in the flour, then dip the beaten eggs and stir in the breadcrumb mixture.
4. Preheat the air fryer.
5. Place the avocados in the preheated air fryer baskets, spray with oil spray and cook at 205°C for 10 minutes. Turn the fried avocado halfway through cooking and sprinkle with cooking oil.

Scrambled Eggs with Beans, Zucchini, Potatoes and Onions

Preparation time: 20 minutes
Cooking Time: 35 Minutes
Servings: 4
Ingredients:
- 300g of beans
- 2 onions
- 1 zucchini
- 4 potatoes
- 8 eggs
- Extra virgin olive oil
- Salt
- Ground pepper
- A splash of soy sauce

Directions:
1. Put the beans taken from their pod to cook in abundant saltwater. Drain when they are tender and reserve.
2. Peel the potatoes and cut into dice. Season and put some threads of oil. Mix and take to the air fryer. Select 1800C, 15 minutes.
3. After that time, add together with the potatoes, diced zucchini, and onion in julienne, mix and select 1800C, 20 minutes.
4. From time to time, mix and stir.
5. Pass the contents of the air fryer together with the beans to a pan.
6. Add a little soy sauce and salt to taste.
7. Sauté and peel the eggs.
8. Do the scrambled.

Cantaloupe & Prosciutto Salad

Preparation time: 10 minutes
Cooking Time: 15 minutes
Servings: 4
Ingredients:

- 6 mozzarella balls, quartered
- 1 medium cantaloupe, peeled and cut into small cubes
- 4 oz. prosciutto, chopped
- 1 tbsp. fresh lime juice
- 1 tbsp. fresh mint, chopped
- What you'll need from store cupboard
- 2 tbsp. extra virgin olive oil
- 1 tsp honey

Directions:
1. In a large bowl, whisk together oil, lime juice, honey, and mint. Season with salt and pepper to taste.
2. Add the cantaloupe and mozzarella and toss to combine. Arrange the mixture on a serving plate and add prosciutto. Serve.

Green Beans

Preparation time: 10 minutes
Cooking Time: 13 minutes
Servings: 4
Ingredients:
1-pound green beans
¾-teaspoon garlic powder
¾-teaspoon ground black pepper
1 ¼-teaspoon salt
½-teaspoon paprika
Directions:
1. Switch on the air fryer, insert fryer basket, grease it with olive oil, then shut with its lid, set the fryer at 400 degrees F, and preheat for 5 minutes.
2. Meanwhile, place beans in a bowl, spray generously with olive oil, sprinkle with garlic powder, black pepper, salt, and paprika and toss until well coated.
3. Open the fryer, add green beans in it, close with its lid and cook for 8 minutes until nicely golden and crispy, shaking halfway through the frying.
4. When air fryer beeps, open its lid, transfer green beans onto a serving plate and serve.

Garden Vegetable Pasta

Preparation time: 23 minutes
Cooking Time: 30 minutes
Servings: 6
Ingredients:

- 2 lbs. fresh cherry tomatoes, halved
- 2 zucchinis, chopped
- 2 ears corn, cut kernels off the cob
- 1 yellow squash, chopped
- ½ cup mozzarella cheese, grated
- ½ cup fresh basil, sliced thin
- What you'll need from store cupboard:
- Homemade Pasta, cook & drain
- 5 tbsp. olive oil, divided
- 2 cloves garlic crushed

- Crushed red pepper flakes, to taste
- Salt, to taste

Directions:
1. Heat 3 tablespoons oil in a large skillet over medium heat. Add garlic and tomatoes. Cover, reduce heat to low, and cook 15 minutes, stirring frequently.
2. In a separate skillet, heat remaining oil over med-high heat. Add zucchini, squash, and corn. Reduce heat to medium and cook until vegetables are tender. Sprinkle with salt.
3. Heat oven to 400 degrees.
4. In a large bowl combine tomato mixture, vegetables, and pasta, toss to mix. Pour into a 9x13-inch baking dish and top with cheese. Bake 10 minutes, or until cheese melts and begins to brown. Serve.

Teriyaki Tofu Burger

Preparation time: 10 minutes
Cooking Time: 15 minutes
Servings: 2
Ingredients:

- 2 3 oz. tofu portions, extra firm, pressed between paper towels 15 minutes
- ¼ red onion, sliced
- 2 tbsp. carrot, grated
- 1 tsp margarine
- Butter leaf lettuce
- What you'll need from store cupboard:
- 2 100% whole wheat sandwich thins
- 1 tbsp. teriyaki marinade
- 1 tbsp. Sriracha
- 1 tsp red chili flakes

Directions:
1. Heat grill, or charcoal, to a medium heat.
2. Marinate tofu in teriyaki marinade, red chili flakes and Sriracha.
3. Melt margarine in a small skillet over med-high heat. Add onions and cook until caramelized, about 5 minutes.
4. Grill tofu for 3-4 minutes per side.
5. To assemble, place tofu on bottom roll. Top with lettuce, carrot, and onion. Add top of the roll and serve.

Tofu Curry

Preparation time: 30 minutes
Cooking Time: 2 hours
Servings: 4
Ingredients:

- 2 cup green bell pepper, diced
- 1 cup firm tofu, cut into cubes
- 1 onion, peeled and diced
- What you'll need from store cupboard:
- 1 ½ cups canned coconut milk
- 1 cup tomato paste
- 2 cloves garlic, diced fine
- 2 tbsp. raw peanut butter
- 1 tbsp. garam masala
- 1 tbsp. curry powder
- 1 ½ tsp salt

Directions:

1. Add all Ingredients, except the tofu to a blender or food processor. Process until thoroughly combined.
2. Pour into a crock pot and add the tofu. Cover and cook on high 2 hours.
3. Stir well and serve over cauliflower rice.

Faux Chow Mein

Preparation time: 10 minutes
Cooking Time: 20 minutes
Servings: 4
Ingredients:

- 1 large spaghetti squash, halved and seeds removed
- 3 stalks celery, sliced diagonally
- 1 onion, diced fine
- 2 cup Cole slaw mix
- 2 tsp fresh ginger, grated
- What you'll need from store cupboard:
- ¼ cup Tamari
- 3 cloves garlic, diced fine
- 3-4 tbsp. water
- 2 tbsp. olive oil
- 1 tbsp. Splenda - ¼ tsp pepper

Directions:
1. Place squash, cut side down, in shallow glass dish and add water. Microwave on high 8-10 minutes, or until squash is soft. Use a fork to scoop out the squash into a bowl.
2. In a small bowl, whisk together Tamari, garlic, sugar, ginger, and pepper.
3. Heat oil in large skillet over med-high heat. Add onion and celery and cook, stirring frequently, 3-4 minutes. Add Cole slaw and cook until heated through, about 1 minute.
4. Add the squash and sauce mixture and stir well. Cook 2 minutes, stirring frequently. Serve.

Roasted Tomato and Bell Pepper Soup

Preparation time: 20 minutes
Cooking Time: 35 Minutes
Servings: 6
Ingredients:

- 2 tablespoons extra-virgin olive oil, plus more for coating the baking dish
- 16 plum tomatoes, cored and halved
- 4 celery stalks, coarsely chopped
- 4 red bell peppers, seeded, halved
- 4 garlic cloves, lightly crushed
- 1 sweet onion, cut into eighths
- Sea salt and freshly ground black pepper, to taste
- 6 cups low-sodium chicken broth
- 2 tablespoons chopped fresh basil
- 2 ounces (57 g) goat cheese, grated

Directions:
1. Preheat the oven to 400°F (205°C). Coat a large baking dish lightly with olive oil.
2. Put the tomatoes in the oiled dish, cut side down. Scatter the celery, bell peppers, garlic, and onion on top of the tomatoes. Drizzle with 2 tablespoons of olive oil and season with salt and pepper.

3. Roast in the preheated oven for about 30 minutes, or until the vegetables are fork-tender and slightly charred.
4. Remove the vegetables from the oven. Let them rest for a few minutes until cooled slightly.
5. Transfer to a food processor, along with the chicken broth, and purée until fully mixed and smooth.
6. Pour the purée soup into a medium saucepan and bring it to a simmer over medium-high heat.
7. Sprinkle the basil and grated cheese on top before serving.

Festive Holiday Salad

Preparation time: 30 minutes
Cooking Time: 1 hour
Servings: 8
Ingredients:

- 1 head broccoli, separated into florets
- 1 head cauliflower, separated into florets
- 1 red onion, sliced thin
- 2 cup cherry tomatoes, halved
- ½ cup fat free sour cream
- What you'll need from store cupboard:
- 1 cup lite mayonnaise
- 1 tbsp. Splenda

Directions:
1. In a large bowl combine vegetable.
2. In a small bowl, whisk together mayonnaise, sour cream, and Splenda. Pour over vegetables and toss to mix.
3. Cover and refrigerate at least 1 hour before serving.

Grilled Vegetable & Noodle Salad

Preparation time: 10 minutes
Cooking Time: 10 minutes
Servings: 4
Ingredients:

- 2 ears corn-on-the-cob, husked
- 1 red onion, cut in ½-inch thick slices
- 1 tomato, diced fine
- 1/3 cup fresh basil, diced
- 1/3 cup feta cheese, crumbled
- What you'll need from store cupboard:
- 1 recipe Homemade Noodles, cook & drain - 4 tbsp. Herb Vinaigrette
- Nonstick cooking spray

Directions:
1. Heat grill to medium heat. Spray rack with cooking spray.
2. Place corn and onions on the grill and cook, turning when needed, until lightly charred and tender, about 10 minutes.
3. Cut corn off the cob and place in a medium bowl. Chop the onion and add to the corn.
4. Stir in noodles, tomatoes, basil, and vinaigrette, toss to mix. Sprinkle cheese over top and serve.

Holiday Apple & Cranberry Salad

Preparation time: 10 minutes
Cooking Time: 15 minutes
Servings: 10
Ingredients:

- 12 oz. salad greens
- 3 Honeycrisp apples, sliced thin

- 1/2 lemon
- ½ cup blue cheese, crumbled
- What you'll need from store cupboard:
- Apple Cider Vinaigrette
- 1 cup pecan halves, toasted
- ¾ cup dried cranberries

Directions:

1. Put the apple slices in a large plastic bag and squeeze the half lemon over them. Close the bag and shake to coat.
2. In a large bowl, layer greens, apples, pecans, cranberries, and blue cheese. Just before serving, drizzle with enough vinaigrette to dress the salad. Toss to coat all Ingredients: evenly.

Zucchini "pasta" Salad

Preparation time: 35 minutes
Cooking Time: 1 Hour
Servings: 5
Ingredients:

- 5 oz. zucchini, spiralized
- 1 avocado, peeled and sliced
- 1/3 cup feta cheese, crumbled
- ¼ cup tomatoes, diced
- ¼ cup black olives, diced
- What you'll need from the store cupboard
- 1/3 cup Green Goddess Salad Dressing
- 1 tsp olive oil
- 1 tsp basil
- Salt and pepper to taste

Directions:

1. Place zucchini on paper towel lined cutting board. Sprinkle with a little bit of salt and let sit for 30 minutes to remove excess water. Squeeze gently.
2. Add oil to medium skillet and heat over med-high heat. Add zucchini and cook, stirring frequently, until soft, about 3 – 4 minutes.
3. Transfer zucchini to a large bowl and add remaining Ingredients, except for the avocado. Cover and chill for 1 hour.
4. Serve topped with avocado.

Homemade Vegetable Chili

Preparation time: 10 minutes
Cooking Time: 15 minutes
Servings: 4
Ingredients:

- 2 tablespoons extra-virgin olive oil
- 1 onion, finely chopped
- 1 green bell pepper, deseeded and chopped
- 1 (14-ounce / 397-g) can kidney beans, drained and rinsed
- 2 (14-ounce / 397-g) cans crushed tomatoes
- 2 cups veggie crumbles
- 1 teaspoon garlic powder
- 1 tablespoon chili powder
- ½ teaspoon sea salt

Directions:

1. Heat the olive oil in a large skillet over medium-high heat until shimmering.

2. Add the onion and bell pepper and sauté for 5 minutes, stirring occasionally.
3. Fold in the beans, tomatoes, veggie crumbles, garlic powder, chili powder, and salt. Stir to incorporate and bring them to a simmer.
4. Reduce the heat and cook for an additional 5 minutes, stirring occasionally, or until the mixture is heated through.
5. Allow the mixture to cool for 5 minutes and serve warm.

Collard Greens with Tomato

Preparation time: 10 minutes
Cooking Time: 20 minutes
Servings: 4
Ingredients:

- 1 cup low-sodium vegetable broth, divided
- ½ onion, thinly sliced
- 2 garlic cloves, thinly sliced
- 1 medium tomato, chopped
- 1 large bunch collard greens including stems, roughly chopped
- 1 teaspoon ground cumin
- ½ teaspoon freshly ground black pepper

Directions:

1. Add ½ cup of vegetable broth to a Dutch oven over medium heat and bring to a simmer.
2. Stir in the onion and garlic and cook for about 4 minutes until tender.
3. Add the remaining broth, tomato, greens, cumin, and pepper, and gently stir to combine.
4. Reduce the heat to low and simmer uncovered for 15 minutes. Serve warm.

Okra

Preparation time: 5 minutes
Cooking Time: 10 minutes
Servings: 4
Ingredients:

 1-cup almond flour
 8 ounces fresh okra
 1/2 teaspoon sea salt
 1-cup milk, reduced-fat
 1 egg, pastured

Directions:

1. Crack the egg in a bowl, pour in the milk and whisk until blended.
2. Cut the stem from each okra, then cut it into ½-inch pieces, add them into egg and stir until well coated.
3. Mix flour and salt and add it into a large plastic bag.
4. Working on one okra piece at a time, drain the okra well by letting excess egg drip off, add it to the flour mixture, then seal the bag and shake well until okra is well coated.
5. Place the coated okra on a grease air fryer basket, coat remaining okra pieces in the same manner and place them into the basket.
6. Switch on the air fryer, insert fryer basket, spray okra with oil, then shut with its lid, set the fryer at 390 degrees F and cook for 10 minutes until nicely golden and cooked, stirring okra halfway through the frying.

Grilled Tofu & Veggie Skewers

Preparation time: 10 minutes
Cooking Time: 15 minutes
Servings: 6
Ingredients:

- 1 block tofu
- 2 small zucchinis, sliced
- 1 red bell pepper, cut into 1-inch cubes
- 1 yellow bell pepper, cut into 1-inch cubes
- 1 red onion, cut into 1-inch cubes
- 2 cups cherry tomatoes
- What you'll need from store cupboard:
- 2 tbsp. lite soy sauce
- 3 tsp barbecue sauce
- 2 tsp sesame seeds
- Salt & pepper, to taste
- Nonstick cooking spray

Directions:
1. Press tofu to extract liquid, for about half an hour. Then, cut tofu into cubes and marinate in soy sauce for at least 15 minutes.
2. Heat the grill to med-high heat. Spray the grill rack with cooking spray.
3. Assemble skewers with tofu alternating with vegetables.
4. Grill 2-3 minutes per side until vegetables start to soften, and tofu is golden brown. At the very end of cooking time, season with salt and pepper and brush with barbecue sauce. Serve garnished with sesame seeds.

Brussels Sprout, Avocado, and Wild Rice Bowl

Preparation time: 15 minutes
Cooking time: 15 minutes
Servings: 4
Ingredients:

- 2 cups sliced Brussels sprouts
- 2 teaspoons extra-virgin olive oil, plus 2 tablespoons
- Juice of 1 lemon
- 1 teaspoon Dijon mustard
- 1 garlic clove, minced
- ½ teaspoon salt
- ¼ teaspoon freshly ground black pepper
- 1 cup cooked wild rice
- 1 cup sliced radishes
- 1 avocado, sliced

Directions:
1. Preheat the oven to 400°F. Line a baking sheet with parchment paper.
2. In a medium bowl, toss the Brussels sprouts with 2 teaspoons of olive oil and spread on the prepared baking sheet. Roast for 12 minutes, stirring once, until lightly browned.
3. In a small bowl, mix the remaining 2 tablespoons of olive oil, lemon juice, mustard, garlic, salt, and pepper. In a large bowl, toss the cooked wild rice, radishes, and roasted Brussels sprouts. Drizzle the dressing over the salad and toss. Divide among 4 bowls and top with avocado slices.

Sweet Potato, Chickpea, and Kale Bowl with Creamy Tahini Sauce

Preparation time: 10 minutes
Cooking time: 15 minutes
Servings: 2
Ingredients:
For The Sauce

- 2 tablespoons plain nonfat Greek yogurt
- 1 tablespoon tahini
- 2 tablespoons hemp seeds
- 1 garlic clove, minced - Pinch salt
- Freshly ground black pepper

For The Bowl

- 1 small sweet potato, peeled and finely diced
- 1 teaspoon extra-virgin olive oil
- 1 cup from 1 (15-ounce) can low-sodium chickpeas, drained and rinsed
- 2 cups baby kale

Directions:
To Make the Sauce
1. In a small bowl, whisk together the yogurt and tahini.
2. Stir in the hemp seeds, garlic, and salt. Season with pepper. Add 2 to 3 tablespoons water to create a creamy yet pourable consistency. Set aside.
To Make the Bowl
1. Preheat the oven to 425°F. Line a baking sheet with parchment paper.
2. Arrange the sweet potato on the prepared baking sheet and drizzle with the olive oil. Toss. Roast for 10 to 15 minutes, stirring once, until tender and browned. In each of 2 bowls, arrange ½ cup of chickpeas, 1 cup of kale, and half of the cooked sweet potato. Drizzle with half the creamy tahini sauce and serve.

Baked Tofu and Mixed Vegetable Bowl

Preparation time: 10 minutes
Cooking time: 20 minutes
Servings: 4
Ingredients:

- Nonstick cooking spray
- 1 (14-ounce) container firm tofu, cut into 1½-inch cubes
- 2 tablespoons low-sodium gluten-free soy sauce or tamari
- 1 tablespoon toasted sesame oil
- 1 teaspoon grated fresh ginger
- 1 teaspoon honey - 2 garlic cloves, minced
- 2 teaspoons cornstarch
- ¼ cup water, plus 2 tablespoons
- 2 teaspoons extra-virgin olive oil
- 2 cups thinly sliced bok choy
- 1 cup sliced shiitake mushrooms
- 1 cup thinly sliced carrots
- 1 (14-ounce) can baby corn, drained, and rinsed - 4 scallions, both white and green parts, chopped

Directions:

1. Preheat the oven to 400°F. Line a baking sheet with parchment paper. Spray the parchment paper with nonstick cooking spray.

2. Place the tofu cubes on the prepared baking sheet and bake for 20 minutes, flipping once, until they are browned.

3. In a small bowl, combine the soy sauce, sesame oil, ginger, honey, and garlic. Stir well to combine.

4. In another small bowl, mix the cornstarch with ¼ cup of water and stir to combine. Add the soy sauce mixture, stir together, and set aside.

5. In a large skillet, heat the oil over medium heat. Add the boy choy, mushrooms, and carrots, and cook for 3 minutes, stirring regularly. Add the remaining 2 tablespoons of water, cover, and steam the vegetables for 3 more minutes until just fork-tender. Add the baby corn. Pour the sauce and cooked tofu into the skillet and bring to a boil. Reduce the heat and simmer for 1 to 2 minutes until the sauce thickens. Divide the tofu and vegetables among 4 bowls. Top with scallions and serve.

Mozzarella and Artichoke Stuffed Spaghetti Squash

Preparation time: 10 minutes
Cooking time: 45 minutes
Servings: 4
Ingredients:

- 1 small spaghetti squash, halved and seeded
- ½ cup low-fat cottage cheese
- ¼ cup shredded mozzarella cheese, divided
- 2 garlic cloves, minced
- 1 cup artichoke hearts, chopped
- 1 cup thinly sliced kale
- 1/8 teaspoon salt
- Pinch freshly ground black pepper

Directions:

1. Preheat the oven to 400°F. Line a baking sheet with parchment paper.

2. Place the cut squash halves on the prepared baking sheet cut-side down, and roast for 30 to 40 minutes, depending on the size and thickness of the squash, until they are fork-tender. Set aside to cool slightly.

3. In a large bowl, mix the cottage cheese, 2 tablespoons of mozzarella cheese, garlic, artichoke hearts, kale, salt, and pepper.

4. Preheat the broiler to high.

5. Using a fork, break apart the flesh of the spaghetti squash into strands, being careful to leave the skin intact. Add the strands to the cheese and vegetable mixture. Toss gently to combine.

6. Divide the mixture between the two hollowed-out squash halves and top with the remaining 2 tablespoons of cheese.

7. Broil for 5 to 7 minutes until browned and heated through.

8. Cut each piece of stuffed squash in half to serve.

Mushroom Cutlets with Creamy Sauce

Preparation time: 15 minutes
Cooking time: 20 minutes

Servings: 4
Ingredients:
For the sauce

- 1 tablespoon extra-virgin olive oil
- 2 tablespoons whole-wheat flour
- 1½ cups unsweetened plain almond milk
- ¼ teaspoon salt
- Dash Worcestershire sauce
- Pinch cayenne pepper
- ¼ cup shredded cheddar cheese

For the cutlets

- 2 eggs
- 2 cups chopped mushrooms
- 1 cup quick oats
- 2 scallions, both white and green parts, chopped
- ¼ cup shredded cheddar cheese
- ½ teaspoon salt
- ¼ teaspoon freshly ground black pepper
- 1 tablespoon extra-virgin olive oil

Directions:
To Make the Sauce

1. In a medium saucepan, heat the oil over medium heat. Add the flour and stir constantly for about 2 minutes until browned.

2. Slowly whisk in the almond milk and bring to a boil. Reduce the heat to low and simmer for 6 to 8 minutes until the sauce thickens.

3. Season with the salt, Worcestershire sauce, and cayenne. Add the cheese and stir until melted. Turn off the heat and cover to keep warm while you make the cutlets.

To Make the Cutlets

1. In a large mixing bowl, beat the eggs. Add the mushrooms, oats, scallions, cheese, salt, and pepper. Stir to combine.

2. using your hands, form the mixture into 8 patties, each about ½ inch thick.

3. In a large skillet, heat the oil over medium-high heat. Cook the patties, in batches, if necessary, for 3 minutes per side until crisp and brown.

4. Serve the cutlets warm with sauce drizzled over the top.

Falafel with Creamy Garlic-Yogurt Sauce

Preparation time: 15 minutes
Cooking time: 10 minutes
Servings: 4
Ingredients:
For the sauce

- ¾ cup plain nonfat Greek yogurt
- 3 garlic cloves, minced
- Juice of 1 lemon
- 1 tablespoon extra-virgin olive oil
- ¼ teaspoon salt

For the falafel

- 1 (15-ounce) can low-sodium chickpeas, drained and rinsed
- 2 garlic cloves, roughly chopped
- 2 tablespoons whole-wheat flour
- 2 tablespoons chopped fresh parsley

- ½ teaspoon ground cumin
- ¼ teaspoon salt
- 2 teaspoons canola oil, divided
- 8 large lettuce leaves, chopped
- 1 cucumber, chopped - 1 tomato, diced

Directions:

To Make the Sauce

1. In a small bowl, combine the yogurt, garlic, lemon juice, olive oil, and salt, and mix well. Cover and refrigerate until ready to serve.

To Make the Falafel

1. In a food processor or blender, combine the chickpeas and garlic, and pulse until chopped well but not creamy. Add the flour, parsley, cumin, and salt. Pulse several more times until incorporated.

2. Using your hands, form the mixture into balls, using about 1 tablespoon of mixture for each ball.

3. In a medium skillet, heat 1 teaspoon of canola oil over medium-high heat. Working in batches, add the falafel to the skillet, cooking on each side for 2 to 3 minutes until browned and crisp. Remove the falafel from the skillet, and repeat with the remaining oil and falafel until all are cooked.

4. Divide the lettuce, cucumber, and tomato among 4 plates. Top each plate with 2 falafel and 2 tablespoons of sauce. Serve immediately.

Lentil Loaf

Preparation time: 15 minutes
Cooking time: 50 minutes
Servings: 8
Ingredients:
For The Glaze

- ¼ cup Low-Carb No-Cook Tomato Ketchup (here)
- 1 tablespoon pure maple syrup
- 1 tablespoon low-sodium gluten-free soy sauce or tamari

For The Loaf

- 1 tablespoon extra-virgin olive oil
- 1 cup finely chopped onion
- 1 cup finely chopped mushrooms
- 1 cup finely chopped celery
- 1 cup shredded carrot
- 3 garlic cloves, minced
- 1½ cups brown lentils
- ½ cup brown rice
- 1 bay leaf
- ½ teaspoon dried thyme
- ¼ cup hemp seeds
- 1 teaspoon ground cumin
- 1 teaspoon dried oregano
- 1 teaspoon paprika
- 2 tablespoons tomato paste
- 2 teaspoons low-sodium gluten-free soy sauce or tamari
- ½ teaspoon salt

Directions:

To Make the Glaze

1. In a small bowl, mix together the ketchup, maple syrup, and soy sauce. Set aside.

To Make the Loaf

1. In an Instant Pot, heat the oil on high. Add the onion, mushrooms, celery, carrot, and garlic, and cook for 2 minutes. Add the lentils, rice, bay leaf, thyme, and 3 cups of water. Cook on high pressure for 10 minutes and release the pressure naturally. Remove the bay leaf.

2. If you don't have an Instant Pot, you can make this on the stove top: Heat the oil in a large pot over medium-high heat. Add the onion, mushrooms, celery, carrot, and garlic, and cook for 2 minutes. Add the lentils, rice, bay leaf, thyme, and 3½ cups of water. Bring to a boil, reduce the heat to low, cover, and simmer for 35 to 45 minutes until the water is absorbed and the lentils and rice are tender. Remove the bay leaf and continue with the recipe.

3. Preheat the oven to 350°F.

4. To the pot, add the hemp seeds, cumin, oregano, paprika, tomato paste, soy sauce, and salt. Stir well.

5. Transfer the mixture to a loaf pan, and bake for 20 minutes.

6. Spread the glaze over the loaf, and bake for 20 minutes more. Serve warm.

Chapter 6

Grains, Beans and Legumes

Black Bean and Tomato Soup with Lime Yogurt

Preparation time: 8 hours 10 minutes
Cooking time: 1 hour 33 minutes
Servings: 8
Ingredients:

- 2 tablespoons avocado oil
- 1 medium onion, chopped
- 1 (10-ounce / 284-g) can diced tomatoes and green chilies
- 1 pound (454 g) dried black beans, soaked in water for at least 8 hours, rinsed
- 1 teaspoon ground cumin
- 3 garlic cloves, minced
- 6 cups chicken bone broth, vegetable broth, or water - Kosher salt, to taste
- 1 tablespoon freshly squeezed lime juice
- ¼ cup plain Greek yogurt

Directions:
1. Heat the avocado oil in a nonstick skillet over medium heat until shimmering.
2. Add the onion and sauté for 3 minutes or until translucent.
3. Transfer the onion to a pot, then add the tomatoes and green chilies and their juices, black beans, cumin, garlic, broth, and salt. Stir to combine well. Bring to a boil over medium-high heat, then reduce the heat to low. Simmer for 1 hour and 30 minutes or until the beans are soft. Meanwhile, combine the lime juice with Greek yogurt in a small bowl. Stir to mix well. Pour the soup in a large serving bowl, then drizzle with lime yogurt before serving.
Tip: If you want to make a thicker soup, remove 1 cup of beans from the pot after the simmering, then pour the remaining soup in a food processor. Process to purée the soup until smooth, then move 1 cup of beans back to the soup and serve.

Classic Texas Caviar

Preparation time: 10 minutes
Cooking time: 0 minutes
Servings: 6
Ingredients:
For the Salad:

- 1 ear fresh corn, kernels removed
- 1 cup cooked lima beans
- 1 cup cooked black-eyed peas
- 1 red bell pepper, chopped
- 2 celery stalks, chopped

- ½ red onion, chopped

For the Dressing:

- 3 tablespoons apple cider vinegar
- 1 teaspoon paprika
- 2 tablespoons extra-virgin olive oil

Directions:
1. Combine the corn, beans, peas, bell pepper, celery, and onion in a large bowl. Stir to mix well.
2. Combine the vinegar, paprika, and olive oil in a small bowl. Stir to combine well.
3. Pour the dressing into the salad and toss to mix well. Let sit for 20 minutes to infuse before serving.
Tip: You can replace the lima beans with the same amount of pinto beans for a distinct flavor.

Lettuce Tomato Salad

Preparation time: 15 minutes
Cooking time: 0 minutes
Servings: 4
Ingredients:

- 4 cups chopped iceberg lettuce
- 1 cucumber, chopped
- 10 cherry tomatoes, halved
- 1 cup crumbled feta cheese
- 1 cup pitted black olives
- ½ red onion, thinly sliced
- ½ cup Greek Vinaigrette

Directions:
1. In a large bowl, combine the lettuce, cucumber, tomatoes, feta, olives, and onion. Toss to combine.
2. Toss with the dressing just before serving.

Chicken Cabbage Salad

Preparation time: 10 minutes
Cooking time: 0 minutes
Servings: 1
Ingredients:

- 1 cup shredded cooked rotisserie chicken meat
- 1 cup shredded cabbage or coleslaw mix
- 1 Asian pear, cored, peeled, and julienned
- 2 scallions, white and green parts, sliced on the bias (cut diagonally into thin slices)
- ¼ cup Asian Vinaigrette

Directions:
1. In a large bowl, combine the chicken, cabbage, pear, and scallions.
2. Toss with the vinaigrette just before serving.

Bell Pepper Black Olive Salad

Preparation time: 10 minutes
Cooking time: 0 minutes
Servings: 2
Ingredients:

- 2 cups chopped iceberg lettuce
- 10 cherry tomatoes, halved
- 1 cup pitted black olives, chopped
- 6 ounces ham, chopped
- ½ red onion, chopped
- 1 red bell pepper, seeded and chopped
- 10 basil leaves, torn
- ¼ cup Italian Vinaigrette

Directions:
1. In a large bowl, combine the lettuce, tomatoes, olives, ham, onion, bell pepper, and basil leaves.
2. Toss with the vinaigrette just before serving.

Chickpea Wraps for Quesadillas

Preparation time: 5 minutes
Cooking time: 10 minutes
Servings: 4
Ingredients:

- 1 cup chickpea flour
- 1 cup water
- ¼ teaspoon salt
- Nonstick cooking spray

Directions:
1. In a large bowl, whisk all together until no lumps remain.
2. Spray a skillet with cooking spray and place over medium-high heat.
3. Pour batter in, ¼ cup at a time, and tilt pan to spread thinly.
4. Cook until golden brown on each side, about 2 minutes per side.
5. Use for taco shells, enchiladas, quesadillas or whatever you desire.

Eggs and Snap Peas Fried Rice

Preparation time: 5 minutes
Cooking time: 15 minutes
Servings: 8
Ingredients:

- 2 cups sugar snap peas
- 2 egg whites
- 1 egg
- 1 cup instant brown rice, cooked according to directions
- 2 tablespoons lite soy sauce

Directions:
1. Add the peas to the cooked rice and mix to combine.
2. In a small skillet, scramble the egg and egg whites.
3. Add the rice and peas to the skillet and stir in soy sauce. Cook, stirring frequently, about 2 to 3 minutes, or until heated through. Serve.

Baked Margarine Cheesy Fish

Preparation time: 10 minutes
Cooking time: 20 minutes

Servings: 4
Ingredients:

- 1 pound (454 g) flounder
- 2 cups green beans
- 4 tablespoons margarine
- 8 basil leaves
  - ounces (50 g) pork rinds
- ½ cup reduced fat Parmesan cheese
- 3 cloves garlic
- Salt and ground black pepper, to taste
- Nonstick cooking spray

Directions:
1. Heat oven to 350°F (180°C). Spray a baking dish with cooking spray.
2. Steam green beans until they are almost tender, about 15 minutes, less if you use frozen or canned beans. Lay green beans in the prepared dish.
3. Place the fish filets over the green beans and season with salt and pepper.
4. Place the garlic, basil, pork rinds, and Parmesan in a food processor and pulse until mixture resembles crumbs. Sprinkle over fish. Cut margarine into small pieces and place on top.
5. Bake 15 to 20 minutes or until fish flakes easily with a fork. Serve.

The Best Ever Veggie Fajitas

Preparation time: 10 minutes
Cooking time: 15 minutes
Servings: 4
Ingredients:
Guacamole:

- 2 small avocados pitted and peeled
- 1 teaspoon freshly squeezed lime juice
- ¼ teaspoon salt
- 9 cherry tomatoes, halved

Fajitas:

- 1 red bell pepper
- 1 green bell pepper
- 1 small white onion
- Avocado oil cooking spray
- 1 cup canned low-sodium black beans, drained and rinsed
- ½ teaspoon ground cumin
- ¼ teaspoon chili powder
- ¼ teaspoon garlic powder
- 4 (6-inch) yellow corn tortillas

Directions:
Make the Guacamole:
1. In a medium bowl, use a fork to mash the avocados with the lime juice and salt.
2. Gently stir in the cherry tomatoes.
Make the Fajitas:
3. Cut the red bell pepper, green bell pepper, and onion into ½-inch slices.
4. Heat a large skillet over medium heat. When hot, coat the cooking surface with cooking spray. Put the peppers, onion, and beans into the skillet.
5. Add the cumin, chili powder, and garlic powder, and stir.
6. Cover and cook for 15 minutes, stirring halfway through.

7. Divide the fajita mixture equally between the tortillas, and top with guacamole and any preferred garnishes.

Weeknight Chickpea Spaghetti Bolognese

Preparation time: 5 minutes
Cooking time: 25 minutes
Servings: 4
Ingredients:

- 1 (3- to 4-pound / 1.4- to 1.8-kg) spaghetti squash
- ½ teaspoon ground cumin
- 1 cup no-sugar-added spaghetti sauce
- 1 (15-ounce / 425-g) can low-sodium chickpeas, drained and rinsed
- 6 ounces (170 g) extra-firm tofu

Directions:
1. Preheat the oven to 400°F (205°C).
2. Cut the squash in half lengthwise. Scoop out the seeds and discard.
3. Season both halves of the squash with the cumin, and place them on a baking sheet cut-side down. Roast for 25 minutes.
4. Meanwhile, heat a medium saucepan over low heat, and pour in the spaghetti sauce and chickpeas.
5. Press the tofu between two layers of paper towels, and gently squeeze out any excess water.
6. Crumble the tofu into the sauce and cook for 15 minutes.
7. Remove the squash from the oven, and comb through the flesh of each half with a fork to make thin strands.
8. Divide the "spaghetti" into four portions, and top each portion with one-quarter of the sauce.

Fat free Sofrito Dumplings

Preparation time: 20 minutes
Cooking time: 15 minutes
Servings: 8 to 10
Ingredients:

- 4 cups water
- 4 cups low-sodium vegetable broth
- 1 cup cassava flour
- 1 cup gluten-free all-purpose flour
- 2 teaspoons baking powder
- 1 teaspoon salt
- 1 cup fat-free milk
- 2 tablespoons bottled chimichurri or sofrito

Directions:
1. In a large pot, bring the water and the broth to a slow boil over medium-high heat.
2. In a large mixing bowl, whisk the cassava flour, all-purpose flour, baking powder, and salt together.
3. In a small bowl, whisk the milk and chimichurri together until combined.
4. Stir the wet Ingredients: into the dry Ingredients: a little at a time to create a firm dough.
5. With clean hands, pinch offs a small piece of dough. Roll into a ball, and gently flatten in the palm of your hand, forming a disk. Repeat until no dough remains.
6. Carefully drop the dumplings one at a time into the boiling liquid. Cover and simmer for 15 minutes, or until the dumplings

are cooked through. You can test by inserting a fork into the dumpling; it should come out clean.
7. Serve warm.

Garlic Zucchini Chicken Soup

Preparation time: 10 minutes
Cooking time: 15 minutes
Servings: 4
Ingredients:

- 2 tablespoons extra-virgin olive oil
- 12 ounces (336 g) chicken breast, chopped
- 1 onion, chopped
- 2 carrots, chopped
- 2 celery stalks, chopped
- 2 garlic cloves
- 6 cups unsalted chicken broth
- 1 teaspoon dried thyme
- 1 teaspoon sea salt
- 2 medium zucchinis cut into noodles (or store-bought zucchini noodles)

Directions:
1. In a large pot over medium-high heat, heat the olive oil until it shimmers.
2. Add the chicken and cook until it is opaque, about 5 minutes. With a slotted spoon, remove the chicken from the pot and set aside on a plate.
3. Add the onion, carrots, and celery to the pot. Cook, stirring occasionally, until the vegetables are soft, about 5 minutes.
4. Add the garlic and cook, stirring constantly, for 30 seconds. Add the chicken broth, thyme, and salt. Bring to a boil, and reduce the heat to medium.
5. Add the zucchini and return the chicken to the pan, adding any juices that have collected on the plate.
6. Cook, stirring occasionally, until the zucchini noodles are soft, 1 to 2 minutes more.

Chestnut Lettuce Wraps

Preparation time: 10 minutes
Cooking time: 0 minutes
Servings: 2
Ingredients:

- 1 tablespoon freshly squeezed lemon juice
- 1 teaspoon curry powder
- 1 teaspoon reduced-sodium soy sauce
- ½ teaspoon sriracha (or to taste)
- ½ cup canned water chestnuts, drained and chopped
- 2 (2.6-ounce/73.7 g) package tuna packed in water, drained
- 2 large butter lettuce leaves

Directions:
1. In a medium bowl, whisk together lemon juice; curry powder, soy sauce, and sriracha.
2. Add the water chestnuts and tuna. Stir to combine.
3. Serve wrapped in the lettuce leaves.

Crispy Cowboy Black Bean Fritters

Preparation time: 10 minutes
Cooking time: 25 minutes
Servings: 20 Fritters

Ingredients:

- 1 ¾ cups all-purpose flour
- ½ teaspoon cumin
- 2 teaspoons baking powder
- 2 teaspoons salt
- ½ teaspoon black pepper
- 4 egg whites, lightly beaten
- 1 cup salsa
- 2 (16-ounce / 454-g) cans no-salt-added black beans, rinsed and drained
- 1 tablespoon canola oil, plus extra if needed

Directions:

1. Combine the flour, cumin, baking powder, salt, and pepper in a large bowl, then mix in the egg whites and salsa. Add the black beans and stir to mix well.
2. Heat the canola oil in a nonstick skillet over medium-high heat.
3. Spoon 1 teaspoon of the mixture into the skillet to make a fritter. Make more fritters to coat the bottom of the skillet. Keep a little space between each two fritters. You may need to work in batches to avoid overcrowding.
4. Cook for 3 minutes or until the fritters are golden brown on both sides. Flip the fritters and flatten with a spatula halfway through the cooking time. Repeat with the remaining mixture. Add more oil as needed.
5. Serve immediately.

Dandelion and Beet Greens

Preparation time: 10 minutes
Cooking time: 15 minutes
Servings: 4
Ingredients:

- 1 tablespoon olive oil
- ½ Vidalia onion, thinly sliced
- 1 bunch dandelion greens, cut into ribbons
- 1 bunch beet greens, cut into ribbons
- ½ cup low-sodium vegetable broth
- 1 (15-ounce / 425-g) can no-salt-added black beans
- Salt and freshly ground black pepper, to taste

Directions:

1. Heat the olive oil in a nonstick skillet over low heat until shimmering.
2. Add the onion and sauté for 3 minutes or until translucent.
3. Add the dandelion and beet greens, and broth to the skillet. Cover and cook for 8 minutes or until wilted.
4. Add the black beans and cook for 4 minutes or until soft. Sprinkle with salt and pepper. Stir to mix well.
5. Serve immediately.

Tip: You can use collard greens, spinach, arugula, or Swiss chard to replace the beet greens or dandelion greens.

Black Bean, Corn, and Chicken Soup

Preparation time: 10 minutes
Cooking time: 25 minutes
Servings: 7
Ingredients:

- 2 tablespoons olive oil

- ½ onion, diced
- 1 pound (454 g) boneless and skinless chicken breast, cut into ½-inch cubes
- ½ teaspoon Adobo seasoning, divided
- ¼ teaspoon black pepper
- 1 (15-ounce / 425-g) can no-salt-added black beans, rinsed and drained
- 1 (14.5-ounce / 411-g) can fire-roasted tomatoes
- ½ cup frozen corn
- ½ teaspoon cumin
- 1 tablespoon chili powder
- 5 cups low-sodium chicken broth

Directions:

1. Grease a stockpot with olive oil and heat over medium-high heat until shimmering.
2. Add the onion and sauté for 3 minutes or until translucent.
3. Add the chicken breast and sprinkle with Adobo seasoning and pepper. Put the lid on and cook for 6 minutes or until lightly browned. Shake the pot halfway through the cooking time.
4. Add the remaining Ingredients. Reduce the heat to low and simmer for 15 minutes or until the black beans are soft.
5. Serve immediately.

Tip: You can use paprika, black pepper, onion powder, dried oregano, cumin, garlic powder, chili powder, and salt to make your own Adobo seasoning.

Kale & Carrot Veggie Soup

Preparation time: 10 minutes
Cooking time: 15 minutes
Servings: 2
Ingredients:

- 2 tablespoons extra-virgin olive oil
- 1 onion, finely chopped
- 1 carrot, chopped
- 1 cup chopped kale (stems removed)
- 3 garlic cloves, minced
- 1 cup canned lentils, drained and rinsed
- 1 cup unsalted vegetable broth
- 2 teaspoons dried rosemary (or 1 tablespoon chopped fresh rosemary)
- ½ teaspoon sea salt
- ¼ teaspoons freshly ground black pepper

Directions:

1. In a large pot over medium-high heat, heat the olive oil until it shimmers.
2. Add the onion and carrot and cook, stirring, until the vegetables begin to soften, about 3 minutes.
3. Add the kale and cook for 3 minutes more. Add the garlic and cook, stirring constantly, for 30 seconds.
4. Stir in the lentils, vegetable broth, rosemary, salt, and pepper. Bring to a simmer. Simmer, stirring occasionally, for 5 minutes more.

Egg Pea Mix wrapped in Kale Leaves

Preparation time: 10 minutes
Cooking time: 0 minutes

Servings: 2

Ingredients:

- 1 teaspoon Dijon mustard
- 1 tablespoon chopped fresh dill
- ½ teaspoon sea salt
- ¼ teaspoon paprika
- 4 hard-boiled large eggs, chopped
- 1 cup shelled fresh peas
- 2 tablespoons finely chopped red onion
- 2 large kale leaves

Directions:

1. In a medium bowl, whisk together mustard, dill, salt, and paprika.

2. Stir in the eggs, peas, and onion.

3. Serve wrapped in kale leaves.

Pepperoni Cheesed Pita

Preparation time: 10 minutes
Cooking time: 0 minutes
Servings: 2
Ingredients:

- ½ cup tomato sauce
- ½ teaspoon oregano
- ½ teaspoon garlic powder
- ½ cup chopped black olives
- 2 canned artichoke hearts, drained and chopped
- 2 ounces pepperoni, chopped
- ½ cup shredded mozzarella cheese
- 1 whole-wheat pita, halved

Directions:

1. In a medium bowl, stir together the tomato sauce, oregano, and garlic powder.

2. Add the olives, artichoke hearts, pepperoni, and cheese. Stir to mix.

3. Spoon the mixture into the pita halves.

Tomato Green Chilies Soup with Lime Yogurt

Preparation time: 8 hours 10 minutes
Cooking time: 1 hour 33 minutes
Servings: 8
Ingredients:

- 2 tablespoons avocado oil
- 1 medium onion, chopped
- 1 (10-ounce / 284-g) can diced tomatoes and green chillies
- 1 pound (454 g) dried black beans, soaked in water for at least 8 hours, rinsed
- 1 teaspoon ground cumin
- 3 garlic cloves, minced
- 6 cup chicken bone broth, vegetable broth, or water
- Kosher salt, to taste
- 1 tablespoon freshly squeezed lime juice
- ¼ cup Low-fat Greek yogurt

Directions:

1. Heat the avocado oil in a nonstick skillet over medium heat until shimmering.

2. Add the onion and sauté for 3 minutes or until translucent.

3. Transfer the onion to a pot, then add the tomatoes and green chilies and their juices, black beans, cumin, garlic, broth, and salt. Stir to combine well.

4. Bring to a boil over medium-high heat, and then reduce the heat to low. Simmer for 1 hour and 30 minutes or until the beans are soft.

5. Meanwhile, combine the lime juice with Greek yogurt in a small bowl. Stir to mix well.

6. Pour the soup in a large serving bowl, and then drizzle with lime yogurt before serving.

Perfect Corn Salad with Paprika Dressing

Preparation time: 10 minutes
Cooking time: 0 minutes
Servings: 6
Ingredients:
Salad:

- 1 ear fresh corn, kernels removed
- 1 cup cooked lima beans
- 1 cup cooked black-eyed peas
- 1 red bell pepper, chopped
- 2 celery stalks, chopped
- ½ red onion, chopped

Dressing:

- 3 tablespoons apple cider vinegar
- 1 teaspoon paprika
- 2 tablespoons extra-virgin olive oil

Directions:

1. Combine the corn, beans, peas, bell pepper, celery, and onion in a large bowl. Stir to mix well.

2. Combine the vinegar, paprika, and olive oil in a small bowl. Stir to combine well.

3. Pour the dressing into the salad and toss to mix well. Let sit for 20 minutes to infuse before serving.

Low Sodium Veggie Greens with Black Beans

Preparation time: 10 minutes
Cooking time: 15 minutes
Servings: 4
Ingredients:

- 1 tablespoon olive oil
- ½ Vidalia onion, thinly sliced
- 1 bunch dandelion greens cut into ribbons
- 1 bunch beet greens, cut into ribbons
- ½ cup low-sodium vegetable broth
- 1 (15-ounce / 425-g) can no-salt-added black beans
- Salt and freshly ground black pepper, to taste

Directions:

1. Heat the olive oil in a nonstick skillet over low heat until shimmering.

2. Add the onion and sauté for 3 minutes or until translucent.

3. Add the dandelion and beet greens, and broth to the skillet. Cover and cook for 8 minutes or until wilted.

4. Add the black beans and cook for 4 minutes or until soft. Sprinkle with salt and pepper. Stir to mix well.

5. Serve immediately.

Classy Chicken Black Bean Soup

Preparation time: 10 minutes
Cooking time: 25 minutes
Servings: 7
Ingredients:

- 2 tablespoons olive oil
- ½ onion, diced
- 1 pound (454 g) boneless and skinless chicken breast, cut into ½-inch cubes
- ½ teaspoon Adobo seasoning, divided
- ¼ teaspoon black pepper
- 1 (15-ounce / 425-g) can no-salt-added black beans, rinsed, and drained
- 1 (14.5-ounce / 411-g) can fire-roasted tomatoes
- ½ cup frozen corn
- ½ teaspoon cumin
- 1 tablespoon chili powder
- 5 cups low-sodium chicken broth

Directions:
1. Grease a stockpot with olive oil and heat over medium-high heat until shimmering.
2. Add the onion and sauté for 3 minutes or until translucent.
3. Add the chicken breast and sprinkle with Adobo seasoning and pepper. Put the lid on and cook for 6 minutes or until lightly browned. Shake the pot halfway through the cooking time.
4. Add the remaining Ingredients. Reduce the heat to low and simmer for 15 minutes or until the black beans are soft.
5. Serve immediately.

Vegetable Broth Kidney Beans Veggie Bowl

Preparation time: 10 minutes
Cooking time: 8 to 12 minutes
Servings: 8
Ingredients:

- 2 tablespoons olive oil
- 1 medium yellow onion, chopped
- 1 cup crushed tomatoes
- 2 garlic cloves, minced
- 2 cups low sodium canned red kidney beans, rinsed
- 1 cup chopped green beans
- ¼ cup low-sodium vegetable broth
- 1 teaspoon smoked paprika
- Salt, to taste

Directions:
1. Heat the olive oil in a nonstick skillet over medium heat until shimmering.
2. Add the onion, tomatoes, and garlic. Sauté for 3 to 5 minutes or until fragrant and the onion is translucent.
3. Add the kidney beans, green beans, and broth to the skillet. Sprinkle with paprika and salt, then sauté to combine well.
4. Cover the skillet and cook for 5 to 7 minutes or until the vegetables are tender. Serve immediately.

Spicy Brown Rice with Red Pepper & Paprika

Preparation time: 15 minutes
Cooking time: 20 minutes
Servings: 4
Ingredients:

- 1 tablespoon extra-virgin olive oil
- 1 bunch collard greens, stemmed and cut into chiffonade
- 1 carrot, cut into 2-inch matchsticks
- 1 red onion, thinly sliced
- ½ cup low-sodium vegetable broth
- 2 tablespoons coconut amino
- 1 garlic clove, minced
- 1 cup cooked brown rice
- 1 large egg
- 1 teaspoon red pepper flakes
- 1 teaspoon paprika
- Salt, to taste

Directions:
1. Heat the olive oil in a Dutch oven or a nonstick skillet over medium heat until shimmering.
2. Add the collard greens and sauté for 4 minutes or until wilted.
3. Add the carrot, onion, broth, coconut amino, and garlic to the Dutch oven, then cover and cook 6 minutes or until the carrot is tender.
4. Add the brown rice and cook for 4 minutes. Keep stirring during the cooking.
5. Break the egg over them, and then cook and scramble the egg for 4 minutes or until the egg is set.
6. Turn off the heat and sprinkle with red pepper flakes, paprika, and salt before serving.

Chicken Rice with Almond Cranberry Salad

Preparation time: 10 minutes
Cooking time: 45 minutes
Servings: 6 Cups
Ingredients:
Rice:

- 2½ cups chicken bone broth, vegetable broth, or water
- 2 cups wild rice blend, rinsed
- 1 teaspoon kosher salt

Dressing:

- Juice of 1 medium orange (about ¼ cup)
- 1½ teaspoons grated orange zest
- ¼ cup white wine vinegar
- 1 teaspoon pure maple syrup
- ¼ cup extra-virgin olive oil

Salad:

- ½ cup sliced almonds, toasted
- ¾ cup unsweetened dried cranberries
- Freshly ground black pepper, to taste

Directions:
Make the Rice:

1. Pour the broth in a pot, then add the rice and sprinkle with salt. Bring to a boil over medium-high heat.

2. Reduce the heat to low. Cover the pot, and then simmer for 45 minutes.

3. Turn off the heat and fluff the rice with a fork. Set aside until ready to use.

Make the Dressing:

4. When cooking the rice, make the dressing: Combine the Ingredients: for the dressing in a small bowl. Stir to combine well. Set aside until ready to use.

Make the Salad:

5. Put the cooked rice, almonds, and cranberries in a bowl, and then sprinkle with black pepper. Add the dressing, then toss to combine well.

6. Serve immediately.

Apple and Almond Butter Spread Pita

Preparation time: 10 minutes
Cooking time: 0 minutes
Servings: 2
Ingredients:
- ½ apple, cored and chopped
- ¼ cup almond butter
- ½ teaspoon cinnamon
- 1 whole-wheat pita, halved

Directions:

1. In a medium bowl, stir together the apple, almond butter, and cinnamon.

2. Spread with a spoon into the pita pocket halves.

Baby Spinach Walnut Salad

Preparation time: 10 minutes
Cooking time: 0 minutes
Servings: 2
Ingredients:
- 4 cups baby spinach
- ½ pear, cored, peeled, and chopped
- ¼ cup whole walnuts, chopped
- 2 tablespoons apple cider vinegar
- 2 tablespoons extra-virgin olive oil
- 1 teaspoon peeled and grated fresh ginger
- ½ teaspoon Dijon mustard
- ½ teaspoon sea salt

Directions:

1. Layer the spinach on the bottom of two mason jars. Top with the pear and walnuts.

2. In a small bowl, whisk together the vinegar, oil, ginger, mustard, and salt. Put in another lidded container. Shake the dressing before serving and add it to the mason jars. Close the jars and shake to distribute the dressing.

Red Kidney Beans with Tomatoes

Preparation time: 10 minutes
Cooking time: 8 to 12 minutes
Servings: 8
Ingredients:
- 2 tablespoons olive oil
- 1 medium yellow onion, chopped
- 1 cup crushed tomatoes
- 2 garlic cloves, minced
- 2 cups low sodium canned red kidney beans, rinsed
- 1 cup chopped green beans
- ¼ cup low-sodium vegetable broth
- 1 teaspoon smoked paprika
- Salt, to taste

Directions:

1. Heat the olive oil in a nonstick skillet over medium heat until shimmering.

2. Add the onion, tomatoes, and garlic. Sauté for 3 to 5 minutes or until fragrant and the onion is translucent.

3. Add the kidney beans, green beans, and broth to the skillet. Sprinkle with paprika and salt, then sauté to combine well.

4. Cover the skillet and cook for 5 to 7 minutes or until the vegetables are tender. Serve immediately.

Tip: You can use the same amount of water to replace the vegetable broth.

Brown Rice with Carrot, and Scrambled Egg

Preparation time: 15 minutes
Cooking time: 20 minutes
Servings: 4
Ingredients:
- 1 tablespoon extra-virgin olive oil
- 1 bunch collard greens, stemmed and cut into chiffonade
- 1 carrot, cut into 2-inch matchsticks
- 1 red onion, thinly sliced
- ½ cup low-sodium vegetable broth
- 2 tablespoons coconut aminos
- 1 garlic clove, minced
- 1 cup cooked brown rice
- 1 large egg
- 1 teaspoon red pepper flakes
- 1 teaspoon paprika
- Salt, to taste

Directions:

1. Heat the olive oil in a Dutch oven or a nonstick skillet over medium heat until shimmering.

2. Add the collard greens and sauté for 4 minutes or until wilted.

3. Add the carrot, onion, broth, coconut aminos, and garlic to the Dutch oven, then cover and cook 6 minutes or until the carrot is tender.

4. Add the brown rice and cook for 4 minutes. Keep stirring during the cooking.

5. Break the egg over them, then cook and scramble the egg for 4 minutes or until the egg is set.

6. Turn off the heat and sprinkle with red pepper flakes, paprika, and salt before serving.

Tip: You can use low-sodium soy sauce to replace the coconut aminos.

Wild Rice and Cranberries Salad

Preparation time: 10 minutes
Cooking time: 45 minutes
Servings: 6 Cups

Ingredients:

For the Rice:

- 2½ cups chicken bone broth, vegetable broth, or water
- 2 cups wild rice blend, rinsed
- 1 teaspoon kosher salt

For the Dressing:

- Juice of 1 medium orange (about ¼ cup)
- 1½ teaspoons grated orange zest
- ¼ cup white wine vinegar
- 1 teaspoon pure maple syrup
- ¼ cup extra-virgin olive oil

For the Salad:

- ½ cup sliced almonds, toasted
- ¾ cup unsweetened dried cranberries
- Freshly ground black pepper, to taste

Directions:

For the Rice

1. Pour the broth in a pot, then add the rice and sprinkle with salt. Bring to a boil over medium-high heat.
2. Reduce the heat to low. Cover the pot, then simmer for 45 minutes.
3. Turn off the heat and fluff the rice with a fork. Set aside until ready to use.

For the Dressing

1. When cooking the rice, make the dressing: Combine the Ingredients: for the dressing in a small bowl. Stir to combine well. Set aside until ready to use.

For the Salad

1. Put the cooked rice, almonds, and cranberries in a bowl, then sprinkle with black pepper. Add the dressing, then toss to combine well.
2. Serve immediately.

Tip: You can combine the Ingredients: for the dressing in a jar and shake to combine. So, you can keep the dressing and undressed salad in the refrigerate for future enjoyment.

Macaroni and Vegetable Pie

Preparation time: 15 minutes
Cooking time: 30 minutes
Servings: 6
Ingredients:

- 1 (1-pound / 454-g) package whole-wheat macaroni
- 2 celery stalks, thinly sliced
- 1 small yellow onion, chopped
- 2 garlic cloves, minced
- Salt, to taste
- ¼ teaspoon freshly ground black pepper
- 2 tablespoons chickpea flour
- 2 cups grated reduced-fat sharp Cheddar cheese
- 1 cup fat-free milk
- 2 large zucchinis, finely grated and squeezed dry
- 2 roasted red peppers, chopped into ¼-inch pieces

Directions:

1. Preheat the oven to 350°F (180°C).
2. Bring a pot of water to a boil, then add the macaroni and cook for 4 minutes or until al dente.
3. Drain the macaroni and transfer to a large bowl. Reserve 1 cup of the macaroni water.
4. Pour the macaroni water in an oven-safe skillet and heat over medium heat.
5. Add the celery, onion, garlic, salt, and black pepper to the skillet and sauté for 4 minutes or until tender.
6. Gently mix in the chickpea flour, then fold in the cheese and milk. Keep stirring until the mixture is thick and smooth.
7. Add the cooked macaroni, zucchini, and red peppers. Stir to combine well.
8. Cover the skillet with aluminum foil and transfer it to the preheated oven.
9. Bake for 15 minutes or until the cheese melts, then remove the foil and bake for 5 more minutes or until lightly browned.
10. Remove the pie from the oven and serve immediately.

Tip: You can use the organic quinoa pasta to replace the macaroni to make this recipe gluten-free.

Chapter 7

Fish and Seafood

Sea Bass and Rice

Preparation time: 10 minutes
Cooking time: 20 minutes
Servings: 4
Ingredients:

- 1pound sea bass fillets, boneless, skinless and cubed 1cup wild rice - 2cups chicken stock - 2scallions, chopped
- 1red bell pepper, chopped
- 1teaspoon turmeric powder
- 1tablespoon chives, chopped
- Salt and black pepper to the taste
- A drizzle of olive oil

Directions:
1. Grease the air fryer's pan with the oil, add the fish, rice, stock and the other Ingredients, toss gently and cook at 380 degrees F and cook for 20 minutes, stirring halfway.
2. Divide between plates and serve.

Sea Bass and Cauliflower

Preparation time: 5 minutes
Cooking time: 20 minutes
Servings: 4
Ingredients:

- 1pound sea bass fillets, boneless and cubed
- 1cup cauliflower florets
- 2tablespoons butter, melted
- 1teaspoon garam masala
- 1/2cup chicken stock
- 1tablespoon parsley, chopped
- Salt and black pepper to the taste

Directions:
1. In your air fryer, combine the fish with the cauliflower and the other Ingredients, toss gently and cook at 380 degrees F for 20 minutes.
2. Divide everything between plates and serve.

Cajun Salmon

Preparation Time: 12 minutes
Cooking Time: 0
Servings: 2
Ingredients:

- 2(4-oz. salmon fillets, skin removed
- 2tbsp. unsalted butter; melted.
- 1tsp. paprika
- 1/4tsp. ground black pepper

- 1/8tsp. ground cayenne pepper
- 1/2tsp. garlic powder.

Directions:
1. Brush each fillet with butter. Combine remaining Ingredients: in a small bowl and then rub onto fish. Place fillets into the air fryer basket
2. Bring the temperature to 390 Degrees F and set the timer for 7 minutes. When fully cooked, internal temperature will be 145 Degrees F. Serve immediately.

Trout and Zucchinis

Preparation Time: 20 minutes
Cooking Time: 0
Servings: 4
Ingredients:

- 3zucchinis, cut in medium chunks
- 4trout fillets; boneless
- 1/4cup tomato sauce
- 1garlic clove; minced
- 1/2cup cilantro; chopped.
- 1tbsp. lemon juice
- 2tbsp. olive oil
- Salt and black pepper to taste.

Directions:
1. In a pan that fits your air fryer, mix the fish with the other Ingredients, toss, introduce in the fryer and cook at 380F for 15 minutes. Divide everything between plates and serve right away

Crab Cakes

Preparation Time: 20 minutes
Cooking Time: 0
Servings: 4
Ingredients:

- 1/2medium green bell pepper; seeded and chopped
- 1/4cup chopped green onion
- 1large egg.
- 2(6-oz. cans lump crabmeat
- 1/4cup blanched finely ground almond flour.
- 1/2tbsp. lemon juice
- 2tbsp. full-fat mayonnaise
- 1/2tsp. Old Bay seasoning
- 1/2tsp. Dijon mustard

Directions:
1. Take a large bowl, merge all Ingredients. Set into four balls and flatten into patties. Place patties into the air fryer basket
2. Adjust the temperature to 350 Degrees F and set the timer for 10 minutes.

3. Flip patties halfway through the cooking time. Serve warm.

Air Fried Catfish

Preparation time: 5 minutes
Cooking time: 20 minutes
Servings: 4
Ingredients:

- 4catfish fillets
- 1tbsp. olive oil
- 1/4 cup fish seasoning
- 1tbsp. fresh parsley, chopped

Directions:
1. Preheat the air fryer to 400 F.
2. Spray air fryer basket with cooking spray.
3. Seasoned fish with seasoning and place into the air fryer basket.
4. Drizzle fish fillets with oil and cook for 10 minutes.
5. Turn fish to another side and cook for 10 minutes more.
6. Garnish with parsley and serve.

Garlic Parmesan Shrimp

Preparation time: 5 minutes
Cooking time: 20 minutes
Servings: 2
Ingredients:

- 1pound shrimp, deveined and peeled
- 1/2 cup parmesan cheese, grated
- 1/4 cup cilantro, diced
- 1 tablespoon olive oil
- 1 teaspoon salt
- 1 teaspoon fresh cracked pepper
- 1 tablespoon lemon juice
- 6 garlic cloves, diced

Directions:
1. Warmth the Air fryer to 350 F and grease an Air fryer basket.
2. Drizzle shrimp with olive oil and lemon juice and season with garlic, salt and cracked pepper.
3. Secure the bowl with plastic wrap and refrigerate for about hours.
4. Stir in the parmesan cheese and cilantro to the bowl and transfer to the Air fryer basket.
5. Cook for about 10 minutes and serve immediately.

Asian Sesame Cod

Preparation Time: 5 Minutes
Cooking Time: 7 to 9 Minutes
Servings: 1
Ingredients:

- 1 Tbsp. reduced-sodium soy sauce
- 2 tsps. Honey
- 1 tsp. sesame seeds
- 6 oz. (170 g.) cod fillet

Directions:
1. In a lesser bowl, put the soy sauce and honey.
2. Sprig the air fryer basket with nonstick cooking spray, then place the cod in the basket, brush with the soy mixture, and sprinkle sesame seeds on top. Roast at 360°F (182°C) for 7 to 9 minutes or until opaque.

3. Remove the fish and allow cooling on a wire rack for 5 minutes before serving.

Easy Tuna Wraps

Preparation Time: 10 Minutes
Cooking Time: 4 to 7 Minutes
Servings: 4
Ingredients:

- 1 lb. (454 g.) fresh tuna steak, cut into 1-inch cubes
- 1 Tbsp. grated fresh ginger
- 2 Garlic cloves, minced
- ½ tsp. toasted sesame oil
- 4 Low-sodium whole-wheat tortillas
- ¼ C. low-fat mayonnaise
- 2 C. shredded romaine lettuce
- 1 Red bell pepper, thinly sliced

Directions:
1. In a medium bowl, mix the tuna, ginger, garlic, and sesame oil. Let it stand for 10 minutes, and then transfer it to the air fryer basket.
2. Air fry at 390°F (199°C) for 4 to 7 minutes, or until done to your liking and lightly browned.
3. Make wraps with tuna, tortillas, mayonnaise, lettuce, and bell pepper. Serve immediately.

Mustard-Crusted Sole

Preparation Time: 5 Minutes
Cooking Time: 8 to 11 Minutes
Servings: 4
Ingredients:
5 tsps. Low-sodium yellow mustard

- 1 Tbsp. freshly squeezed lemon juice
- 4 (31/2-oz./99-g.) Sole fillets
- ½ tsp. dried thyme
- ½ tsp. dried marjoram
- 1/8 tsp. freshly ground black pepper
- 1 Slice low-sodium whole-wheat bread, crumbled

2 tsps. Olive oil
Directions:
1. In a small bowl, blend the mustard and lemon juice. Spread this evenly over the fillets. Place them in the air fryer basket.
2. In another small bowl, mix the thyme, marjoram, pepper, bread crumbs, and olive oil. Mix until combined.
3. Gently but firmly press the spice mixture onto each fish fillet's top.
4. Bake at 320°F (160°C) for 8 to 11 minutes, or until the fish grasps an inner temperature of at least 145°F (63°C) on a meat thermometer and the topping is browned and crisp. Serve immediately.

Baked Salmon with Garlic Parmesan Topping

Preparation Time: 5 Minutes
Cooking Time: 20 Minutes
Servings: 4
Ingredients:

- 1 lb. Wild-caught salmon filets
- 2 Tbsps. margarine

- ¼ C. reduced-fat parmesan cheese, grated
- ¼ C. light mayonnaise
- 2-3 Garlic cloves, diced
- 2 Tbsps. parsley
- Salt and pepper

Directions:

1. Heat the oven to 350°F and line a baking pan with parchment paper.

2. Place the salmon on the pan and season with salt and pepper.

3. In a medium skillet, over medium heat, melt butter. Add garlic and cook, stirring 1 minute.

4. Reduce heat to low and add the remaining Ingredients. Stir until everything is melted and combined.

5. Spread all evenly over the salmon and bake 15 minutes for thawed fish or 20 for frozen. Salmon is done when it flakes easily with a fork.

Blackened Shrimp

Preparation Time: 5 Minutes
Cooking Time: 5 Minutes
Servings: 4
Ingredients:

- 1 ½ lb. Shrimps, peeled and deveined
- 4 Lime wedges
- 4 Tbsps. cilantro, chopped
- 4 Garlic cloves, diced
- 1 Tbsp. chili powder
- 1 Tbsp. paprika
- 1 Tbsp. olive oil
- 2 tsps. Splenda brown sugar
- 1 tsp. cumin
- 1 tsp. oregano
- 1 tsp. garlic powder
- 1 tsp. salt
- ½ tsp. pepper

Directions:

1. In a small bowl, combine seasonings and Splenda brown sugar.

2. Heat oil in a skillet over med-high heat. Add the shrimps in a single layer, and cook 1 to 2 minutes per side.

3. Add seasonings, and cook, stirring, 30 seconds. Serve garnished with cilantro and lime wedges.

Cajun Catfish

Preparation Time: 5 Minutes
Cooking Time: 15 Minutes
Servings: 4
Ingredients:

- 4 (8 oz.) Catfish fillets
- 2 Tbsps. olive oil
- 2 tsps. Garlic salt
- 2 tsps. Thyme
- 2 tsps. Paprika
- ½ tsp. cayenne pepper
- ½ tsp. red hot sauce
- ¼ tsp. black pepper
- Nonstick cooking spray

Directions:

1. Heat the oven to 450°F. Spray a 9x13-inch baking dish with cooking spray.

2. In a small bowl, whisk everything together but the catfish. Brush both sides of fillets, using all the spices mixed.

3. Bake 10 to 13 minutes or until fish flakes easily with a fork.

Cajun Flounder and Tomatoes

Preparation Time: 10 Minutes
Cooking Time: 15 Minutes
Servings: 4
Ingredients:

- 4 Flounder fillets
- 2 ½ C. tomatoes, diced
- ¾ C. onion, diced
- ¾ C. green bell pepper, diced
- 2 Garlic cloves, finely diced
- 1 Tbsp. Cajun seasoning
- 1 tsp. olive oil

Directions:

1. Heat oil in a large skillet over med-high heat. Add onion and garlic and cook 2 minutes, or until soft. Add tomatoes, peppers, and spices. Cook 2 to 3 or minutes until tomatoes soften.

2. Lay fish over the top. Cover, reduce the heat to medium, and cook, 5 to 8 minutes, or until fish flakes easily with a fork—transfer the fish to serving plates and top with sauce.

Crispy Calamari

Preparation time: 5 minutes
Cooking time: 15 minutes
Servings: 4
Ingredients:

- 1lb. fresh squid
- Salt and pepper
- 2cups flour
- 1cup water
- 2cloves garlic, minced
- 1/2cup mayonnaise

Directions:

1. Detach the skin from the squid and discard any ink. Slice the squid into rings and season with some salt and pepper.

2. Put the flour and water in separate bowls. Dip the squid firstly in the flour, then into the water, then into the flour again, ensuring that it is entirely covered with flour.

3. Pre-heat the air fryer at 400F. Put the squid inside and cook for six minutes.

4. In the meantime, prepare the aioli by combining the garlic with the mayonnaise in a bowl.

5. Once the squid is ready, plate up and serve with the aioli.

Cilantro Salmon

Preparation time: 5 minutes
Cooking time: 15 minutes
Servings: 4

- Ingredients:
- 4salmon fillets, boneless
- Juice of 1/2 lemon
- 1/4cup chives, chopped
- 4cilantro springs, chopped
- 3tablespoons olive oil

- Salt and black pepper to the taste

Directions:

1. In a bowl, mix the salmon with all the other Ingredients: and toss. Put the fillets in your air fryer's basket and cook at 370 degrees F for minutes, flipping the fish halfway. Divide everything between plates and serve with a side salad.

Sesame Salmon

Preparation time: 5 minutes
Cooking time: 15 minutes
Servings: 6
Ingredients:

- 18oz. salmon fillet
- 2tablespoons swerve
- 1tablespoon apple cider vinegar
- 6teaspoons liquid aminos
- 1teaspoon minced ginger
- 1tablespoon sesame seeds
- 2tablespoons lemon juice
- 1/2teaspoon minced garlic
- 1tablespoon avocado oil

Directions:

1. Cut the salmon fillet on 8 servings and sprinkle with apple cider vinegar, minced ginger, lemon juice, minced garlic, and liquid aminos. Leave the fish for -15 minutes to marinate. After this, sprinkle the fish with avocado oil and put in the preheated to 380F air fryer in one layer. Cook the fish fillets for 7 minutes. Then sprinkle them with swerve and sesame seeds and cook for 2 minutes more at 400F.

Old Bay Crab Sticks with Garlic Mayo

Preparation time: 5 minutes
Cooking time: 20 minutes
Servings: 4
Ingredients:

- 1tbsp. old bay seasoning
- 1/3cup panko breadcrumbs
- 1egg
- 1/4cup mayonnaise
- 2garlic cloves, minced
- 1lime, juiced
- 1tsp. flour

Directions:

1. Warmth your Air Fryer to 390 F. Spray the air fryer basket with cooking spray.
2. Beat the eggs in a bowl. In a separate bowl, merge panko breadcrumbs with old bay seasoning. In a third bowl, pour the flour.
3. Dip the crab sticks in the flour and then in the eggs, and finally in the breadcrumb mixture. Spray with cooking spray and arrange on the cooking basket. Cook for 12 minutes, flipping halfway through.
4. Meanwhile, mix well all the mayonnaise with garlic and lime juice. Serve with crab sticks.

Mango Shrimp Skewers

Preparation time: 5 minutes

Cooking time: 20 minutes
Servings: 2
Ingredients:

- 2 tbsp. olive oil
- 1/2 tsp. garlic powder
- 1tsp. dry mango powder
- 2tbsp. fresh lime juice
- Salt and black pepper to taste

Directions:

1. In a bowl, mix well the garlic powder, mango powder, lime juice, salt, and pepper. Add the shrimp and toss to coat. Cover and allow to marinate for minutes.
2. Warmth your Air Fryer to 390 F. Spray the air fryer basket with cooking spray. Transfer the marinated shrimp to the cooking basket and drizzle the olive oil.

Cook for 5 minutes, slide out the fryer basket and shake the shrimp; cook for 5 minutes. Leave to cool and serve.

Salmon with Fennel and Carrot

Preparation Time: 15 Minutes
Cooking Time: 13 to 14 Minutes
Servings: 2
Ingredients:

- 1 Fennel bulb, thinly sliced
- 1 large carrot, peeled and sliced
- 1 Small onion, thinly sliced
- ¼ C. low-fat sour cream
- ¼ tsp. coarsely ground pepper
- 2 (5-oz. /142-g.) salmon fillets

Directions:

1. Combine the fennel, carrot, and onion in a bowl and toss.
2. Put the vegetable mixture into a baking pan. Prepare in the air fryer at 400°F (204°C) for 4 minutes or until the vegetables are crisp-tender.
3. Remove the pan from the air fryer. Stir in the sour cream and sprinkle the vegetables with the pepper.
4. Top with the salmon fillets.
5. Return the pan to the air fryer. Roast for another 9 to 10 minutes or until the salmon just barely flakes when tested with a fork.

Ranch Tilapia Fillets

Preparation Time: 7 Minutes
Cooking Time: 17 Minutes
Servings: 2 fillets
Ingredients:

- 2 Tbsps. flour
- 1 Egg, lightly beaten
- 1 C. crushed cornflakes
- 2 Tbsps. ranch seasoning
- 2 Tilapia fillets
- Olive oil spray

Directions:

1. Place a parchment liner in the air fryer basket.
2. Scoop the flour out onto a plate; set it aside.
3. Put the beaten egg in a medium shallow bowl.
4. Place the cornflakes in a zip-top bag and crush them with a rolling pin or another small, blunt object.

5. on another plate, mix to combine the crushed cereal and ranch seasoning.

6. Dredge the tilapia fillets in the flour, then dip in the egg, and then press into the cornflake mixture.

7. Place the prepared fillets on the liner in the air fryer in a single layer.

8. Spray lightly with olive oil and air fry at 400°F (204°C) for 8 minutes. Carefully flip the fillets and spray with more oil. Air fry for an additional 9 minutes, until golden and crispy, and serve.

Cilantro Lime Grilled Shrimp

Preparation Time: 5 Minutes
Cooking Time: 5 Minutes
Servings: 6
Ingredients:

- 1 1/2 lbs. large shrimp raw, peeled, deveined with tails on
- Juice and zest of 1 lime
- 2 Tbsps. fresh cilantro chopped
- ¼ C. olive oil
- 2 Cloves garlic, diced fine
- 1 tsp. smoked paprika
- ¼ tsp. cumin
- ½ tsp. salt
- ¼ tsp. cayenne pepper

Directions:

1. Place the shrimps in a large Ziploc bag.

2. Mix the remaining Ingredients: in a small bowl and pour over the shrimps. Let them marinate for 20-30 minutes.

3. Heat up the grill. Skewer the shrimps and cook 2 to 3 minutes, per side, just until they turn pink. Be careful not to overcook them. Serve garnished with cilantro.

Crab Frittata

Preparation Time: 10 Minutes
Cooking Time: 50 Minutes
Servings: 4
Ingredients:

- 4 Eggs
- 2 C.s lump crabmeat
- 1 C. half-n-half
- 1 C. green onions, diced
- 1 C. reduced fat parmesan cheese, grated
- 1 tsp. salt
- 1 tsp. pepper
- 1 tsp. smoked paprika
- 1 tsp. Italian seasoning
- Nonstick cooking spray

Directions:

1. Heat the oven to 350°F. Spray an 8-inch springform pan or pie plate with cooking spray.

2. In a large bowl, whisk together the eggs and half-n-half. Add seasonings and parmesan cheese, stir to mix.

3. Stir in the onions and the crabmeat. Pour into the prepared pan and bake 35 to 40 minutes, or until the eggs are set and the top is lightly browned.

4. Let cool for 10 minutes, then slice and serve warm or at room temperature.

Crunchy Lemon Shrimp

Preparation Time: 5 Minutes
Cooking Time: 10 Minutes
Servings: 4
Ingredients:

- 1 lb. raw shrimps, peeled and deveined
- 2 Tbsps. Italian parsley, roughly chopped
- 2 Tbsps. lemon juice, divided
- 2/3 C. panko bread crumbs
- 2 ½ Tbsp. olive oil, divided
- Salt and pepper, to taste

Directions:

1. Heat the oven to 400°F.

2. Place the shrimps evenly in a baking dish and sprinkle with salt and pepper. Drizzle on one Tbsp. lemon juice and one Tbsp. of olive oil. Set aside.

3. In a medium bowl, combine parsley, the remaining lemon juice, bread crumbs, the remaining olive oil, and ¼ tsp. each of salt and pepper. Layer the panko mixture evenly on top of the shrimps.

4. Bake for 8 to 10 minutes or until the shrimps are cooked through and the panko is golden brown.

Grilled Tuna Steaks

Preparation Time: 5 Minutes
Cooking Time: 10 Minutes
Servings: 6
Ingredients:

- 6 (6 oz.) Tuna steaks
- 3 Tbsps. fresh basil, diced
- 4 ½ Tsps. olive oil
- ¾ tsp. salt
- ¼ tsp. pepper
- Nonstick cooking spray

Directions:

1. Place a grill on medium heat. Apply cooking spray.

2. Drizzle both sides of the tuna with oil. Sprinkle with basil, salt, and pepper.

3. Place the tuna on the grill and cook 5 minutes per side; the tuna should be slightly pink in the center.

Chilean Sea Bass with Green Olive Relish

Preparation Time: 10 Minutes
Cooking Time: 16 to 20 Minutes
Servings: 4
Ingredients:

- Olive oil spray
- 2 (6-oz. /170-g.) Chilean sea bass fillets or other firm-fleshed white fish
- 3 Tbsps. extra-virgin olive oil
- ½ tsp. ground cumin
- ½ tsp. kosher salt
- ½ tsp. black pepper
- 1/3 C. pitted green olives, diced
- ¼ C. finely diced onion
- 1 tsp. chopped capers

Directions:

1. Spray the air fryer basket with olive oil spray. Drizzle the fillets with olive oil and sprinkle with cumin, salt, and pepper. Place the fish in the air fryer basket. Bake at 325°F (163°C) for 10 minutes or until the fish flakes easily with a fork.
2. In the meantime, in a lesser bowl, stir together the olives, onion, and capers.
3. Serve the fish topped with the relish.

Ginger and Green Onion Fish

Preparation Time: 15 Minutes
Cooking Time: 15 Minutes
Servings: 2
Ingredients:
For the Bean Sauce:

- 2 Tbsps. low-sodium soy sauce
- 1 Tbsp. rice wine
- 1 Tbsp. doubanjiang (Chinese black bean paste)
- 1 tsp. minced fresh ginger
- 1 Clove garlic, minced

For the vegetables and fish:

- 1 Tbsp. peanut oil
- ¼ C. julienned green onions
- ¼ C. chopped fresh cilantro
- 2 Tbsps. julienned fresh ginger
- 2 (6-oz. /170-g.) white fish fillets, such as tilapia

Directions:

1. For the sauce, in a small bowl, combine all the Ingredients: and stir until well combined; set aside.
2. For the vegetables and fish, in a medium bowl, combine the peanut oil, green onions, cilantro, and ginger. Toss to combine.
3. Cut two squares of parchment large enough to hold one fillet and half of the vegetables. Place one fillet on each parchment square, top with the vegetables, and pour over the sauce. Bend over the parchment paper and tuck the sides in small, tight folds to hold the fish, vegetables, and sauce securely inside the packet.
4. Place the packets in a single layer in the air fryer basket—roast at 350F (177C) for 15 minutes.
5. Transfer each packet to a dinner plate. Cut open with scissors just before serving.

Cilantro Lime Shrimp

Preparation Time: 15 Minutes
Cooking Time: 8 Minutes
Servings: 4
Ingredients:

- 1 tsp. extra virgin olive oil
- ½ tsp. garlic clove, minced
- 1 lb. (454 g.) large shrimps, peeled and deveined
- ¼ C. chopped fresh cilantro or more to taste
- 1 Lime, zested and juiced
- ¼ tsp. salt
- 1/8 tsp. black pepper

Directions:

1. In a large, heavy skillet, heat the olive oil over medium-high heat.
2. Add the minced garlic and cook for 30 seconds until fragrant.

3. Toss in the shrimps and cook for about 5 to 6 minutes, stirring occasionally, or until they turn pink and opaque.
4. Remove from the heat to a bowl. Add the cilantro, lime zest and juice, salt, and pepper to the shrimps, and toss to combine. Serve immediately.

Panko Coconut Shrimp

Preparation Time: 12 Minutes
Cooking Time: 8 Minutes
Servings: 4
Ingredients:

- 2 Egg whites
- 1 Tbsp. water
- ½ C. whole-wheat panko bread crumbs
- ¼ C. unsweetened coconut flakes
- ½ tsp. turmeric
- ½ tsp. ground coriander
- ½ tsp. ground cumin
- 1/8 tsp. salt
- 1 lb. (454 g.) large raw shrimps, peeled, deveined, and patted dry
- Nonstick cooking spray

Directions:

1. Preheat the air fry to 400°F (205°C).
2. In a shallow dish, beat the egg whites and water until slightly foamy. Set aside.
3. In a separate shallow dish, mix the bread crumbs, coconut flakes, turmeric, coriander, cumin, and salt, and stir until well combined.
4. Dredge the shrimps in the egg mixture, shaking off any excess, then coat them in the crumb-coconut mixture. Spritz the air fryer basket with nonstick cooking spray and arrange the coated shrimps in the basket. Air fry the shrimps for 6 to 8 minutes, flipping once during cooking, or until golden brown and cooked through.

Shrimp Coleslaw

Preparation Time: 10 Minutes
Cooking Time: 0 Minutes
Servings: 4
Ingredients:

- 1 lb. (454 g.) frozen cooked shrimps, thawed
- 1 (8-oz. /227-g.) package shredded cabbage
- 3 Tangerines, peeled and sectioned
- 3 Scallions, sliced
- 3 Tbsps. olive oil
- 2 tsps. Grated fresh ginger root
- 2 Tbsps. white rice vinegar
- 1/8 tsp. red pepper flakes
- 1 Avocado, peeled, pitted, and sliced
- ¼ C. toasted slivered almonds (optional)
- 3 Tbsps. chopped fresh cilantro

Directions:

1. Stir together the shrimps, cabbage, tangerines, scallions, olive oil, ginger root, vinegar, and red pepper flakes in a large bowl.
2. Transfer to the refrigerator to chill for at least 30 minutes.
3. When ready to serve, sprinkle the avocado slices, almonds (if desired), and cilantro on top. Serve immediately.

Easy Creamy Shrimp Nachos

Preparation time: 5 minutes
Cooking time: 15 minutes
Servings: 4
Ingredients:

- 1pound shrimp, cleaned and deveined
- 1tablespoon olive oil
- 2tablespoons fresh lemon juice
- 1teaspoon paprika
- 1/4teaspoon cumin powder
- 1/2teaspoon shallot powder
- 1/2teaspoon garlic powder
- Coarse sea salt and black pepper, to flavor
- 1(9-ounce bag corn tortilla chips
- 1/4cup pickled jalapeño, minced
- 1cup Pepper Jack cheese, grated
- 1/2cup sour cream

Directions:
1. Set the shrimp with the olive oil, lemon juice, paprika, cumin powder, shallot powder, garlic powder, salt, and black pepper.
2. Cook in the preheated Air Fryer at 390 degrees F for 5 minutes.
3. Place the tortilla chips on the aluminum foil-lined cooking basket. Top with the shrimp mixture, jalapeño and cheese. Cook another 2 minutes or until cheese has melted.
4. Serve garnished with sour cream and enjoy!

Roasted Red Snapper

Preparation Time: 20 minutes
Cooking Time: 0
Servings: 4
Ingredients:

- 4red snapper fillets; boneless
- 2garlic cloves; minced
- 1tbsp. hot chili paste
- 2tbsp. olive oil
- 2tbsp. coconut aminos
- 2tbsp. lime juice
- A pinch of salt and black pepper

Directions:
1. Take a bowl and merge all the Ingredients: except the fish and whisk well
2. Rub the fish with this mix, place it in your air fryer's basket and cook at 380°F for 15 minutes
3. Serve with a side salad.

Swordfish Steaks and Tomatoes

Preparation Time: 15 minutes
Cooking Time: 0
Servings: 2
Ingredients:

- 30oz. canned tomatoes; chopped.
- 2 1-inch-thick swordfish steaks
- 2tbsp. capers, drained
- 1tbsp. red vinegar
- 2tbsp. oregano; chopped.
- Pinch of salt and black pepper

Directions:
1. In a pan that fits the air fryer, combine all the Ingredients, toss, put the pan in the fryer and cook at 390F for 10 minutes, flipping the fish halfway
2. Divide the mix between plates and serve

Buttery Cod

Preparation Time: 13 minutes
Cooking Time: 0
Servings: 2
Ingredients:

- 2 (4-oz.cod fillets
- 1/2 medium lemon, sliced
- 2 tbsp. salted butter; melted.
- 1tsp. Old Bay seasoning

Directions:
1. Place cod fillets into a 6-inch round baking dish. Brush each fillet with butter and sprinkle with Old Bay seasoning. Lay two lemon slices on each fillet
2. Secure the dish with foil and place into the air fryer basket. Adjust the temperature to 350 Degrees F and set the timer for 8 minutes
3. Flip halfway through the cooking time. When cooked, internal temperature should be at least 145 Degrees F. serve warm.

Lemon Scallops with Asparagus

Preparation Time: 10 Minutes
Cooking Time: 7 to 10 Minutes
Servings: 4
Ingredients:

- ½ lb. (227 g.) asparagus, ends trimmed and cut into 2-inch pieces
- 1 C. sugar snap peas
- 1 lb. (454 g.) sea scallops
- 1 Tbsp. lemon juice
- 2 tsps. Olive oil
- ½ tsp. dried thyme
- Pinch salt
- Freshly ground black pepper, to taste

Directions:
1. Place the asparagus and sugar snap peas in the air fryer basket. Air fry at 400°F (204°C) for 2 to 3 minutes or until the vegetables are just getting tender.
2. Meanwhile, check the scallops for a small muscle Added to the side, pull it off, and discard.
3. In a medium bowl, toss the scallops with lemon juice, olive oil, thyme, salt, and pepper. Place into the air fryer basket on top of the vegetables.
4. Air fry for 5 to 7 minutes, tossing the basket once during the cooking time, and the vegetables are tender. Serve immediately.

Honey Lemon Snapper with Fruit

Preparation Time: 15 Minutes
Cooking Time: 9 to 13 Minutes
Servings: 4
Ingredients:

- 4 (4-oz. /113-g.) Red snapper fillets
- 2 tsps. Olive oil

- 3 Nectarines, halved and pitted
- 3 Plums, halved and pitted
- 1 C. red grapes
- 1 Tbsp. freshly squeezed lemon juice
- 1 Tbsp. honey
- ½ tsp. dried thyme

Directions:

1. Put the red snapper in the air fryer basket and drizzle with the olive oil. Air fry at 390°F (199°C) for 4 minutes.
2. Remove the basket and add the nectarines and plums. Scatter the grapes overall.
3. Drizzle with the lemon juice and honey and sprinkle with thyme.
4. Return the basket to the air fryer and air fry for 5 to 9 more minutes, or till the fish flakes when tested with a fork and the fruit is tender. Serve immediately.

Fresh Rosemary Trout

Preparation Time: 5 Minutes
Cooking Time: 8 Minutes
Servings: 2
Ingredients:

- 4 to 6 Fresh rosemary sprigs
- 8 oz. (227 g.) trout fillets, about ¼ inch thick; rinsed and patted dry
- ½ tsp. olive oil
- 1/8 tsp. salt - 1/8 tsp. pepper
- 1 tsp. fresh lemon juice

Directions:

1. Preheat the oven to 350°F (180°C).
2. Put the rosemary sprigs in a small baking pan in a single row. Spread the fillets on the top of the rosemary sprigs.
3. Brush both sides of each piece of fish with olive oil. Sprinkle with salt, pepper, and lemon juice.
4. Bake in the preheated oven for 7 to 8 minutes, or until the fish is opaque and flakes easily.
5. Divide the fillets between two plates and serve hot.

Asian-Inspired Swordfish Steaks

Preparation Time: 10 Minutes
Cooking Time: 6 to 11 Minutes
Servings: 4
Ingredients:

- 4 (4-oz. /113-g.) Swordfish steaks
- ½ tsp. toasted sesame oil
- 1 Jalapeño pepper, finely minced
- 2 Garlic cloves, grated
- 1 Tbsp. grated fresh ginger
- ½ tsp. Chinese five-spice powder
- 1/8 tsp. freshly ground black pepper
- 2 Tbsps. freshly squeezed lemon juice

Directions:

1. Place the swordfish steaks on a work surface and drizzle with the sesame oil.
2. In a small bowl, mix the jalapeño, garlic, ginger, five-spice powder, pepper, and lemon juice. Rub this mixture into the fish and let it stand for 10 minutes. Put in the air fryer basket.

3. Roast at 380°F (193°C) for 6 to 11 minutes, or until the swordfish reaches an inner temperature of at least 140°F (60°C) on a meat thermometer. Serve immediately.

Fish Tacos

Preparation Time: 15 Minutes
Cooking Time: 9 to 12 Minutes
Servings: 4
Ingredients:

- 1 lb. (454 g.) white fish fillets, such as snapper
- 1 Tbsp. olive oil
- 3 Tbsps. freshly squeezed lemon juice, divided
- 1½ C. chopped red cabbage
- ½ C. of salsa
- 1/3 C. sour cream
- 6 Whole-wheat tortillas
- 2 Avocados, peeled and chopped

Directions:

1. Skirmish the fish with olive oil and sprinkle with one Tbsp. of lemon juice. Set in the air fryer basket and air fry at 400°F (204°C) meant for 9 to 12 minutes.
2. Meanwhile, combine the remaining two Tbsps. of lemon juice, cabbage, salsa, and sour cream in a medium bowl.
3. As soon as the fish is cooked, remove it from the air fryer basket and break it into large pieces.
4. Let everyone assemble their taco combining the fish, tortillas, cabbage mixture, and avocados.

Lime Baked Salmon

Preparation Time: 22 minutes
Cooking Time: 0
Servings: 2
Ingredients:

- 2(3-oz. salmon fillets, skin removed
- 1/4cup sliced pickled jalapeños
- 1/2medium lime, juiced
- 2tbsp. chopped cilantro
- 1tbsp. salted butter; melted.
- 1/2tsp. finely minced garlic
- 1tsp. chili powder

Directions:

1. Place salmon fillets into a 6-inch round baking pan. Brush each with butter and sprinkle with chili powder and garlic
2. Place jalapeño slices on top and around salmon. Pour half of the lime juice over the salmon and cover with foil. Place pan into the air fryer basket. Adjust the temperature to 370 Degrees F and set the timer for 12 minutes
3. When fully cooked, salmon should flake easily with a fork and reach an internal temperature of at least 145 Degrees F.
4. To serve, spritz with remaining lime juice and garnish with cilantro.

Lime Trout and Shallots

Preparation Time: 17 minutes
Cooking Time: 0
Servings: 4
Ingredients:

- 4 trout fillets; boneless
- 3garlic cloves; minced

- 6shallots; chopped.
- 1/2cup butter; melted
- 1/2cup olive oil
- Juice of 1 lime
- A pinch of salt and black pepper

Directions:

1. In a pan that fits the air fryer, combine the fish with the shallots and the rest of the Ingredients, toss gently
2. Put the pan in the machine and cook at 390F for 12 minutes, flipping the fish halfway.
3. Cut between plates and serve with a side salad.

Chapter 8

Vegetables Sides

Delicious Golden Onion Rings

Preparation time: 5 minutes
Cooking time: 15 minutes
Servings: 4
Ingredients:

- 1 large onion, slice ½-inch thick
- 1 egg
- ¼ cup sunflower oil
- 2 tablespoons coconut flour
- 2 tablespoons reduced fat Parmesan cheese
- 1/4 teaspoon parsley flakes
- 1/8 teaspoon garlic powder
- 1/8 teaspoon cayenne pepper
- Salt, to taste
- Ketchup, for serving

Directions:
1. Heat oil in a large skillet over medium-high heat.
2. In a shallow bowl, combine flour, Parmesan, and seasonings.
3. Beat the egg.
4. Separate onion slices into individual rings and place in large bowl, adds beaten egg and toss to coat well. Let rest 1 to 2 minutes.
5. In small batches, coat onion in flour mixture and add to skillet. Cook 1 to 2 minutes per side, or until golden brown. Transfer to paper towel lined cookie sheet.
6. Serve with ketchup.

Whole Wheat Bread Zucchini Bake

Preparation time: 5 minutes
Cooking time: 10 minutes
Servings: 6
Ingredients:

- 1 large zucchini, sliced into ¼-inch circle
- ¼ cup reduced fat, Parmesan cheese, grated fine - 3 tablespoons low-fat milk
- 1/3 cup whole wheat breadcrumbs
- ½ teaspoon garlic powder
- 1/8 Teaspoon cayenne pepper
- Nonstick cooking spray

Directions:
1. After slicing zucchini pat dry with paper towels. Let sit for 60 minutes before using. Then pat dry again.
2. Heat oven to 425°F (220°C). Spray a wire rack with cooking spray and place on cookie sheet.
3. In a medium bowl combine all except milk and zucchini. Pour milk into a shallow bowl.

4. Dip zucchini into milk the coat with bread crumb mixture. Place on wire rack and bake 10 to 15 minutes or until browned and crisp. Serve immediately.

Rainbow Vegetable Fritters

Preparation Time: 20 Minutes
Cooking Time: 10 Minutes
Servings: 2
Ingredients:

- 1 Zucchini, grated and squeezed
- 1 C. corn kernels
- ½ C. canned green peas
- 4 Tbsps. all-purpose flour
- 2 Tbsps. fresh shallots, minced
- 1 tsp. fresh garlic, minced
- 1 Tbsp. peanut oil
- Sea salt and pepper, to taste
- 1 tsp. cayenne pepper

Directions:
1. In a mixing bowl, thoroughly combine all Ingredients: until everything is well incorporated.
2. Shape the mixture into patties. Spritz the Air Fryer carrier with cooking spray.
3. Cook in the preheated Air Fryer at 365°F for 6 minutes. Place on top and cook for another 6 minutes. Serve immediately and enjoy!

Mediterranean Vegetable Skewers

Preparation Time: 30 Minutes
Cooking Time: 10 Minutes
Servings: 4
Ingredients:

- 2 Medium-sized zucchinis, cut into 1-inch pieces
- 2 Red bell peppers, cut into 1-inch pieces
- 1 Green bell pepper, cut into 1-inch pieces
- 1 Red onion, cut into 1-inch pieces
- 2 Tbsps. olive oil
- Sea salt, to taste
- ½ tsp. black pepper, preferably freshly cracked
- ½ tsp. red pepper flakes

Directions:
1. Soak the wooden skewers in water for 15 minutes.
2. Thread the vegetables on skewers; drizzle olive oil all over the vegetable skewers; sprinkle with spices. 3. Cook in the preheated Air Fryer at 400°F for 13 minutes. Serve warm and enjoy!

Roasted Veggies with Yogurt-Tahini Sauce

Preparation Time: 20 Minutes
Cooking Time: 10 Minutes
Servings: 4
Ingredients:

- 1 lb. Brussels sprouts
- 1 lb. button mushrooms
- 2 Tbsps. olive oil
- ½ tsp. white pepper
- ½ tsp. dried dill weed
- ½ tsp. cayenne pepper
- ½ tsp. celery seeds
- ½ Tsp. mustard seeds
- Salt, to taste

For the yogurt tahini sauce:

- 1 C. plain yogurt
- 2 Heaping Tbsps. tahini paste
- 1 Tbsp. lemon juice
- 1 Tbsp. extra-virgin olive oil
- ½ tsp. Aleppo pepper, minced

Directions:
1. Toss the Brussels sprouts and mushrooms with olive oil and spices. Preheat your Air Fryer to 380°F.
2. Add the Brussels sprouts to the cooking basket and cook for 10 minutes.
3. Add the mushrooms, turn the temperature to 390°F and cook for six more minutes.
4. While the vegetables are cooking, make the sauce by whisking all Ingredients. Serve the warm vegetables with the sauce on the side. Bon appétit!

Swiss cheese and Vegetable Casserole

Preparation Time: 50 Minutes
Cooking Time: 10 Minutes
Servings: 4
Ingredients:

- 1 lb. Potatoes, peeled and sliced (¼-inch thick
- 2 Tbsps. olive oil
- ½ tsp. red pepper flakes, crushed
- ½ tsp. freshly ground black pepper
- Salt, to taste
- 3 Bell peppers, thinly sliced
- 1 Serrano pepper, thinly sliced
- 2 Medium-sized tomatoes, sliced
- 1 Leek, thinly sliced
- 2 Garlic cloves, minced
- 1 C. Swiss cheese, shredded

Directions:
1. Start by warming your Air Fryer to 350°F. Spritz a casserole dish with cooking oil.
2. Place the potatoes in the casserole dish in an even layer; drizzle one Tbsp. of olive oil over the top. Then swell the red pepper, black pepper, and salt.

3. Add two bell peppers and half of the leeks. Add the tomatoes and the remaining Tbsp. of olive oil.
4. Add the remaining peppers, leeks, and minced garlic. Top with the cheese.
5. Cover the casserole with foil and bake for 32 minutes. Remove the foil and increase the temperature to 400°F; bake an additional 16 minutes. Bon appétit!

American-Style Brussels Sprout Salad

Preparation Time: 35 Minutes
Cooking Time: 10 Minutes
Servings: 4
Ingredients:

- 1 lb. Brussels sprouts
- 1 Apple, cored and diced
- ½ C. mozzarella cheese, crumbled
- ½ C. pomegranate seeds
- 1 Small-sized red onion, chopped
- 4 Eggs, hardboiled and sliced

For the dressing:

- ¼ C. olive oil - 2 Tbsps. champagne vinegar
- 1 tsp. Dijon mustard
- 1 tsp. honey
- Sea salt and ground black pepper, to taste

Directions:
1. Start by preheating your Air Fryer to 380°F.
2. Add the Brussels sprouts to the cooking basket. Spritz with cooking spray and cook for 15 minutes. Let it cool to room temperature for about 15 minutes.
3. Toss the Brussels sprouts with apple, cheese, pomegranate seeds, and red onion.
4. Mix all Ingredients: for the dressing and toss to combine well. Serve topped with the hardboiled eggs. Bon appétit!

Sundried Tomato with Brussels sprouts Roast

Preparation time: 15 minutes
Cooking time: 20 minutes
Servings: 4
Ingredients:

- 1 pound (454 g) Brussels sprouts, trimmed and halved
- 1 tablespoon extra-virgin olive oil
- Sea salt and freshly ground black pepper, to taste
- ½ cup sun-dried tomatoes, chopped
- 2 tablespoons freshly squeezed lemon juice
- 1 teaspoon lemon zest

Directions:
1. Preheat the oven to 400°F (205°C). Line a large baking sheet with aluminum foil.
2. Toss the Brussels sprouts in the olive oil in a large bowl until well coated. Sprinkle with salt and pepper.
3. Spread out the seasoned Brussels sprouts on the prepared baking sheet in a single layer.
4. Roast in the preheated oven for 20 minutes, shaking the pan halfway through, or until the Brussels sprouts are crispy and browned on the outside. Remove from the oven to a serving bowl.

6. Add the tomatoes, lemon juice, and lemon zest, and stir to incorporate. Serve immediately.

Cardamom Spiced Swiss chard

Preparation time: 10 minutes
Cooking time: 10 minutes
Servings: 4
Ingredients:

- 2 tablespoons extra-virgin olive oil
- 1 pound (454 g) Swiss chard, coarse stems removed and leaves chopped
- 1 pound (454 g) kale, coarse stems removed and leaves chopped
- ½ teaspoon ground cardamom
- 1 tablespoon freshly squeezed lemon juice
- Sea salt and freshly ground black pepper, to taste

Directions:
1. Heat the olive oil in a large skillet over medium-high heat.
2. Add the Swiss chard, kale, cardamom, and lemon juice to the skillet, and stir to combine. Cook for about 10 minutes, stirring continuously, or until the greens are wilted. Sprinkle with the salt and pepper and stir well. Serve the greens on a plate while warm.

Japanese Tempura Bowl

Preparation Time: 20 Minutes
Cooking Time: 10 Minutes
Servings: 3
Ingredients:

- 1 C. all-purpose flour
- Kosher salt and ground black pepper, to taste
- ½ tsp. paprika
- 2 Eggs
- 3 Tbsps. soda water
- 1 C. panko crumbs
- 2 Tbsps. olive oil
- 1 C. green beans
- 1 Onion, cut into rings
- 1 Zucchini, cut into slices
- 2 Tbsps. soy sauce
- 1 Tbsp. mirin
- 1 tsp. dashi granules

Directions:
1. In a shallow bowl, mix the flour, salt, black pepper, and paprika. In a separate bowl, whisk the eggs and soda water. In a third shallow bowl, combine the panko crumbs with olive oil.
2. Dip the vegetables in the flour mixture, then in the egg mixture; lastly, roll over the panko mixture to coat evenly.
3. Cook in the preheated Air Fryer at 400°F for 10 minutes, shaking the basket halfway through the cooking time. Work in batches until the vegetables are crispy and golden brown.
4. Then, make the sauce by whisking the soy sauce, mirin, and dashi granules. Bon appétit!

Balsamic Root Vegetables

Preparation Time: 25 Minutes
Cooking Time: 10 Minutes
Servings: 3
Ingredients:

- 2 Potatoes, cut into 1 ½-inch piece
- 2 Carrots, cut into 1 ½-inch piece
- 2 Parsnips, cut into 1 ½-inch piece
- 1 Onion, cut into 1 ½-inch piece
- Pink Himalayan salt and ground black pepper, to taste
- ¼ tsp. smoked paprika
- 1 tsp. garlic powder
- ½ tsp. dried thyme
- ½ tsp. dried marjoram
- 2 Tbsps. olive oil
- 2 Tbsps. balsamic vinegar

Directions:
1. Toss all Ingredients: in a large mixing dish.
2. Roast in the preheated Air Fryer at 400°F for 10 minutes. Shake the basket and cook for 7 more minutes.
3. Serve with some extra fresh herbs if desired. Bon appétit!

Winter Vegetable Braise

Preparation Time: 25 Minutes
Cooking Time: 10 Minutes
Servings: 2
Ingredients:

- 4 Potatoes, peeled and cut into 1-inch pieces
- 1 Celery root, peeled and cut into 1 inch pieces
- 1 C. winter squash
- 2 Tbsps. unsalted butter, melted
- ½ C. chicken broth
- ¼ C. tomato sauce
- 1 tsp. parsley
- 1 tsp. rosemary
- 1 tsp. thyme

Directions:
1. Start by preheating your Air Fryer to 370°F. Add all Ingredients: to a lightly greased casserole dish. Stir to combine well.
2. Bake in the preheated Air Fryer for 10 minutes. Gently stir the vegetables with a large spoon and increase the temperature to 400°F; cook for 10 more minutes.
3. Serve in individual bowls with a few drizzles of lemon juice. Bon appétit!

Aromatic Thyme Spiced Button Mushrooms

Preparation time: 10 minutes
Cooking time: 12 minutes
Servings: 4
Ingredients:

- 1 tablespoon butter
- 2 teaspoons extra-virgin olive oil
- 2 pounds (907 g) button mushrooms, halved
- 2 teaspoons minced fresh garlic
- 1 teaspoon chopped fresh thyme
- Sea salt and freshly ground black pepper, to taste

Directions:
1. Heat the butter and olive oil in a large skillet over medium-high heat.

2. Add the mushrooms and sauté for 10 minutes, stirring occasionally, or until the mushrooms are lightly browned and cooked though.
3. Stir in the garlic and thyme and cook for an additional 2 minutes.
4. Season with salt and pepper and serve on a plate.

Peppery Bok Choy with Toasted Sliced Almonds

Preparation time: 15 minutes
Cooking time: 7 minutes
Servings: 4
Ingredients:
- 2 teaspoons sesame oil
- 2 pounds (907 g) bok choy, cleaned and quartered
- 2 teaspoons low-sodium soy sauce
- Pinch red pepper flakes
- ½ cup toasted sliced almonds

Directions:
1. Heat the sesame oil in a large skillet over medium heat until hot.
2. Sauté the bok choy in the hot oil for about 5 minutes, stirring occasionally, or until tender but still crisp.
3. Add the soy sauce and red pepper flakes and stir to combine. Continue sautéing for 2 minutes.
4. Transfer to a plate and serve topped with sliced almonds.

Spicy Asparagus Cashews Bake

Preparation time: 10 minutes
Cooking time: 15 to 20 minutes
Servings: 4
Ingredients:
- 2 pounds (907 g) asparagus, woody ends trimmed
- 1 tablespoon extra-virgin olive oil
- Sea salt and freshly ground black pepper, to taste
- ½ cup chopped cashews
- Zest and juice of 1 lime

Directions:
1. Preheat the oven to 400°F (205°C). Line a baking sheet with aluminum foil.
2. Toss the asparagus with the olive oil in a medium bowl. Sprinkle the salt and pepper to season.
3. Arrange the asparagus on the baking sheet and bake for 15 to 20 minutes, or until lightly browned and tender.
4. Remove the asparagus from the oven to a serving bowl.
5. Add the cashews, lime zest and juice, and toss to coat well. Serve immediately.

Gingery Eggplant with Green Onions

Preparation time: 10 minutes
Cooking time: 40 minutes
Servings: 4
Ingredients:
- 1 large eggplant, sliced into fourths
- 3 green onions, diced, green tips only
- 1 teaspoon fresh ginger, peeled and diced fine
- ¼ cup plus 1 teaspoon cornstarch

- 1½ tablespoons soy sauce
- 1½ tablespoons sesame oil
- 1 tablespoon vegetable oil
- 1 tablespoon fish sauce
- 2 teaspoons Splenda
- ¼ teaspoon salt

Directions:
1. Place eggplant on paper towels and sprinkle both sides with salt. Let for 1 hour to remove excess moisture. Pat dry with more paper towels.
2. In a small bowl, whisk together soy sauce, sesame oil, fish sauce, Splenda, and 1 teaspoon cornstarch.
3. Coat both sides of the eggplant with the ¼ cup cornstarch, use more if needed.
4. Heat oil in a large skillet, over medium-high heat.
5. Add ½ the ginger and 1 green onion, then lay 2 slices of eggplant on top. Use ½ the sauce mixture to lightly coat both sides of the eggplant. Cook 8 to 10 minutes per side. Repeat.
6. Serve garnished with remaining green onions.

Peppery Egg Butternut Fritters

Preparation time: 15 minutes
Cooking time: 15 minutes
Servings: 6
Ingredients:
- 5 cup butternut squash, grated
- 2 large eggs
- 1 tablespoon fresh sage, diced fine
- 2/3 cup flour - 2 tablespoons olive oil
- Salt and pepper, to taste

Directions:
1. Heat oil in a large skillet over medium-high heat.
2. In a large bowl, combine squash, eggs, sage and salt and pepper to taste. Fold in flour.
3. Drop ¼ cup mixture into skillet, keeping fritters at least 1 inch apart. Cook till golden brown on both sides, about 2 minutes per side.
4. Transfer to paper towel lined plate. Repeat. Serve immediately with your favorite dipping sauce.

The Best Cauliflower Tater Tots

Preparation Time: 25 Minutes
Cooking Time: 10 Minutes
Servings: 4
Ingredients:
- 1 lb. cauliflower florets
- 2 Eggs
- 1 Tbsp. olive oil
- 2 Tbsps. scallions, chopped
- 1 Garlic clove, minced
- 1 C. Colby cheese, shredded
- ½ C. breadcrumbs
- Sea salt and ground black pepper, to taste
- ¼ tsp. dried dill weed
- 1 tsp. paprika

Directions:
1. Blanch the cauliflower in salted boiling water for about 3 to 4 minutes until al dente. Drain well and pulse in a food processor.

2. Add the remaining Ingredients; mix to combine well. Shape the cauliflower mixture into bite-sized tots.

3. Spritz the Air Fryer basket with cooking spray.

4. Cook in the preheated Air Fryer at 375°F for 16 minutes, shaking halfway through the cooking time. Serve with your favorite sauce for dipping Bon appétit!

Three-Cheese Stuffed Mushrooms

Preparation Time: 15 Minutes
Cooking Time: 10 Minutes
Servings: 3
Ingredients:

- 9 large button mushrooms, stems removed
- 1 Tbsp. olive oil
- Salt and ground black pepper, to taste
- ½ tsp. dried rosemary
- 6 Tbsps. Swiss cheeses shredded
- 6 Tbsps. Romano cheese, shredded
- 6 Tbsps. cream cheese
- 1 tsp. soy sauce
- 1 tsp. garlic, minced
- 3 Tbsps. green onion, minced

Directions:

1. Brush the mushroom caps with olive oil; sprinkle with salt, pepper, and rosemary.

2. In a mixing bowl, thoroughly combine the remaining Ingredients, combine them well, and divide the filling mixture among the mushroom caps.

3. Cook in the preheated Air Fryer at 390°F for 7 minutes.

4. Let the mushrooms cool slightly before serving Bon appétit!

Sweet Corn Fritters with Avocado

Preparation Time: 20 Minutes
Cooking Time: 10 Minutes
Servings: 3
Ingredients:

- 2 C. sweet corn kernels
- 1 Small-sized onion, chopped
- 1 Garlic clove, minced
- 2 Eggs, whisked
- 1 tsp. baking powder
- 2 Tbsps. fresh cilantro, chopped
- Sea salt and ground black pepper, to taste
- 1 Avocado, peeled, pitted, and diced
- 2 Tbsps. sweet chili sauce

Directions:

1. In a mixing bowl, thoroughly combine the corn, onion, garlic, eggs, baking powder, cilantro, salt, and black pepper.

2. Shape the corn mixture into six patties and transfer them to the lightly greased Air Fryer basket.

3. Cook in the preheated Air Fry at 370°F for 8 minutes; turn them over and cook for 7 minutes longer.

4. Serve the cakes with avocado and chili sauce.

Greek-Style Vegetable Bake

Preparation Time: 35 Minutes
Cooking Time: 10 Minutes
Servings: 4
Ingredients:

- 1 Eggplant, peeled and sliced
- 2 Bell peppers, seeded and sliced
- 1 Red onion, sliced
- 1 tsp. fresh garlic, minced
- 4 Tbsps. olive oil
- 1 tsp. mustard
- 1 tsp. dried oregano
- 1 tsp. smoked paprika
- Salt and ground black pepper, to taste
- 1 Tomato, sliced
- 6 oz. halloumi cheese, sliced lengthways

Directions:

1. Start by preheating your Air Fryer to 370°F. Spritz a baking pan with non-stick cooking spray.

2. Place the eggplant, peppers, onion, and garlic on the baking pan's bottom. Add the olive oil, mustard, and spices. Transfer to the cooking basket and cook for 14 minutes.

3. Top with the tomatoes and cheese; increase the temperature to 390°F and cook for five more minutes until bubbling. Let it sit on a cooling rack for 10 minutes before serving.

4. Bon appétit!

Grandma's Citrusy Broccoli Tofu

Preparation time: 15 minutes
Cooking time: 2 hours
Servings: 4
Ingredients:

- 1 package extra firm tofu, pressed for at least 15 minutes, cut into cubes
- 2 cups broccoli florets, fresh
- 1 tablespoon margarine
- ¼ cup orange juice
- ¼ cup reduced sodium soy sauce
- ¼ cup honey
- 2 cloves garlic, diced fine

Directions:

1. Melt butter in a medium skillet, over medium high heat. Add tofu and garlic and cook, stirring occasionally until tofu starts to brown, about 5 to 10 minutes. Transfer to crock pot.

2. Whisk the wet together in a small bowl. Pour over tofu and add the broccoli.

3. Cover and cook on high 90 minutes, or on low 2 hours.

4. Serve warm.

One Pan Spiced Tofu with Spinach

Preparation time: 15 minutes
Cooking time: 1 hour 25 minutes
Servings: 4
Ingredients:

- 1 package extra firm tofu, pressed 15 minutes and cut into cubes
- 1 package fresh baby spinach
- 2 limes
- 1 tablespoon margarine
- ½ cup raw peanut butter
- 2 tablespoons lite soy sauce
- 3 cloves garlic, chopped fine

- ½ teaspoon ginger
- ¼ teaspoon red pepper flakes

Directions:

1. Melt margarine in a large saucepan. Add tofu and garlic and cook, stirring occasionally, 5 to 10 minutes, or until tofu starts to brown.

2. Add remaining, except spinach and bring to simmer. Reduce heat, cover and cook, stirring occasionally 30 to 35 minutes.

3. Stir in the spinach and cook 15 minutes more. Serve.

Chicken Broth Cauliflower Soup

Preparation time: 10 minutes
Cooking time: 15 minutes
Servings: 6
Ingredients:

- 2½ pounds (1.1 kg) cauliflower florets
- ½ leek, white and pale green part, halved
- 4 tablespoons butter
- 2 teaspoons fresh parsley, diced
- 2 tablespoons low sodium chicken broth
- 2 teaspoons extra virgin olive oil
- 4 cloves garlic, diced fine
- ¼ teaspoon salt - ¼ teaspoon pepper

Directions:

1. Place the cauliflower in a steamer basket over boiling water. Cover and steam 10 to 15 minutes or until fork tender.

2. Rinse the leek under water and pat dry. Chop into thin slices.

3. Heat oil in a large skillet over medium-low heat. Add the leek and cook 2 to 3 minutes, or until soft. Add the garlic and cook 1 minute more.

4. Add all to a food processor and pulse until almost smooth. Serve warm, or refrigerate for a later use.

Cheese Coated Egg Muffins

Preparation time: 10 minutes
Cooking time: 20 minutes
Servings: 4
Ingredients:

- 4 egg whites
- ½ teaspoon fresh parsley, diced fine
- 3 tablespoons reduced fat Parmesan cheese, divided
- 2 teaspoons water
- ½ teaspoon salt
- Truffle oil to taste
- Nonstick cooking spray

Directions:

1. Heat oven to 400°F (205°C). Spray two muffin pans with cooking spray.

2. In a small bowl, whisk together egg whites, water, and salt until combined.

3. Spoon just enough egg white mixture into each muffin cup to barely cover the bottom. Sprinkle a small pinch of Parmesan on each egg white.

4. Bake 10 to 15 minutes or until the edges are dark brown, be careful not to burn them.

5. Let cool in the pans 3 to 4 minutes then transfer to a small bowl and drizzle lightly with truffle oil.

6. Add parsley and ½ tablespoon Parmesan and toss to coat. Serve.

Cardamom spiced Kale and Chard

Preparation time: 10 minutes
Cooking time: 10 minutes
Servings: 4
Ingredients:

- 2 tablespoons extra-virgin olive oil
- 1 pound (454 g) kale, coarse stems removed and leaves chopped
- 1 pound (454 g) Swiss chard, coarse stems removed and leaves chopped
- 1 tablespoon freshly squeezed lemon juice
- ½ teaspoon ground cardamom
- Sea salt to taste
- Freshly ground black pepper

Directions:

1. Place a large skillet over medium-high heat and add the olive oil.

2. Add the kale, chard, lemon juice, and cardamom to the skillet. Use tongs to toss the greens continuously until they are wilted, about 10 minutes or less.

3. Season the greens with salt and pepper. Serve immediately.

Sautéed Peppery Mushrooms

Preparation time: 10 minutes
Cooking time: 12 minutes
Servings: 4
Ingredients:

- 1 tablespoon butter
- 2 teaspoons extra-virgin olive oil
- 2 pounds button mushrooms, halved
- 2 teaspoons minced fresh garlic
- 1 teaspoon chopped fresh thyme
- Sea salt to taste
- Freshly ground black pepper

Directions:

1. Place a large skillet over medium-high heat and add the butter and olive oil.

2. Sauté the mushrooms, stirring occasionally, until they are lightly caramelized and tender, about 10 minutes.

3. Add the garlic and thyme and sauté for 2 more minutes.

4. Season the mushrooms with salt and pepper before serving.

Low Sugar Bok Choy Bowl

Preparation time: 15 minutes
Cooking time: 7 minutes
Servings: 4
Ingredients:

- 2 teaspoons sesame oil
- 2 pounds (907 g) bok choy, cleaned and quartered
- 2 teaspoons low-sodium soy sauce
- Pinch red pepper flakes
- ½ cup toasted sliced almonds

Directions:

1. Place a large skillet over medium heat and add the oil.

2. When the oil is hot, sauté the bok choy until tender-crisp, about 5 minutes.

3. Stir in the soy sauce and red pepper flakes and sauté 2 minutes more.

4. Remove the bok choy to a serving bowl and top with the sliced almonds.

Nutrition: Calories: 119 fats: 8g protein: 6g carbs: 8 g fiber: 4g sugar: 3g sodium: 294mg

Chapter 9

Pork, Beef and Lamb

Zucchini Lasagna

Preparation time: 30 minutes
Cooking Time: 1 Hour
Servings: 4
Ingredients:

- 1 lb. lean ground beef
- 2 medium zucchinis, julienned
- 3 tomatoes, blanch in hot water, remove skins and dice
- 1 onion, diced
- 1 serrano chili, remove seeds and dice
- 1 cup mushrooms, remove stems and dice
- ½ cup low-fat mozzarella, grated
- What you'll need from store cupboard:
- 2 cloves garlic, diced fine
- ½ cube chicken bouillon
- 1 tsp. paprika
- 1 tsp. dried thyme
- 1 tsp. dried basil
- Salt and pepper
- Nonstick cooking spray

Directions:
1. Lay zucchini on paper towel lined cutting board and sprinkle lightly with salt. Let sit for 10 minutes.
2. Heat oven to broil. Blot zucchini with paper towels and place on baking sheet. Broil 3 minutes. Transfer to paper towels again to remove excess moisture.
3. Lightly coat a deep skillet with cooking spray and place over med-high heat. Add garlic, onion, and chili and cook 1 minute.
4. Add the tomatoes and mushrooms and cook, stirring frequently, about 4 minutes. Transfer vegetables to a bowl.
5. Add the beef to the skillet with the paprika and cook until no longer pink. Add the vegetables and bouillon to the beef along with remaining spices and let simmer over low heat 25 minutes.
6. Heat oven to 375 degrees. Line a small baking dish with parchment paper and place 1/3 of the zucchini in an even layer on the bottom. Top with 1/3 of the meat mixture. Repeat layers.
7. Sprinkle cheese over top and bake 35 minutes. Let rest 10 minutes before serving.

Roasted Duck Legs with Balsamic Mushrooms

Preparation time: 45 minutes
Cooking Time: 1 Hour
Servings: 4

Ingredients:

- 4 bone-in, skin-on duck legs
- 1/2 lb. cremini mushrooms, remove stems and cut caps into thick slices
- 1 green onion, sliced thin
- 1 small shallot, sliced thin
- 3-4 fresh thyme sprigs, crushed lightly
- What you'll need from store cupboard:
- 5 Tbs. extra-virgin olive oil
- 5 Tbs. balsamic vinegar
- 2 cloves garlic, sliced thin
- ½ tsp fresh thyme, chopped
- Kosher salt and freshly ground pepper

Directions:
1. Rinse duck and pat dry with paper towels.
2. In a shallow glass bowl, large enough to hold the duck, combine 3 tablespoons oil, 3 tablespoons vinegar, garlic, shallot, thyme sprigs, ½ teaspoon salt and some pepper. Add the duck, turning to coat. Cover and chill 3-4 hours turning legs once or twice.
3. Remove the duck from the marinade. Pour the marinade into a saucepan and bring to a boil over high heat. Remove from heat.
4. Place a footed rack on the bottom of a large pot, tall enough that the duck legs can stand 2 inches from the bottom. Add about 1 inch of water. Place the duck, skin side up on the rack. Cover and bring to a boil over med-high heat. Let steam until the skin is translucent, about 20 minutes.
5. While duck is steaming, heat the oven to 450 degrees. Line a roasting pan large enough to hold the duck with foil. Place a flat rack in the pan.
6. When the duck is ready, transfer it skin side up to the prepared rack. Brush the skin with the glaze and roast, until skin is brown and crisp, about 20 minutes. Remove from oven and glaze the duck again. Let rest for 5 minutes.
7. In a large skillet, over med-high heat, heat the remaining oil. Add mushrooms, green onions, and cook, stirring frequently about 2 minutes. Add the remaining vinegar, chopped thyme, salt and pepper to taste. Cook until mushrooms are soft and most of the liquid has evaporated.
8. To serve, place duck leg on a plate and spoon mushrooms over.

Russian Steaks with Nuts and Cheese

Preparation time: 30 minutes
Cooking Time: 20 Minutes
Servings: 4

Ingredients:

- 800g of minced pork
- 200g of cream cheese
- 50g peeled walnuts
- 1 onion
- Salt
- Ground pepper
- 1 egg
- Breadcrumbs
- Extra virgin olive oil

Directions:

1. Put the onion cut into quarters in the Thermo mix glass and select 5 seconds speed 5.
2. Add the minced meat, cheese, egg, salt, and pepper.
3. Select 10 seconds, speed 5, turn left.
4. Add the chopped and peeled walnuts and select 4 seconds, turn left, speed 5.
5. Pass the dough to a bowl.
6. Make Russian steaks and go through breadcrumbs.
7. Paint the Russian fillets with extra virgin olive oil on both sides with a brush.
8. Put in the basket of the air fryer, without stacking the Russian fillets.
9. Select 1800C, 15 minutes.

Pork Paprika

Preparation time: 1 hour, plus 20 minutes soaking
Cooking Time: 40 Minutes
Servings: 6
Ingredients:

- 1 lb. pork loin, trim fat and cut into 1-inch cubes
- 1 onion, diced fine
- 1 cup mushrooms, sliced thick
- 2/3 cup fat free sour cream
- What you'll need from store cupboard:
- 1 can petite tomatoes, diced
- ½ cup low sodium chicken broth
- 2 tbsp. olive oil
- 2 tbsp. sweet paprika, divided
- 1 tbsp. garlic, diced fine
- ½ tsp thyme
- ½ tsp caraway seeds, ground
- Salt & pepper to taste

Directions:

1. Place pork in large bowl and sprinkle 1 tablespoon paprika, salt and pepper over meat, toss to coat.
2. Heat 1 tablespoon oil in a large, deep skillet over med-high heat. Add pork and cook, stirring frequently until brown on all sides, about 5-6 minutes. Transfer to a plate.
3. Add remaining tablespoon of oil to skillet and the mushrooms. Cook, stirring, till browned and no more liquid remains in the pan, about 5 minutes. Add the mushrooms to the pork.
4. Add more oil if needed and the onion. Cook about 3-5 minutes, or they just start to brown. Add garlic and spices and cook another 1-2 minutes. Add tomatoes with juice and broth, cook, stirring frequently, until mixture starts to thicken, about 5 minutes.

5. Stir the pork and mushrooms into the sauce. Reduce heat, cover, and simmer 15 minutes, or until pork is tender. Serve.

Beef Goulash Soup

Preparation time: 30 minutes
Cooking time: 20 minutes
Servings: 4
Ingredients:

- Boneless beef top sirloin steak – 6 oz.
- Olive oil – 1 tsp.
- Chopped onion – ½ cup
- Water – 2 cups
- Beef broth – 1 (14.5 oz.) can
- No-salt-added diced tomatoes – 1 (14.5 oz.) can, undrained
- Thinly sliced carrot – ½ cup
- Unsweetened cocoa powder – 1 tsp.
- Garlic – 1 clove, minced
- Thinly sliced cabbage – 1 cup
- Dried wide noodles – ½ cup
- Paprika – 2 tsps.
- Light sour cream – ¼ cup
- Snipped fresh parsley

Directions:

1. Cut meat into ½-inch cubes. In a saucepan, cook and stir meat in hot oil until browned, for about 6 minutes. Add onion, cook and stir until onion softens, about 3 minutes.
2. Stir in the next six Ingredients: (through garlic). Bring to a boil. Reduce heat. Simmer, uncovered, for about 15 minutes or until meat is tender.
3. Stir in paprika, noodles, and cabbage. Simmer, uncovered, until noodles are tender but still firm, for about 5 to 7 minutes. Remove from heat.
4. Top each serving with sour cream.
5. Sprinkle with parsley and additional paprika.
6. Serve.

Beef-Vegetable Ragout

Preparation time: 30 minutes
Cooking time: 8 hours
Servings: 8
Ingredients:

- Beef chuck roast – 1 ½ lb.
- Sliced fresh button or cremini mushrooms – 3 cups
- Chopped onion – 1 cup
- Garlic – 4 cloves, minced
- Salt – ½ tsp.
- Black pepper – ½ tsp.
- Quick-cooking tapioca -1/4 cup, crushed
- 50% less-sodium beef broth – 2 (14.5 oz.) cans
- Dry sherry – ½ cup
- Sugar snap pea pods – 4 cups
- Cherry tomatoes – 2 cups, halved
- Hot cooked multigrain noodles – 4 cups

Directions:

1. Cut meat into ¾-inch pieces.
2. Coat a skillet with cooking spray. Cook meat, half at a time, in the hot skillet until browned.

3. Combine the next five Ingredients: (through pepper) in a slow cooker. Sprinkle with tapioca. Add meat and pour in broth and dry sherry.

4. Cover and cook on low for 8 to 10 hours or high for 4 to 5 hours. If slow cooker is on low, turn to high. Stir in sugar snap peas. Cover and cook for 5 minutes. Stir in cherry tomatoes. Serve meat mixture over hot cooked noodles.

Fried Pork Chops

Preparation time: 10 minutes
Cooking Time: 35 Minutes
Servings: 2
Ingredients:

- 3 cloves of ground garlic
- 2 tbsp. olive oil - 1 tbsp. of marinade
- 4 thawed pork chops

Directions:
1. Mix the cloves of ground garlic, marinade, and oil. Then apply this mixture on the chops.
2. Put the chops in the air fryer at 3600C for 35 minutes

Pork on a Blanket

Preparation time: 10 minutes
Cooking Time: 10 Minutes
Servings: 4
Ingredients:

- ½ puff pastry sheet, defrosted
- 16 thick smoked sausages
- 15 ml of milk

Directions:
1. Preheat la air fryer to 200°C and set the timer to 5 minutes.
2. Cut the puff pastry into 64 x 38 mm strips.
3. Place a cocktail sausage at the end of the puff pastry and roll around the sausage, scaling the dough with some water.
4. Brush the top (with the seam facing down) of the sausages wrapped in milk and place them in the preheated air fryer.
5. Cook at 200°C for 10 minutes or until golden brown.

Greek Flat Iron Steaks

Preparation time: 10 minutes
Cooking time: 15 minutes
Servings: 4
Ingredients:

- Lemon – 1 - Boneless beef shoulder top blade steaks (flat iron) – 2 (6 to 8 oz.)
- Salt – ¼ tsp.
- Black pepper – ¼ tsp.
- Dried rosemary – 1 tsp. crushed
- Olive oil – 4 tsp.
- Grape tomatoes – 2 cups, halved
- Garlic – 2 cloves, minced
- Pitted green olives – 1/3 cup, halved
- Crumbled feta cheese – ¼ cup
- Lemon wedges

Directions:
1. Remove 1 tsp. zest from the lemon. Set zest aside. Cut steaks in half and season with salt and pepper. Sprinkle rosemary on both sides of the steaks.

2. Heat 2 tsps. Oil in a skillet. Add steaks and cook until medium rare, about 8 to 10 minutes. Turning once. Remove and set aside.

3. Add remaining 2 tsps. Oil to the skillet. Add garlic and tomatoes. Cook until tomatoes are soft and burst, for about 3 minutes. Remove from heat. Stir in the lemon zest and olives. Serve steaks with tomato relish. Sprinkle with cheese and serve with the reserved lemon wedges.

Spiced Burgers with Cilantro Cucumber Sauce

Preparation time: 25 minutes
Cooking time: 15 minutes
Servings: 4
Ingredients:

- Plain fat-free Greek yogurt – 1 (5.3 to 6 oz.) container
- Finely chopped cucumber – 2/3 cup
- Snipped fresh cilantro – ¼ cup
- Garlic – 2 cloves, minced
- Salt – 1/8 tsp.
- Black pepper – 1/8 tsp.
- Canned garbanzo beans – ½ cup, rinsed and drained
- Lean ground beef – 1 lb.
- Finely chopped red onion – ¼ cup
- Chopped jalapeno pepper – 2 Tbsps.
- Salt – ½ tsp.
- Ground cumin – ¼ tsp.
- Ground coriander – ¼ tsp.
- Cinnamon – 1/8 tsp.
- Black pepper – 1/8 tsp.
- Radicchio – 1 head, shredded

Directions:
1. To make the sauce: in a bowl, stir together the first six Ingredients: (through black pepper). Cover and keep in the refrigerator.
2. In a bowl, mash garbanzo beans with a fork. Add the next eight Ingredients: (through black pepper), mix well. Form meat mixture into four ¾ inch thick patties.
3. Grill burgers, covered, over medium 14 to 18 minutes or until done (160F). Turning once.
4. Toss radicchio with additional fresh cilantro leaves.
5. Serve burgers on radicchio, top with sauce.

Sunday Brisket

Preparation time: 4 hours
Cooking time: 8 hours
Servings: 10
Ingredients:

- 1 teaspoon coarsely ground pepper
- 2 tablespoons cold water
- 3 tablespoons olive oil, divided
- 1 tablespoon tapioca flour
- 4 cups onions, sliced
- 1/2 teaspoon paprika
- 4 garlic cloves, minced
- 1 teaspoon Worcestershire sauce
- 1 tablespoon brown sugar

- 2 teaspoons Italian seasoning
- 1 fresh beef brisket (4 to 5 lbs.)
- 2 tablespoons tomato paste
- 1/3 cup all-purpose flour
- 1 can (14-1/2 ounces) reduced-sodium beef broth
- 1 teaspoon salt
- 4 tablespoons balsamic vinegar

Directions:

1. Preheat a tablespoon of oil in a skillet over medium heat; add and sauté sliced onions until softened. Then sprinkle with a 1 tablespoon of brown sugar and garlic.
2. Turn the heat down and cook until onions become brown, with occasional stirring, for about 10 minutes.
3. Transfer cooked onions to a slow cooker. Cut brisket into half and sprinkle with 1/3 cup all-purpose flour.
4. Preheat leftover oil in a skillet and then add brisket; cook both sides until browned and sprinkle with pepper and salt.
5. Transfer cooked brisket to the cooker over onions. Now add 4 tablespoons balsamic vinegar and cook over high heat.
6. Then stir in 2 tablespoons tomato paste, 1 can (14-1/2 ounces) broth, 1 teaspoon Worcestershire sauce, 2 teaspoons Italian seasoning and 1/2 teaspoon paprika until blended; pour this mixture over brisket.
7. Cover the cooker and cook for about 8-10 hours on low, until meat is completely cooked through.
8. Then take the brisket out from the cooker. Transfer cooking juices from the cooker to the pan; skim fat if any and boil it lightly.
9. Take a bowl and add 1 tablespoon tapioca flour and 2 tablespoons cold water; mix well until smooth and transfer to cooking juices with stirring. Cook for about 1-2 minutes until thickened.
10. Cut the brisket into thin slices. Serve the brisket with sauce and enjoy!

Pork Rind

Preparation time: 10 minutes
Cooking Time: 1h
Servings: 4
Ingredients:

- 1kg of pork rinds
- Salt
- ½ tsp. black pepper coffee

Directions:

1. Preheat the air fryer. Set the time of 5 minutes and the temperature to 2000C.
2. Cut the bacon into cubes - 1 finger wide.
3. Season with salt and a pinch of pepper.
4. Place in the basket of the air fryer. Set the time of 45 minutes and press the power button.
5. Shake the basket every 10 minutes so that the pork rinds stay golden brown equally.
6. Once they are ready, drain a little on the paper towel so they stay dry. Transfer to a plate and serve.

Ginger Chili Broccoli

Preparation time: 10 minutes
Cooking Time: 25 Minutes
Servings: 5
Ingredients:

- 8 cups broccoli florets
- 1/2 cup olive oil
- 2 fresh lime juice
- 2 tbsp. fresh ginger, grated
- 2 tsp chili pepper, chopped

Directions:

1. Add broccoli florets into the steamer and steam for 8 minutes.
2. Meanwhile, for dressing in a small bowl, combine lime juice, oil, ginger, and chili pepper.
3. Add steamed broccoli in a large bowl then pour dressing over broccoli. Toss well.

Pork Tenderloin

Preparation time: 10 minutes
Cooking time: 45 minutes
Servings: 2-4
Ingredients:

- 2 large eggs
- ¼ cup milk
- 2 cups seasoned breadcrumbs
- Salt and pepper to taste
- Nonstick cooking spray

Directions:

1. Slice the tenderloin into ½-inch slices.
2. Place the slices between two plastic sheets and tap them until each piece is ¼ inch thick.
3. In a large container, mix the eggs and milk.
4. In a separate container or dish, pour the breadcrumbs.
5. Introduce each piece of pork in the mixture of eggs and milk, letting the excess drain.
6. Then introduce the pork in the breadcrumbs, covering each side.
7. Place the covered pork on a wire rack for 30 minutes to make sure the cover adheres.
8. Preheat the air fryer to 400°F (204 °C).
9. Spray the basket of the air fryer with nonstick cooking spray. Place the covered sirloin in the basket in a single layer.
10. Cook the sirloin for 10 minutes, then take it out, turn it over and sprinkle with more nonstick spray.
11. Cook for 5-minutes more or until both sides are crispy and golden brown.

Chestnut Stuffed Pork Roast

Preparation time: 1 hour 30 minutes
Cooking time: 1 hour 35 minutes
Servings: 15
Ingredients:

- 5 lb. pork loin roast, boneless, double tied
- ½ lb. ground pork
- ½ cup celery, diced fine
- ½ cup onion, diced fine
- 2 tbsp. fresh parsley, diced, divided
- 1 tbsp. margarine
- What you'll need from store cupboard:
- 15 oz. can chestnuts, drained
- 2 cup low sodium chicken broth
- 3 tbsp. flour
- 2 tbsp. brandy, divided

- ½ tsp salt
- ½ tsp pepper
- 1/8 tsp allspice
- Salt & black pepper, to taste

Directions:

1. Heat oven to 350 degrees.
2. Untie roast, open and pound lightly to even thickness.
3. Melt margarine in a skillet over med-high heat. Add celery and onion and cook until soft.
4. In a large bowl, combine ground pork, 1 tablespoon parsley, 1 tablespoon brandy and seasonings. Mix in celery and onion. Spread over roast.
5. Lay a row of chestnuts down the center. Roll meat around filling and tie securely with butcher string. Roast in oven 1 ½ hours or until meat thermometer reaches 145 degrees. Remove and let rest 10 minutes.
6. Measure out 2 tablespoons of drippings, discard the rest, into a saucepan. Place over medium heat and whisk in flour until smooth. Add broth and cook, stirring, until mixture thickens. Chop remaining chestnuts and add to gravy along with remaining brandy and parsley. Season with salt and pepper if desired. Slice the roast and serve topped with gravy.

Beef, Tomato, and Pepper Tortillas

Preparation time: 20 minutes
Cooking time: 0 minutes
Servings: 6
Ingredients:

- 6 whole wheat flour tortillas (10-inch)
- 6 large romaine lettuce leaves
- 12 ounces (340 g) cooked deli roast beef, thinly sliced
- 1 cup diced red bell peppers
- 1 cup diced tomatoes
- 1 tablespoon red wine vinegar
- 1 teaspoon cumin
- 1/4 teaspoon freshly ground black pepper
- 1 tablespoon olive oil

Directions:

1. Unfold the tortillas on a clean work surface, then top each tortilla with a lettuce leaf. Divide the roast beef over the leaf.
2. Combine the remaining Ingredients: in a bowl. Stir to mix well. Pour the mixture over the beef.
3. Fold the tortillas over the fillings, then roll them up. Serve immediately.

Nutrition: calories: 295 fats: 6.0g protein: 19.0g carbs: 43.0g fiber: 6.0g sugar: 3.0g sodium: 600mg
Preparation time: 10 minutes
Cooking time: 20 minutes
Servings: 4
Ingredients:

- 4 (5-ounce / 142-g) pork chops, about 1 inch thick
- 1 tablespoon chipotle chili powder
- Juice and zest of 1 lime
- 2 teaspoons minced garlic
- 1 teaspoon ground cinnamon
- 1 tablespoon extra-virgin olive oil
- Pinch sea salt
- Lime wedges, for garnish

Directions:

1. Combine all the Ingredients, except for the lemon wedges, in a large bowl. Toss to combine well.
2. Wrap the bowl in plastic and refrigerate to marinate for at least 4 hours.
3. Preheat the oven to 400°F (205°C). Set a rack on a baking sheet.
4. Remove the bowl from the refrigerator and let sit for 15 minutes. Discard the marinade and place the pork on the rack.
5. Roast in the preheated oven for 20 minutes or until well browned. Flip the pork halfway through the cooking time.
6. Serve immediately with lime wedges.

Salted Biscuit Pie Turkey Chops

Preparation time: 15 minutes
Cooking time: 20 minutes
Servings: 4
Ingredients:

- 8 large turkey chops
- 300 gr of crackers
- 2 eggs
- Extra virgin olive oil
- Salt
- Ground pepper

Directions:

1. Put the turkey chops on the worktable, and salt and pepper.
2. Beat the eggs in a bowl.
3. Crush the cookies in the Thermo mix with a few turbo strokes until they are made grit, or you can crush them with the blender.
4. Put the cookies in a bowl.
5. Pass the chops through the beaten egg and then passed them through the crushed cookies. Press well so that the empanada is perfect.
6. Paint the empanada with a silicone brush and extra virgin olive oil.
7. Put the chops in the basket of the air fryer, not all will enter. They will be done in batches.
8. Select 200 degrees, 15 minutes.
9. When you have all the chops made, serve.

Roasted Pork

Preparation time: 10 minutes
Cooking Time: 30 Minutes
Servings: 2-4
Ingredients:

- 500-2000g Pork meat (To roast)
- Salt
- Oil

Directions:

1. Join the cuts in an orderly manner.
2. Place the meat on the plate
3. Varnish with a little oil.
4. Place the roasts with the fat side down.
5. Cook in air fryer at 1800C for 30 minutes.
6. Turn when you hear the beep.
7. Remove from the oven. Drain excess juice.
8. Let stand for 10 minutes on aluminum foil before serving.

Homemade Flamingos

Preparation time: 30 minutes

Cooking Time: 20 Minutes
Servings: 4
Ingredients:
1. 400g of very thin sliced pork fillets c / n
2. 2 boiled and chopped eggs
3. 100g chopped Serrano ham
4. 1 beaten egg
5. Breadcrumbs
Directions:
1. Make a roll with the pork fillets. Introduce half-cooked egg and Serrano ham. So that the roll does not lose its shape, fasten with a string or chopsticks. Pass the rolls through beaten egg and then through the breadcrumbs until it forms a good layer. Preheat the air fryer a few minutes at 180° C.
2. Insert the rolls in the basket and set the timer for about 8 minutes at 180o C.

Meatloaf Reboot

Preparation time: 20 minutes
Cooking Time: 9 Minutes
Servings: 2
Ingredients:
- 4 slices of leftover meatloaf, cut about 1-inch thick.
Directions:
1. Preheat your air fryer to 350 degrees.
2. Spray each side of the meatloaf slices with cooking spray. Add the slices to the air fryer and cook for about 9 to 10 minutes. Don't turn the slices halfway through the cooking cycle, because they may break apart. Instead, keep them on one side to cook to ensure they stay together

Turkey Enchiladas

Preparation time: 45 minutes
Cooking time: 35 minutes
Servings: 8
Ingredients:
- 3 cup turkey, cooked and cut in pieces
- 1 onion, diced
- 1 bell pepper, diced
- 1 cup fat free sour cream
- 1 cup reduced fat cheddar cheese, grated
- What you'll need from store cupboard:
- 8 6-inch flour tortillas
- 14 ½ oz. low sodium chicken broth
- ¾ cup salsa
- 3 tbsp. flour
- 2 tsp olive oil
- 1 ¼ tsp coriander
- ¼ tsp pepper
- Nonstick cooking spray
Directions:
1. Spray a large saucepan with cooking spray and heat oil over med-high heat. Add onion and bell pepper and cook until tender.
2. Sprinkle with flour, coriander and pepper and stir until blended. Slowly stir in broth. Bring to a boil and cook, stirring, 2 minutes or until thickened.
3. Remove from heat and stir in sour cream and ¾ cup cheese.

4. Heat oven to 350 degrees. Spray a 13x9-inch pan with cooking spray.
5. In a large bowl, combine turkey, salsa, and 1 cup of cheese mixture. Spoon 1/3 cup mixture down middle of each tortilla and roll up. Place seam side down in prepared dish.
6. Pour remaining cheese mixture over top of enchiladas. Cover and bake 20 minutes. Uncover and sprinkle with remaining cheese. Bake another 5-10 minutes until cheese is melted and starts to brown.

Mexican Meat Loaf

Preparation time: 30 minutes
Cooking time: 4 hours
Servings: 8
Ingredients:
- 6 garlic cloves, minced
- 2 pounds lean ground beef (90% lean)
- 6 tablespoons ketchup, divided
- 1/8 teaspoon cayenne pepper
- 2 tablespoons Worcestershire sauce
- 1/2 teaspoon pepper
- 12 saltines, crushed
- 1/2 teaspoon salt
- 1 medium onion, finely chopped
- 1 teaspoon paprika
Directions:
1. Make 3 strips of foil; crisscross the strips. Place these strips into a slow cooker at the bottom.
2. Now spray the strips with cooking spray. Take a bowl and add 2 tablespoons Worcestershire sauce, 12 crushed saltines, 2 tablespoons of ketchup, 1 finely chopped onion, 1/2 teaspoon salt, 1 teaspoon paprika, 1/8 teaspoon cayenne pepper, 1/2 teaspoon pepper and 6 minced cloves of garlic; combine well.
3. Add beef into the mixture and toss well until coated. Shape into a loaf. Place this round loaf over strips in the center.
4. Cover the cooker and cook for about 4-5 hours on low. Once done, take the meat out and transfer to a serving platter. Spread ketchup over Mexican meatloaf and enjoy!

Beef Daube Provencal

Preparation time: 1 hour 30 minutes
Cooking time: 5 hours
Servings: 8
Ingredients:
- 2 teaspoons olive oil
- 1 cup dry red wine
- Hot cooked pasta or mashed potatoes
- 1 (about 2 pounds) boneless beef chuck roast or venison roast, cut into 1-inch cubes
- 1-1/2 teaspoons salt, divided
- 1 bay leaf
- 1/2 teaspoon coarsely ground pepper, divided
- 1 teaspoon fresh thyme, chopped
- 2 cups carrots, chopped
- 1 teaspoon fresh rosemary, chopped
- 1-1/2 cups onion, chopped
- 1/2 cup beef broth
- 12 garlic cloves, crushed

- 1 can (14-1/2 ounces) diced tomatoes
- 1 tablespoon tomato paste
- Fresh thyme leaves (optional)
- Dash ground cloves

Directions:

1. Preheat oil in a skillet over medium heat; sprinkle meat with ¼ teaspoon of pepper and ½ teaspoon of salt.

2. Transfer meat to a skillet and cook both sides until browned; then transfer to a slow cooker.

3. Add 1-1/2 cups chopped onion, 12 crushed cloves of garlic, 2 cups of chopped carrots and remaining pepper and salt into the skillet; cook for about 4-6 minutes until golden brown.

4. Add 1 tablespoon of tomato paste; cook for about a minute until fragrant. Then add 1 cup dry red wine and boil it lightly.

5. Transfer the mixture into the slow cooker. Cover the cooker and cook for about 5-7 hours, until tender. Serve beef daube Provencal with mashed potatoes and cooked pasta. Sprinkle fresh thyme over top and enjoy!

Boeuf Bourguignon

Preparation time: 15 minutes
Cooking time: 8 hours
Servings: 12 servings (2/3 cup each)
Ingredients:

- 3 pounds beef stew meat
- 1 teaspoon salt
- 1-3/4 cups dry red wine
- 1/3 cup all-purpose flour
- 3 tablespoons olive oil
- 2 garlic cloves, minced
- 1/4 teaspoon pepper
- 3 tablespoons dried onion, minced
- 24 (about 2 cups) pearl onions, peeled
- 2 tablespoons dried parsley flakes
- 1-pound whole fresh mushrooms, quartered
- 8 bay leaves
- 8 bacon strips, chopped
- 1 teaspoon dried thyme

Directions:

1. Add 3 lbs. beef stew meat into a large plastic bag; then add 3 tablespoons olive oil, 1-3/4 cups dry red wine and all the seasonings. Seal this bag and shake lightly to coat the meat, refrigerate for 12 hours or overnight.

2. Cook bacon in a skillet over medium heat with occasional stirring until crisp. Drain on a plate cover with paper towels.

3. Discard dripping, if any. (Reserve only a tablespoon in the pan).

4. Add 1-pound whole fresh quartered mushrooms and 3 tablespoons of dried minced onion; cook over medium heat with stirring for a minute.

5. Now drain the marinade and reserve it. Transfer beef to a slow cooker.

6. Sprinkle with 1/3 cup all-purpose flour and 1 teaspoon salt; toss well until coated.

7. Top with the mixture of mushrooms and bacon along with reserved marinade.

8. Cover the cooker and cook for about 8-10 hours on low, until tender. Remove the bay leaf.

9. Serve Boeuf Bourguignon with noodles!

Pork and Pumpkin Stew

Preparation time: 30 minutes
Cooking time: 4 hours
Servings: 8
Ingredients:

- 1 onion, diced
- 1 (14.5-ounce) can black beans, drained and rinsed
- 16 oz. pork shoulder, trimmed of all visible fat, and cut into cubes of 1-inch
- 1 bay leave
- ½ teaspoon black pepper
- 4 sprig fresh thyme
- 1 teaspoon seasoning (salt-free, such as Mrs. Dash)
- 4 clove garlic, minced
- 1 tablespoon olive oil
- 1 small sugar/pie pumpkin, peeled, seeded, and diced
- 2 tablespoons tomato paste
- 3 carrots, peeled and diced
- 1 cup beef broth
- 4 celery stalks, diced
- 1/4 teaspoon ground cinnamon

Directions:

1. Season pork with salt, seasoning and pepper.

2. Preheat oil to a skillet over medium heat; cook pork for about 8 minutes until browned. Once browned, take it out and keep it aside.

3. Add 2 tablespoons tomato paste, 1/4 teaspoon ground cinnamon and 1 cup beef broth to a pan; whisk well.

4. Now add cooked browned meat along with leftover Ingredients: and liquid into slow cooker; stir well. Add to the slow cooker.

5. Cook for about 7 hours and 40 minutes on low or for 3 hours and 40 minutes on high.

6. Stir in 1 (14.5-ounce) can black beans and cook further for 20 minutes.

7. Before serving, remove bay leaf.

Crockpot Chipotle Steak

Preparation time: 15 minutes
Cooking time: 2 hours
Servings: 6
Ingredients:

- 2 cups canned crushed tomatoes
- 1 teaspoon garlic, finely minced
- 1 1/2 lbs. London broil, cubed
- 1 1/2 cup poblano pepper, cut into 1-inch squares
- ½ teaspoon salt free Mexican seasoning
- 1 1/2 cup red onion, cut into 1-inch squares
- 1/4 teaspoon kosher salt
- 3 teaspoons olive oil, divided
- 2 peppers chipotle chili in adobo
- 1 tablespoon light or dark brown sugar, packed
- ½ tablespoon adobo sauce from chipotle pepper can
- 1 tablespoon Worcestershire sauce

Directions:

1. In a bowl, mix steak cubes with salt and seasoning; toss well until coated and keep it aside.
2. Take out 2 chipotle peppers from the can and chop them finely. Transfer them to a bowl. Add 2 cups crushed tomatoes, 1 tablespoon Worcestershire sauce, 1 tablespoon brown sugar and 1/2 tablespoon of the sauce from can; stir well and keep it aside.
3. Preheat a teaspoon of oil in a nonstick pan; then add 1 1/2 cup red onion, 1 1/2 cup poblano pepper, and 1 teaspoon of finely minced garlic. Spread all these Ingredients: evenly in a pan and cook with stirring occasionally until crisp-tender. Once cooked, transfer into a Crockpot.
4. Again, preheat a teaspoon of oil in a pan. Then add half seasoned cubes of beef and cook each side for a minute, until browned. Once cooked, transfer these cubes into Crockpot.
5. Then stir in the adobo and crushed tomato mixture. Simmer in the crockpot on low for about 2-4 hours.
6. Serve right away!

Chuck and Veggies
Preparation time: 15 minutes
Cooking time: 9 hours
Servings: 2
Ingredients:

- ¼ cup dry red wine - ¼ teaspoon salt
- 8 oz. boneless lean chuck roast
- ¼ teaspoon black pepper
- 8 oz. frozen pepper stir-fry
- 1 teaspoon Worcestershire sauce
- 8 oz. whole mushrooms
- 1 teaspoon instant coffee granules
- 1 1/4 cups fresh green beans, trimmed
- 1 dried bay leaf

Directions:
1. Mix all the Ingredients: except salt in a bowl; combine well and then transfer to a slow cooker.
2. Cover the cooker and cook for about 9 hours on low and 4 1/2 hours on high, until beef is completely cooked through and tender.
3. Stir in ¼ teaspoon salt gently. Take out the vegetables and beef and transfer to 2 shallow bowls.
4. Pour liquid into the skillet; boil it lightly and cook until liquid reduces to ¼ cup, for about 1 1/2 minutes.
5. Pour over veggies and beef. Discard bay leaf and serve.

Southwest Turkey Lasagna
Preparation time: 50 minutes
Servings: 8
Cooking Time: 20 Minutes
Ingredients:

- 1 lb. lean ground turkey
- 1 onion, diced
- 1 green bell pepper, diced
- 1 red pepper, diced
- 8 oz. fat free cream cheese
- 1 cup Mexican cheese blend, grated
- ½ cup fat free sour cream
- What you'll need from store cupboard:
- 6 8-inch low carb whole wheat tortillas

- 10 oz. enchilada sauce
- ½ cup salsa
- 1 tsp chili powder
- Nonstick cooking spray

Directions:
1. Heat oven to 400 degrees. Spray a 13x9-inch baking dish with cooking spray.
2. In a large skillet, over medium heat, cook turkey, onion, and peppers until turkey is no longer pink. Drain fat.
3. Stir in cream cheese and chili powder.
4. Pour enchilada sauce into a shallow dish. Dip tortillas in sauce to coat. Place two tortillas in prepared dish. Spread with ½ the turkey mixture and sprinkle 1/3 of the cheese over turkey. Repeat layer. Top with remaining tortillas and cheese.
5. Cover with foil and bake 20-25 minutes, or until heated through. This can also be frozen up to 3 months.
6. Let rest 10 minutes before cutting. Serve topped with salsa and sour cream.

Balsamic Chicken & Vegetable Skillet
Preparation time: 10 minutes
Cooking time: 20 minutes
Servings: 4
Ingredients:

- 1 lb. chicken breasts, cut in 1-inch cubes
- 1 cup cherry tomatoes, halved
- 1 cup broccoli florets
- 1 cup baby Bella mushrooms, sliced
- 1 tbsp. fresh basil, diced
- What you'll need from store cupboard:
- 1/2 recipe homemade pasta, cooked and drain well
- ½ cup low sodium chicken broth
- 3 tbsp. balsamic vinegar
- 2 tbsp. olive oil, divided
- 1 tsp pepper
- ½ tsp garlic powder
- ½ tsp salt
- ½ tsp red pepper flakes

Directions:
1. Heat oil in a large, deep skillet over med-high heat. Add chicken and cook until browned on all sides, 8-10 minutes.
2. Add vegetables, basil, broth, and seasonings. Cover, reduce heat to medium and cook 5 minutes, or vegetables are tender.
3. Uncover and stir in cooked pasta and vinegar. Cook until heated through, 3-4 minutes. Serve.

Deconstructed Philly Cheesesteaks
Preparation time: 10 minutes
Cooking Time: 20 Minutes
Servings: 4
Ingredients:

- 1 lb. lean ground beef
- 5-6 mushrooms, halved
- 4 slices provolone cheese
- 3 green bell peppers, quartered
- 2 medium onions, quartered
- What you'll need from store cupboard:

- ½ cup low sodium beef broth
- 1-2 tbsp. Worcestershire sauce
- 1 tsp olive oil
- Salt & pepper, to taste

Directions:
1. Heat oven to 400 degrees.
2. Place vegetables in a large bowl and add oil. Toss to coat. Dump out onto a large baking sheet and bake 10-15 minutes, or until tender-crisp.
3. Place beef in a large skillet and cook over med-high heat until no longer pink. Drain off fat.
4. Add broth and Worcestershire. Cook, stirring occasionally, until liquid is absorbed, about 5 minutes. Salt and pepper beef if desired. Top with sliced cheese, remove from heat and cover until cheese melts.
5. Divide vegetables evenly between 4 bowls. Top with beef and serve.

Ham & Brie Turnovers
Preparation time: 30 minutes
Cooking Time: 25 Minutes
Servings: 8
Ingredients:

- 8 slices ham, diced
- 3 oz. brie cheese
- 1 egg
- What you'll need from store cupboard:
- 2 9-inch pie crusts, unbaked
- 2 tbsp. sugar free fig pre servings
- 2 tbsp. stone ground mustard
- 1 tbsp. water
- 1/8 tsp salt
- 1/8 tsp pepper

Directions:
1. Heat oven to 400 degrees. Line two cookie sheets with parchment paper.
2. On a lightly floured surface unroll one pie crust and cut 4 4-inch circles and place on prepared pan.
3. Gather up remaining dough, roll out and cut 4 more 4-inch circles and set aside
4. In a small bowl, combine fig preserves, mustard, salt, and pepper. Place a heaping teaspoon of fig mustard mixture in the center of dough on the pan and shape into a half dollar size
5. Use your hands to make a smaller circle of the brie and place on top of fig mixture. Place ham on top of the cheese, leaving ¼-inch edge.
6. In another small bowl, beat egg and water together. Brush around edge and top with 4-inch circle of dough. Repeat. Use a fork to seal the edges and cut a small X in the top. Brush with remaining egg wash.
7. Bake 25 minutes, or until golden brown. Remove from oven and cool on wire rack at least 5 minutes before serving. Repeat these steps with the second pie crust.

Shredded Green Chili Beef
Preparation time: 10 minutes
Cooking time: 7 hours
Servings: 12
Ingredients:

- 1 teaspoon chili powder
- 2 large sweet onions, halved and thinly sliced
- 1 can (28 ounces) green enchilada sauce
- 4 tablespoons packed brown sugar, divided
- 2 tablespoons canola oil
- 1 tablespoon paprika
- 1 (about 3 lbs.) boneless beef chuck roast
- 1-1/2 teaspoons salt
- 1/2 teaspoon pepper
- 1 teaspoon cayenne pepper
- 1 teaspoon garlic powder

Directions:
1. Add 3 tablespoons brown sugar along with thinly sliced onion into a slow cooker.
2. Combine leftover sugar with 1 teaspoon cayenne pepper, 1 tablespoon paprika, 1-1/2 teaspoons salt, 1 teaspoon chili powder, 1/2 teaspoon pepper and 1 teaspoon garlic powder; coat beef with this mixture completely.
3. Preheat some oil in a skillet and add beef; cook each side for about 1-2 minutes, until browned. Once cooked, transfer to the cooker.
4. Pour 1 can (28 ounces) green enchilada sauce over beef. Cover the cooker and cook for about 7-9 hours on low, until completely cooked through.
5. Once cooked, take the beef out and shred it with forks; transfer shredded beef back to the cooker and heat through.
6. Serve over potatoes, if needed and enjoy!

Chinese Pot Roast
Preparation time: 3 hours
Cooking time: 9 hours
Servings: 6
Ingredients:

- 2 onions, chopped
- 1/2 teaspoon ground ginger
- 3 pounds boneless pot roast
- 4 tablespoons cup water
- 2 tablespoons flour
- 4 tablespoons light soy sauce
- 1 tablespoon canola oil

Directions:
1. Fill the small bowl with 2 tablespoons flour; dip roast into it.
2. Preheat oil in a pan and cook the roast until browned. Then transfer it to a slow cooker followed by 2 large chopped onions on top.
3. Now combine 4 tablespoons cup water, 4 tablespoons light soy sauce and 1/2 teaspoon ground ginger; mix well and pour over roast in the cooker.
4. Cover the cooker and cook for about 10 minutes on high. Turn the heat down and cook for about 8-10 hours on low.
5. Slice the beef and serve along with rice. Enjoy the meal!

Tuscan Pork Chops
Preparation time: 30 minutes
Cooking time: 8 hours
Servings: 6
Ingredients:

- 6 (about 2-1/2 lbs.) bone-in pork chops, cut 1/2-inch think

- 4 ounces cooked orzo, kept warm
- 2 teaspoons Italian seasoning
- 2 tablespoons cold water
- 4 cloves garlic, minced
- 2 tablespoons cornstarch
- 1/2 teaspoon salt
- 2 zucchinis, cut into 1-inch pieces
- 1/4 teaspoon pepper
- 2 tablespoons balsamic vinegar
- 1 onion, chopped
- 2 (14-1/2-ounce) cans no-salt-added diced tomatoes, undrained

Directions:
1. Take a bowl and mix 1/4 teaspoon pepper, 1/2 teaspoon salt, 2 teaspoons Italian seasoning and garlic in it; stir well.
2. Add chopped onion to a slow cooker along with half of pork chops. Sprinkle half of the mixture of seasoning over pork chops.
3. Again, layer pork chops followed by remaining seasoning mixture on top.
5. Top last layer of seasoning with 2 tablespoons balsamic vinegar and undrained tomatoes. Then add pieces of zucchini.
6. Cover the cooker and cook for about 4-5 hours on high or for 8-9 hours on low.
7. Once cooked, transfer veggies along with meat to a platter.
8. Add 2 tablespoons cornstarch and 2 tablespoons cold water to a saucepan; cook well with stirring. Then add juices present from cooker into the pan slowly and gradually. Cook until thickened for about 2-3 minutes.
9. Serve Tuscan pork chops over veggies and meat. You can also serve it with orzo!

Crockpot Flank Steak

Preparation time: 10 minutes
Cooking time: 4 hours
Servings: 6
Ingredients:

- 2 tablespoons vinegar
- 1/8 teaspoon pepper
- 1 flank steak (about 1-1/2 lbs.), cut in half
- 1/2 teaspoon salt
- 1 tablespoon canola oil
- 1/2 teaspoon sugar
- 1 large onion, sliced
- 1 teaspoon garlic powder
- 1/3 cup water
- 1-1/4 teaspoons chili powder
- 1 can (4 oz.) green chiles, chopped

Directions:
1. Preheat some oil in a skillet and brown steak in it. Transfer browned steak into a slow cooker.
2. Add and sauté onion in the same skillet for about a minute. Start adding 1/3 cups of water gradually.
3. Add leftover Ingredients: and boil lightly. Pour this mixture over steak in cooker.
4. Cover the cooker and cook for about 4-5 hours on low, until meat is tender.

5. Before serving, slice the steak and serve along with pan juices and onion!

Pot Roast Soup

Preparation time: 10 minutes
Cooking Time: 7 hours
Servings: 6
Ingredients:

- Beef shoulder roast boneless 2 ½ pounds (1 kg 134 g)
- Onions, chopped 2 cups
- Diced tomatoes 15 oz. (425 g)
- Hash brown potatoes, cubed 1 cup
- Beef broth 1 cup
- Minced garlic 1 tbsp.
- Dried thyme leaves 1 tsp
- Pepper ¼ tsp
- Broccoli slaw 2 cups
- Frozen peas ½ cup

Directions:
1. Cut roast into equal pieces.
2. Place in a slow cooker and add onions, tomatoes, broth, thyme, garlic, and pepper.
3. Cover and cook for 5 to 6 hours on high until beef is tender.
4. Add in broccoli and potatoes, and cook for half an hour.
5. Add in peas and cook for 20 more minutes or until the peas are done.
6. Serve after done.

Beef and Zucchini Meatballs

Preparation time: 5 minutes
Cooking Time: 25 minutes
Servings: 4
Ingredients:

- Ground beef 1 pound (454 g)
- Grated zucchini 1 cup
- Salt ¼ tsp
- Pepper ¼ tsp

Directions:
1. Preheat oven to 400 F (204 °C).
2. In a bowl, mix all Ingredients: and shape them into 20 meatballs.
3. Place on a baking sheet and bake for 23-25 minutes.
4. Serve hot.

Meatballs with Spaghetti

Preparation time: 15 minutes
Cooking Time: 30 minutes
Servings: 6
Ingredients:

- Grounded turkey breast 1 pound (454 g)
- Chopped onion ½ cup
- Egg, beaten 1
- Plain bread crumbs ¼ cup
- Garlic powder 1 tsp
- Salt ½ tsp
- Black pepper ½ tsp
- Canola oil 1 tbsp.
- Sliced mushrooms 8 oz. (227 g)

- Marinara sauce 26 oz. (737 g)
- Spaghetti, cooked 12 oz. (340 g) - dried
- Dried basil leaves ½ tsp

Directions:

1. Combine turkey with onions, breadcrumbs, eggs, salt, pepper, and garlic powder. Mix well and form in meatballs.
2. In a skillet, brown meatballs on all sides for about 5-8 minutes and remove them. Then cook mushrooms for about 5-8 minutes. Add in meatballs, then cover with marinara sauce and basil. Cook for 11-12 minutes.
3. Serve with spaghetti.

Irish Beef Pot Pie

Preparation time: 10 minutes
Cooking Time: 30 minutes
Servings: 6
Ingredients:

- Beef flat iron steaks 1 ½ pound (680 g)
- Cremini mushrooms, sliced 8 oz. (227 g)
- Frozen sliced carrots 1 ½ cups
- Frozen peas 1 ½ cups
- Fresh thyme, chopped 2 tsp, divided
- Minced garlic 1 tsp, divided
- Salt and pepper to taste
- Cornstarch 3 tbsp.
- Beef broth 14 oz. (397 g)
- Refrigerated pie crust 7 oz. (198 g)

Directions:

1. Preheat oven to 425 F (218 °C).
2. Cut the steaks into strips.
3. In a skillet, add the mushrooms and cook for 3 minutes.
4. Add in carrots, peas, thyme, and garlic, and cook for another 4-5 minutes. Remove from skillet.
5. Add beef to the skillet and cook for 2 minutes. Season with salt and pepper and take out.
6. Take an empty skillet, mix cornstarch into the broth and cook until slightly thick. Add in beef and veggies.
7. Place defrosted pie crust into the pie plate, fill in the beef mixture and bake for 19-20 minutes. You can cover the pie with the remaining crust if you want.
8. Serve when done.

Spicy Beef Sloppy Joes

Preparation time: 20 minutes
Cooking time: 8 hours
Servings: 12
Ingredients:

- Lean ground beef – 2 lb.
- Lower-sodium salsa – 2 ½ cups
- Coarsely chopped fresh mushrooms – 3 cups
- Shredded carrots – 1 ¼ cups
- Finely chopped red and green sweet peppers – 1 ¼ cups
- No-salt added tomato paste – ½ (6-oz.) can
- Garlic – 4 cloves, minced
- Dried basil – 1 tsp. crushed
- Salt – ¾ tsp.
- Dried oregano – ½ tsp. crushed

- Cayenne pepper – ¼ tsp.
- Whole wheat hamburger buns – 12, split and toasted

Directions:

1. Cook ground beef in a skillet until browned. Drain off fat.
2. In a slow cooker, add the meat and combine the next 10 Ingredients: (through cayenne pepper).
3. Cover and cook on low for 8 to 10 hours or on high for 4 to 5 hours.
4. Spoon ½-cup of the meat mixture onto each bun.
5. Serve.

Roasted Steak and Tomato Salad

Preparation time: 20 minutes
Cooking time: 20 minutes
Servings: 4
Ingredients:

- Beef tenderloin steaks – 2 (8 oz.), trimmed
- Cracked black pepper – 1 tsp.
- Kosher salt – ¼ tsp.
- Small tomatoes – 6, halved
- Olive oil – 2 tsps.
- Shredded Parmesan cheese – ¼ cup
- Dried oregano – ½ tsp. crushed
- Torn romaine lettuce – 8 cups
- Artichoke hearts – 1 (14-oz.) can, drained and quartered
- Red onion slivers – 1/3 cup
- Balsamic vinegar – 3 Tbsp.
- Olive oil – 1 Tbsp.

Directions:

1. Preheat the oven to 400F.
2. Season the meat with salt and pepper and rub. Let stand for 20 minutes at room temperature.
3. Arrange tomato halves on a baking sheet (cut side down).
4. Heat 2 tsps. Oil in a skillet. Add meat and cook until well browned on all sides, about 8 minutes. Transfer meat to other side of baking sheet.
5. Roast for 8 to 10 minutes for medium (145F). Remove meat from oven. Cover with foil and let stand. Move oven rack for broiling.
6. Turn oven to broil. Turn tomatoes cut sides up. Combine oregano and Parmesan. Sprinkle over tomatoes. Broil 4 to 5 inches from heat for about 2 minutes, or until cheese is melted and golden.
7. In a bowl, combine onion, artichoke hearts, and lettuce. Drizzle with vinegar and 1 tbsp. oil. Toss to coat.
8. Arrange on plates. Slice steak and arrange over lettuce with tomato halves.

Lamb Fatteh with Asparagus

Preparation time: 10 minutes
Cooking time: 20 minutes
Servings: 4
Ingredients:

- Olive oil – 1 Tbsp.
- Medium onion – 1, sliced
- Garlic – 4 cloves, minced
- Boneless lamb leg – 12 oz. cut into smaller pieces
- 50% less sodium beef broth – 1 (14.5 oz.) can

- Whole wheat pearl couscous - 1 cup
- Dried oregano – ½ tsp. crushed
- Ground cumin – ½ tsp.
- Salt – ¼ tsp.
- Black pepper – ¼ tsp.
- Thin asparagus spears – 1 lb. sliced into 2-inch pieces
- Chopped red sweet pepper – ¾ cup
- Snipped fresh oregano and lemon wedges

Directions:

1. Heat oil in a skillet. Add onion and cook for 3 minutes.
2. Add garlic and cook for 1 minute.
3. Add lamb and cook until browned on all sides, about 3 to 5 minutes.
4. Stir in the next six Ingredients: (through black pepper). Bring to a boil. Lower heat and simmer, covered, for 10 minutes. Stirring occasionally.
5. Stir in sweet pepper and asparagus. Cover and simmer until vegetables are crisp-tender, about 3 to 5 minutes.
6. Fluff lamb mixture lightly with a fork. Top with fresh oregano.
7. Serve with lemon wedges.

Fruity Pork Roast

Preparation time: 25 minutes
Cooking time: 5 hours
Servings: 8
Ingredients:

- 1/2 teaspoon ground mustard
- 1/2 cup packed fresh parsley sprigs
- 1/2 lemon, sliced
- 1 apple, peeled and sliced
- 1/2 cup dried cranberries
- 1/8 to 1/4 teaspoon ground ginger
- 1/3 cup golden raisins
- 1/4 teaspoon pepper
- 1/3 cup unsweetened apple juice
- 1/2 teaspoon salt
- 3 tablespoons sherry or additional unsweetened apple juice
- 1 (3 lbs.) boneless pork loin roast
- 1 teaspoon garlic, minced

Directions:

1. Take a bowl and mix 1/3 cup golden raisins, 1/2 cup dried cranberries, 1/2 medium sliced lemon, 1/3 cup unsweetened apple juice, 1/3 cup unsweetened apple juice, 1/2 teaspoon ground mustard and 3 tablespoons of additional unsweetened apple juice in it; mix well and keep it aside.
2. Cut the roast in half; season with ginger, pepper and salt.
3. Transfer seasoned roast into a slow cooker followed by fruit mixture. Add parsley and apple around the roast.
4. Cover the cooker and cook for about 5-6 hours on low.
5. Once done, let it cool and then slice and serve!

Crust Less Pizza

Preparation time: 10 minutes
Cooking Time: 25 Minutes
Servings: 4
Ingredients:

- Pepperoni, ham, sausage, mushrooms, or toppings of your choice
- 8 oz. fat free cream cheese, soft
- 1 ½ cup mozzarella cheese, grated
- 2 eggs
- What you'll need from store cupboard:
- ½ cup lite pizza sauce
- ¼ cup reduced fat parmesan cheese
- 1 tsp garlic powder
- ¼ tsp pepper

Directions:

1. Heat oven to 350 degrees. Spray and 9x13-inch baking dish with cooking spray.
2. In a large bowl, beat cream cheese, eggs, pepper, garlic powder, and parmesan until combined. Spread in prepared dish and bake 12-15 minutes or until golden brown. Let cool 10 minutes.
3. Spread pizza sauce over crust. Top with cheese and your favorite pizza toppings. Sprinkle lightly with garlic powder. Bake 8-10 minutes or until cheese melts. Cool 5 minutes before serving.

North Carolina Style Pork Chops

Preparation time: 10 minutes
Cooking Time: 10 Minutes
Servings: 2
Ingredients:

- 2 boneless pork chops
- 15 ml of vegetable oil
- 25g dark brown sugar, packaged
- 6g of Hungarian paprika
- 2g ground mustard
- 2g freshly ground black pepper
- 3g onion powder
- 3g garlic powder
- Salt and pepper to taste

Directions:

1. Preheat the air fryer a few minutes at 1800C.
2. Cover the pork chops with oil.
3. Put all the spices and season the pork chops abundantly, almost as if you were making them breaded.
4. Place the pork chops in the preheated air fryer.
5. Select Steak, set the time to 10 minutes.
6. Remove the pork chops when it has finished cooking. Let it stand for 5 minutes and serve.

Chapter 10

Soups and Stews

Asparagus and Chicken Soup

Preparation time: 30 minutes
Cooking time: 20 minutes
Servings: 4
Ingredients:

- 2 chicken breast fillets, cooked and diced
- 2-3 leeks, finely cut
- 1 bunch asparagus, trimmed and cut
- 4 cups chicken broth
- 2 tbsp. extra virgin olive oil
- 1/2 cup fresh parsley, finely chopped
- Salt and black pepper, to taste
- Lemon juice, to serve

Directions:
1. Heat the olive oil in a large soup pot. Add in the leeks and gently sauté, stirring, for 2-3 minutes. Add chicken broth, the diced chicken, and bring to a boil. Reduce heat and simmer for 15 minutes.
2. Add in asparagus, parsley, salt and black pepper, and cook for 5 minutes more. Serve with lemon juice.

Mediterranean Fish and Quinoa Soup

Preparation time: 30 minutes
Cooking time: 20 minutes
Servings: 4-5
Ingredients:

- 1 lb. cod fillets, cubed
- 1 onion, chopped
- 3 tomatoes, chopped
- 1/2 cup quinoa, rinsed
- 1 red pepper, chopped
- 1 carrot, chopped
- 1/2 cup black olives, pitted and sliced
- 1 garlic clove, crushed
- 3 tbsp. extra virgin olive oil
- A pinch of cayenne pepper
- 1 bay leaf
- 1 tsp dried thyme
- 1 tsp dried dill
- ½ tsp pepper
- ½ cup white wine
- 4 cups water
- Salt and black pepper, to taste
- 1/2 cup fresh parsley, finely cut

Directions:
1. Heat the olive oil over medium heat and sauté the onion, red pepper, garlic and carrot until tender.
2. Stir in the cayenne pepper, bay leaf, herbs, salt and pepper. Add the white wine, water, quinoa and tomatoes and bring to a boil.
3. Reduce heat, cover, and cook for 10 minutes. Stir in olives and the fish and cook for another 10 minutes. Stir in parsley and serve hot.

Alkalizing Green Soup

Preparation time: 20 minutes
Cooking time: 20 minutes
Servings: 4-5
Ingredients:

- 2 cups broccoli, cut into florets and chopped
- 2 zucchinis, peeled and chopped
- 2 cups chopped kale
- 1 small onion, chopped
- 2-3 garlic cloves, chopped
- 4 cups vegetable broth
- 2 tbsp. extra virgin olive oil
- 1/2 tsp ground ginger
- 1/2 tsp ground coriander
- 1 lime, juiced, to serve

Directions:
1. Gently heat olive oil in a large saucepan over medium-high heat. Cook onion and garlic for 3-4 minutes until tender. Add ginger and coriander and stir to coat well.
2. Add in broccoli, zucchinis, kale and vegetable broth. Bring to the boil, then reduce heat and simmer for 15 minutes, stirring from time to time. Set aside to cool and blend until smooth. Return to pan and cook until heated through. Serve with lime juice.

Lentil, Ground Beef and Quinoa Soup

Preparation Time: 45 minutes
Cooking time: 40 minutes
Servings: 4-5
Ingredients:

- 1 lb. ground beef
- 1/2 cup quinoa
- 1/1 cup green lentils
- 1 carrot, chopped
- 1 onion, chopped
- 1 small potato, peeled and diced

- 2-3 garlic cloves, chopped
- 2 tomatoes, grated or pureed
- 5 cups water
- 1 tsp summer savory or dried mint
- 1 tsp paprika
- 2 tbsp. olive oil
- 1 tsp salt
- Ground black pepper, to taste

Directions:

1. Heat olive oil in a large soup pot. Brown the ground beef, breaking it up with a spoon. Add in paprika and garlic and stir. Add lentils, washed quinoa, remaining vegetables, water and spice.

2. Bring the soup to a boil. Reduce heat to low and simmer, covered, for about 40 minutes, or until the lentils are tender. Stir occasionally.

Hearty Lamb and Root Vegetables Soup

Preparation Time: 45 minutes

Cooking time: 20 minutes

Servings: 6-7

Ingredients:

- 2 cups roasted lamb, shredded
- 3 cups chicken or vegetable broth
- 1 cup water
- 1 cup canned tomatoes, diced, undrained
- 1 onion, chopped
- 1 large carrot, chopped
- 1 medium parsnip, peeled and chopped
- 1 small turnip, chopped
- 1 celery rib
- 3 tbsp. olive oil
- Salt and black pepper, to taste

Directions:

1. Gently heat olive oil in a large saucepan and sauté onion, carrot, parsnip, celery and turnip, stirring, for 5 minutes, or until softened.

2. Add in lamb, broth, tomatoes, and a cup of water. Bring to the boil then reduce heat and simmer for 20 minutes, or until vegetables are tender. Season with salt and black pepper to taste.

Spicy Red Pepper and Potato Soup

Preparation time: 30 minutes

Cooking time: 20 minutes

Servings: 4

Ingredients:

- 1 onion, chopped
- 2 garlic cloves, minced
- 2 carrots, chopped
- 2 red bell peppers, chopped
- 2 cups, diced potatoes
- 4 cups vegetable broth
- 3 tbsp. extra virgin olive oil
- 1/2 tsp smoked paprika
- 1/4 tsp ginger

- 1/2 tsp dried sage
- 1/2 tsp cinnamon
- 1/2 tsp nutmeg
- Salt, to taste
- Black pepper, to taste

Directions:

1. Gently heat olive oil in a large saucepan over medium-high heat. Cook onion, garlic, carrot and the peppers together with all the spices for 3-4 minutes, stirring.

2. Add in potatoes and the broth. Season with salt and black pepper to taste. Cover and simmer for 20 minutes or until the potatoes and carrots are tender.

Creamy Brussels Sprout Soup

Preparation time: 30 minutes

Cooking time: 25 minutes

Servings: 4-5

Ingredients:

- 1 lb. frozen Brussels sprouts, thawed
- 2 potatoes, peeled and chopped
- 1 large onion, chopped
- 3 garlic cloves, minced
- 1 cup raw cashews
- 4 cups vegetable broth
- 3 tbsp. extra virgin olive oil
- 1/2 tsp curry powder
- Salt and black pepper, to taste

Directions:

1. Soak cashews in a bowl covered with water for at least 4 hours. Drain water and blend cashews with 1 cup of vegetable broth until smooth. Set aside.

2. Gently heat olive oil in a large saucepan over medium-high heat. Cook onion and garlic and for 3-4 minutes until tender. Add in Brussels sprouts, potato, curry and vegetable broth.

3. Cover and bring to a boil, then reduce heat and simmer for 20 minutes, stirring from time to time. Remove from heat and stir in cashew mixture. Blend until smooth, return to pan and cook until heated through.

Tuscan Chicken Stew

Preparation time: 15 minutes

Cooking time: 6 hours

Servings: 6

Ingredients:

- 1 medium eggplant, cubed
- 3 zucchinis, cubed
- 1 cup chopped onion
- 2 cans great northern beans
- 2 cans diced tomatoes (no salt added)
- 1 tsp sugar
- 2 tbsp. Italian seasoning
- 1 tsp garlic powder
- Salt and pepper to taste
- 2 lbs. of chicken breasts (boneless, skinless)
- 3 cups chicken stock

Directions:
1. Put tomatoes, chicken, broth seasonings and sugar into the slow cooker. Cook on low for 6 hours or 8 if using frozen chicken breasts.
2. During the last 1 1/2 hours, add eggplant, zucchini and beans in, and stir.

Zucchini Vegetable Stew

Preparation time: 15 minutes
Cooking time: 10-15 minutes
Servings: 6
Ingredients:

- 1 (1 lb.) eggplant, peeled, cubed
- 1 zucchini, sliced
- 1/2 cup reduced-sodium pasta sauce
- 1 package (12 oz.) frozen mixed stew vegetables (celery, onion, peppers)

Directions:
1. Combine eggplant, vegetable blend, zucchini and 2 tablespoons water in large heavy pan. Heat until mixture boils, then reduce heat to low and cover.
2. Cook for about 10 to 15 minutes or until vegetables are tender and drain.
3. Return eggplant mixture to pan. Add pasta sauce and stir until sauce heats through.

Creamy Chicken Soup

Preparation time: 35 minutes
Cooking time: 30 minutes
Servings: 4
Ingredients:

- 4 chicken breasts
- 1 carrot, chopped
- 1 cup zucchini, peeled and chopped
- 2 cups cauliflower, broken into florets
- 1 celery rib, chopped
- 1 small onion, chopped
- 5 cups water
- 1/2 tsp salt
- Black pepper, to taste

Directions:
1. Place chicken breasts, onion, carrot, celery, cauliflower and zucchini in a deep soup pot. Add in salt, black pepper and 5 cups of water. Stir and bring to a boil.
2. Simmer for 30 minutes then remove chicken from the pot and let it cool slightly.
3. Blend soup until completely smooth. Shred or dice the chicken meat, return it back to the pot, stir, and serve.

Broccoli and Chicken Soup

Preparation time: 35 minutes
Cooking time: 30 minutes
Servings: 4
Ingredients:

- 4 boneless chicken thighs, diced
- 1 small carrot, chopped
- 1 broccoli head, broken into florets
- 1 garlic clove, chopped
- 1 small onion, chopped
- 4 cups water
- 3 tbsp. extra virgin olive oil
- 1/2 tsp salt
- Black pepper, to taste

Directions:
1. In a deep soup pot, heat olive oil and gently sauté broccoli for 2-3 minutes, stirring occasionally. Add in onion, carrot, chicken and cook, stirring, for 2-3 minutes. Stir in salt, black pepper and water.
2. Bring to a boil. Simmer for 30 minutes then remove from heat and set aside to cool.
3. In a blender or food processor, blend soup until completely smooth. Serve and enjoy!

Warm Chicken and Avocado Soup

Preparation time: 6-7 minutes
Cooking time: 25 minutes
Servings: 4
Ingredients:

- 2 ripe avocados, peeled and chopped
- 1 cooked chicken breast, shredded
- 1 garlic clove, chopped
- 3 cups chicken broth
- Salt and black pepper, to taste
- Fresh coriander leaves, finely cut, to serve
- 1/2 cup sour cream, to serve

Directions:
1. Combine avocados, garlic, and chicken broth in a blender. Process until smooth and transfer to a saucepan.
2. Add in chicken and cook, stirring, over medium heat until the mixture is hot. Serve topped with sour cream and finely cut coriander leaves.

Quick Clam Chowder

Preparation time: 10 minutes
Cooking time: 15 minutes
Servings: 4
Ingredients:

- 2 tablespoons extra-virgin olive oil
- 3 slices pepper bacon, chopped
- 1 onion, chopped
- 1 red bell pepper, seeded and chopped
- 1 fennel bulb, chopped
- 3 tablespoons flour
- 5 cups low-sodium or unsalted chicken broth
- 6 ounces (170 g) chopped canned clams, undrained
- ½ teaspoon sea salt
- ½ cup milk

Directions:
1. In a large pot over medium-high heat, heat the olive oil until it shimmers. Add the bacon and cook, stirring, until browned, about 4 minutes. Remove the bacon from the fat with a slotted spoon, and set it aside on a plate.
2. Add the onion, bell pepper, and fennel to the fat in the pot. Cook, stirring occasionally, until the vegetables are soft, about 5 minutes. Add the flour and cook, stirring constantly, for 1 minute. Add the broth, clams, and salt. Bring to a simmer. Cook, stirring, until the soup thickens, about 5 minutes more.

3. Stir in the milk and return the bacon to the pot. Cook, stirring, 1 minute more.

Beef Barley Soup

Preparation time: 20 minutes
Cooking time: 30 minutes
Servings: 4
Ingredients:

- 2 teaspoons extra-virgin olive oil
- 1 sweet onion, chopped
- 1 tablespoon minced garlic
- 4 celery stalks, with greens, chopped
- 2 carrots, peeled, diced
- 1 sweet potato, peeled, diced
- 8 cups low-sodium beef broth
- 1 cup cooked pearl barley
- 2 cups diced cooked beef
- 2 bay leaves
- 2 teaspoons hot sauce
- 2 teaspoons chopped fresh thyme
- 1 cup shredded kale
- Sea salt and freshly ground black pepper, to taste

Directions:
1. Place a large stockpot over medium-high heat and add the oil.
2. Sauté the onion and garlic until softened and translucent, about 3 minutes.
3. Stir in the celery, carrot, and sweet potato, and sauté for a further 5 minutes.
4. Stir in the beef broth, barley, beef, bay leaves, and hot sauce.
5. Bring the soup to a boil, then reduce the heat to low.
6. Simmer until the vegetables are tender, about 15 minutes.
7. Remove the bay leaves and stir in the thyme and kale.
8. Simmer for 5 minutes, and season with salt and pepper.

Seafood Stew

Preparation time: 20 minutes
Cooking time: 30 minutes
Servings: 6
Ingredients:

- 1 tablespoon extra-virgin olive oil
- 1 sweet onion, chopped
- 2 teaspoons minced garlic
- 3 celery stalks, chopped
- 2 carrots, peeled and chopped
- 1 (28-ounce / 794-g) can sodium-free diced tomatoes, undrained
- 3 cups low-sodium chicken broth
- ½ cup clam juice
- ¼ cup dry white wine
- 2 teaspoons chopped fresh basil
- 2 teaspoons chopped fresh oregano
- 2 (4-ounce / 113-g) haddock fillets, cut into 1-inch chunks

1-pound (454 g) mussels, scrubbed, debearded
8 ounces (227 g) shrimp, peeled, deveined, quartered
Sea salt and freshly ground black pepper, to taste
2 tablespoons chopped fresh parsley

Directions:
1. Place a large saucepan over medium-high heat and add the olive oil.
2. Sauté the onion and garlic until softened and translucent, about 3 minutes.
3. Stir in the celery and carrots and sauté for 4 minutes.
4. Stir in the tomatoes, chicken broth, clam juice, white wine, basil, and oregano.
5. Bring the sauce to a boil, then reduce the heat to low. Simmer for 15 minutes.
6. Add the fish and mussels, cover, and cook until the mussels open, about 5 minutes.
7. Discard any unopened mussels. Add the shrimp to the pan and cook until the shrimp are opaque, about 2 minutes.
8. Season with salt and pepper. Serve garnished with the chopped parsley.

Potlikker Soup

Preparation time: 15 minutes
Cooking time: 20 minutes
Servings: 6
Ingredients:

- 3 cups chicken broth, divided
- 1 medium onion, chopped
- 3 garlic cloves, minced
- 1 bunch collard greens or mustard greens including stems, roughly chopped
- 1 fresh ham bone
- 5 carrots, peeled and cut into 1-inch rounds
- 2 fresh thyme sprigs
- 3 bay leaves
- Freshly ground black pepper, to taste

Directions:
1. Select the Sauté setting on an electric pressure cooker, and combine ½ cup of chicken broth, the onion, and garlic and cook for 3 to 5 minutes, or until the onion and garlic are translucent.
2. Add the collard greens, ham bone, carrots, remaining 2½ cups of broth, the thyme, and bay leaves.
3. Close and lock the lid and set the pressure valve to sealing.
4. Change to the Manual setting, and cook for 15 minutes.
5. Once cooking is complete, quick-release the pressure. Carefully remove the lid. Discard the bay leaves.
6. Serve with Skillet Bivalves.

Roasted Carrot Soup with Basil

Preparation Time: 10 minutes
Cooking Time: 10 minutes
Servings: 8
Ingredients:

- 3 pounds' carrots, peeled and cut into 2- to 3-inch pieces
- 2 onions, peeled and quartered
- 6 cloves garlic, unpeeled
- 1 (1 inch) piece fresh ginger, peeled and sliced
- 2 tablespoons coconut oil
- 3 cups unsweetened coconut milk
- 1-1/2 cups low-sodium vegetable broth
- 1 teaspoon coarsely ground black pepper

- 1-1/2 cups water
- 1 teaspoon Shredded carrot
- 2 Fresh basil leaves

Directions:

1. Preheat the oven to 400 degrees. In a large bowl, combine the carrot pieces, onions, garlic and ginger. Drizzle with coconut oil; toss to coat. Place vegetables in a 15 x 10 x 1-inch baking dish in a single layer. Bake for 50 to 60 minutes or until carrots are very tender. Let cool slightly.

2. In a food processor or blender, press the garlic cloves out of the skin. Add the grilled carrots, onions and ginger; Cover and process or turn on / off in several turns until vegetables are chopped. Add the coconut milk, broth and pepper. Cover and mix or stir until smooth.

3. Transfer to a medium saucepan. Add the water. Cook and stir until heated through. Garnish with grated carrots and basil leaves if desired.

Asparagus Carrot Soup

Preparation Time: 10 minutes
Cooking Time: 10 minutes
Servings: 6
Ingredients:

- ½ tablespoon butter
- ½ tablespoon olive oil
- 1pounds' fresh asparagus, trimmed and cut into 1-inch pieces
- ½ medium onion, chopped
- ½ medium carrot, thinly sliced
- ¼ teaspoon salt
- 1/8 teaspoon pepper
- 1/8 teaspoon dried thyme
- 2/3 cup uncooked long grain brown rice
- 3 cups vegetable broth
- Reduced-fat sour cream, optional

Directions:

1. Heat the pot, Add butter and oil over medium heat. Add vegetables and spices; cook until vegetables are tender, 8 to 10 minutes, stirring occasionally.

2. Add the brown rice and broth; bring to a boil. Reduce the heat; Cook, covered, over low heat for 40 to 45 minutes, stirring occasionally, until the rice is tender.

3. Puree the soup with a hand blender or allow it to cool slightly and puree the soup in batches in a blender. Return to the pot and heat. Serve with sour cream and croutons if desired.

Meatball and Chickpea Soup

Preparation Time: 30 minutes
Cooking time: 30 minutes
Servings: 4-5
Ingredients:

- 1 lb. lean ground beef
- 3-4 tbsp. flour
- 1 small onion, chopped
- 1 garlic clove, chopped
- 1 can tomatoes, diced and undrained
- 1 can chickpeas, drained
- 1 green pepper, chopped

- 4 cups water
- ½ bunch of parsley, finely cut
- 3 tbsp. olive oil
- ½ tsp black pepper
- 1 tsp dried mint
- 1 tsp paprika - 1 tsp salt

Directions:

1. Combine ground meat, paprika, black pepper and salt in a large bowl. Mix well with hands and roll teaspoonfuls of the mixture into balls. Put flour in a small bowl and roll each meatball in the flour, coating entire surface then set aside on a large plate.

2. Heat olive oil into a large soup pot and gently sauté onion, garlic and pepper until tender. Add water and tomatoes and bring to the boil over high heat. Add in meatballs and chickpeas.

3. Reduce heat to low and simmer, uncovered, for 25 minutes. Add mint and stir. Serve with lemon juice.

Beef Noodle Soup

Preparation Time: 30 minutes
Cooking time: 15 minutes
Servings: 7-8
Ingredients:

- 8 oz. fillet steak, thinly sliced
- 6 oz. rice stick noodles
- 2 carrots, peeled, halved, sliced diagonally
- 1 red pepper, deseeded, thinly sliced diagonally
- 7-8 spring onions, chopped
- 8 oz. green beans, sliced diagonally
- 3 tbsp. sweet chili sauce
- 4 cups beef broth
- 1 tbsp. olive oil

Directions:

1. In a skillet, heat olive oil and cook beef, stirring, until medium rare.

2. Place broth and half the onions in a saucepan over high heat. Bring to the boil, cover, reduce heat to low. Simmer for 5 minutes then add carrots, pepper and beans. Bring to the boil, uncovered. Cook for 2 minutes or until vegetables are tender. Remove from heat.

3. Stir in remaining onions and sweet chili sauce.

4. Place noodles in a heatproof bowl. Cover with boiling water. Stand for 5 minutes or until tender. Drain. Divide noodles between bowls. Top with beef. Ladle over boiling soup mixture. Serve.

Cabbage, Beef and Buckwheat Soup

Preparation Time: 30 minutes
Cooking time: 35 minutes
Servings: 7-8
Ingredients:

- 3/4 – 1 lb. beef, chuck (boneless, cut into 1-inch cubes)
- 1 cup buckwheat
- 2 cups chopped cabbage
- 1 small onion, chopped

- 2 carrots, peeled, halved, sliced diagonally
- 1 red pepper, deseeded, thinly sliced diagonally
- 1 tbsp. paprika
- 4 cups beef broth
- 1 tbsp. olive oil
- 1/2 cup sour cream, to serve, optional
- Salt and black pepper, to taste

Directions:

1. In a deep soup pot, heat olive oil and cook beef, stirring, until lightly browned.

2. Add broth, paprika, onion and carrot and bring to the boil. Cover, reduce heat to low and simmer for 20 minutes then add the pepper, cabbage and buckwheat.

3. Bring to the boil and cook for 15 minutes or until vegetables are tender. Remove from heat.

4. Season with salt and pepper to taste and serve with sour cream.

Italian Wedding Soup

Preparation Time: 30 minutes
Cooking time: 40 minutes
Servings: 4-5
Ingredients:

- 1 lb. lean ground beef
- 1/3 cup breadcrumbs
- 1 egg, lightly beaten
- 1 onion, grated
- 2 carrots, chopped
- 1 small head escarole, trimmed and cut into 1/2-inch strips
- 1 cup baby spinach leaves
- 1 cup small pasta
- 2 tbsp. Parmesan cheese, grated
- 2 tbsp. parsley, finely cut
- 1 tsp salt
- 1 tsp ground black pepper
- 3 tbsp. olive oil
- 3 cups chicken broth
- 3 cups water
- 1 tsp dried oregano

Directions:

1. Combine ground beef, egg, onion, breadcrumbs, cheese, parsley, 1/2 teaspoon of the salt and 1/2 teaspoon of the black pepper. Mix well with hands. Using a tablespoon, make walnut sized meatballs. Heat olive oil in a large skillet and brown meatballs in batches. Place aside on a plate.

2. In a large soup pot boil broth and water together with carrots, oregano, and the remaining salt and pepper. Gently add meatballs. Reduce heat and simmer for 30 minutes. Add pasta, spinach and escarole and simmer 10 minutes more.

Italian Meatball Soup

Preparation Time: 5 minutes
Cooking time: 15 minutes
Servings: 6-7
Ingredients:

- 1 lb. lean ground beef
- 1 small onion, grated

- 1 onion, chopped
- 2 garlic cloves, crushed
- ½ cup breadcrumbs
- 3-4 basil leaves, finely chopped
- 1/3 cup Parmesan cheese, grated
- 1 egg, lightly beaten
- 2 cups tomato sauce with basil
- 3 cups water
- ½ cup small pasta
- 1 zucchini, diced
- ½ cup green beans, trimmed, cut into thirds
- 2 tbsp. olive oil

Directions:

1. Combine ground meat, grated onion, garlic, breadcrumbs, basil, Parmesan and egg in a large bowl. Season with salt and pepper. Mix well with hands and roll tablespoonfuls of the mixture into balls. Place on a large plate.

2. Heat olive oil into a large deep saucepan and sauté onion and garlic until transparent. Add tomato sauce, water, and bring to the boil over high heat. Add meatballs.

3. Reduce heat to medium-low and simmer, uncovered, for 10 minutes. Add in pasta and cook for 5 more minutes. Add the zucchini and beans. Cook until pasta and vegetables are tender. Serve sprinkled with Parmesan.

Spicy Chick Pea Stew

Preparation time: 15 minutes
Cooking time: 3-4 hours
Servings: 6
Ingredients:

- 1 tablespoon vegetable oil
- 2 onions, peeled and finely chopped
- 4 garlic cloves, finely chopped
- 2 tablespoons minced fresh gingerroot
- 2 teaspoons ground coriander
- 1 teaspoon cumin seed
- 1 teaspoon salt
- 1/2 teaspoon fresh ground black pepper
- 1/2 teaspoon cayenne pepper
- 2 teaspoons balsamic vinegar
- 2 cups coarsely chopped tomatoes (canned or fresh)
- 2 (19 ounce) cans chickpeas, rinsed and drained

Directions:

1. In a skillet over medium heat, cook onions, stirring, just until they begin to brown; then add garlic and all spices and cook, stirring, for 1 minute.

2. Add vinegar and tomatoes and bring to a boil, then place mixture in your slow cooker; add chickpeas and combine well.

3. Cover and cook on Low for 6 to 8 hours or on High for 3 to 4 hours, or until the mixture is hot and bubbling.

Easy Salsa Chicken Stew

Preparation time: 15 minutes
Cooking time: 6-8 hours
Servings: 6

Ingredients:
- 4 boneless skinless chicken breasts
- 32 ounces salsa
- 1 (14 1/2 ounce) can corn, drained
- 1 (14 1/2 ounce) can black beans, drained

Directions:
1. Place Ingredients: in slow cooker and cook on low 6-8 hours.
2. 30-60 minutes prior to serving, remove chicken, shred, and return to slow cooker.

Moroccan Eggplant Stew

Preparation time: 20 minutes
Cooking time: 3 minutes
Servings: 4
Ingredients:
- 2 tablespoons avocado oil
- 1 large onion, minced
- 2 garlic cloves, minced
- 1 teaspoon ras el hanout spice blend or curry powder
- ¼ teaspoon cayenne pepper
- 1 teaspoon kosher salt
- 1 cup vegetable broth or water
- 1 tablespoon tomato paste
- 2 cups chopped eggplant
- 2 medium gold potatoes, peeled and chopped
- 4 ounces (113 g) tomatillos, husks removed, chopped
- 1 (14-ounce / 397-g) can diced tomatoes

Directions:
1. Set the electric pressure cooker to the Sauté setting. When the pot is hot, pour in the avocado oil.
2. Sauté the onion for 3 to 5 minutes, until it begins to soften. Add the garlic, ras el hanout, cayenne, and salt. Cook and stir for about 30 seconds. Hit Cancel.
3. Stir in the broth and tomato paste. Add the eggplant, potatoes, tomatillos, and tomatoes with their juices.
4. Close and lock the lid of the pressure cooker. Set the valve to sealing.
5. Cook on high pressure for 3 minutes.
6. When the cooking is complete, hit Cancel and allow the pressure to release naturally.
7. Once the pin drops, unlock and remove the lid.
8. Stir well and spoon into serving bowls.

Cheeseburger Soup

Preparation time: 5 minutes
Cooking time: 25 minutes
Servings: 4
Ingredients:
- Avocado oil cooking spray
- ½ cup diced white onion
- ½ cup diced celery
- ½ cup sliced portobello mushrooms
- 1 pound (454 g) 93% lean ground beef
- 1 (15-ounce / 425-g) can no-salt-added diced tomatoes
- 2 cups low-sodium beef broth
- 1/3 cup half-and-half
- ¾ cup shredded sharp Cheddar cheese

Directions:
1. Heat a large stockpot over medium-low heat. When hot, coat the cooking surface with cooking spray. Put the onion, celery, and mushrooms into the pot. Cook for 7 minutes, stirring occasionally.
2. Add the ground beef and cook for 5 minutes, stirring and breaking apart as needed.
3. Add the diced tomatoes with their juices and the broth. Increase the heat to medium-high and simmer for 10 minutes.
4. Remove the pot from the heat and stir in the half-and-half.
5. Serve topped with the cheese.

Taco Soup

Preparation time: 5 minutes
Cooking time: 20 minutes
Servings: 4
Ingredients:
- Avocado oil cooking spray
- 1 medium red bell pepper, chopped
- ½ cup chopped yellow onion
- 1 pound (454 g) 93% lean ground beef
- 1 teaspoon ground cumin
- ½ teaspoon salt
- ½ teaspoon chili powder
- ½ teaspoon garlic powder
- 2 cups low-sodium beef broth
- 1 (15-ounce / 425-g) can no-salt-added diced tomatoes
- 1½ cups frozen corn
- 1/3 cup half-and-half

Directions:
1. Heat a large stockpot over medium-low heat. When hot, coat the cooking surface with cooking spray. Put the pepper and onion in the pan and cook for 5 minutes.
2. Add the ground beef, cumin, salt, chili powder, and garlic powder. Cook for 5 to 7 minutes, stirring and breaking apart the beef as needed.
3. Add the broth, diced tomatoes with their juices, and corn. Increase the heat to medium-high and simmer for 10 minutes.
4. Remove from the heat and stir in the half-and-half.

Lentil Vegetable Soup

Preparation time: 10 minutes
Cooking time: 15 minutes
Servings: 4
Ingredients:
- 2 tablespoons extra-virgin olive oil
- 1 onion, finely chopped
- 1 carrot, chopped
- 1 cup chopped kale (stems removed)
- 3 garlic cloves, minced
- 1 cup canned lentils, drained and rinsed
- 5 cups unsalted vegetable broth
- 2 teaspoons dried rosemary (or 1 tablespoon chopped fresh rosemary)
- ½ teaspoon sea salt
- ¼ teaspoon freshly ground black pepper

Directions:

1. In a large pot over medium-high heat, heat the olive oil until it shimmers. Add the onion and carrot and cook, stirring, until the vegetables begin to soften, about 3 minutes. Add the kale and cook for 3 minutes more. Add the garlic and cook, stirring constantly, for 30 seconds.

2. Stir in the lentils, vegetable broth, rosemary, salt, and pepper. Bring to a simmer. Simmer, stirring occasionally, for 5 minutes more.

Broccoli Soup

Preparation time: 15 minutes
Cooking time: 7 minutes
Servings: 6
Ingredients:

- 1-pound fresh broccoli (1 medium-sized head)
- 14 ounces low-sodium fat free chicken broth
- 2 tablespoons margarine
- 2 tablespoons all-purpose flour
- 2 cups skim milk
- 1/4 teaspoon pepper
- 1 cup reduced-fat shredded cheddar cheese

Directions:

1. Clean the broccoli, then chop the florets and thinly slice the stems.

2. In a medium-sized saucepan, combine the broccoli and chicken broth; heat to a boil. Reduce heat and simmer, covered, for about 7 minutes or until the broccoli is fork-tender.

3. Transfer to a food processor or blender. Process until fairly smooth.

4. In the same saucepan, melt the margarine over medium heat; add the flour. Cook, stirring constantly, until it starts to bubble. Add the milk and pepper; heat to a boil, stirring constantly.

5. Reduce heat to medium and add the broccoli purée. Stir in the cheese; heat just until the cheese melts - do not boil, keep stirring constantly.

Chicken and Potato Stew

Preparation time: 15 minutes
Cooking time: 6 hours
Servings: 6
Ingredients:

- 1 1/2 cups russet potatoes, peeled cut into bite-size pieces, and washed
- 1 1/2 cups carrots, peeled, cut into bite-size pieces, and washed
- 1/2 cup finely chopped onion
- 1/4 teaspoon garlic powder (to taste)
- 1/2 teaspoon salt (to taste)
- 3/4 teaspoon ground black pepper (to taste)
- 1/2 teaspoon sage (to taste)
- 1/4 teaspoon thyme (to taste)
- 2 boneless skinless chicken breast halves
- 1 (10 3/4 ounce) can cream of chicken soup

Directions:

1. Place vegetables in the bottom of a 2 1/2-quart slow cooker. Sprinkle seasonings evenly over the vegetables.

2. Top with chicken, then cover with soup. Cook on low for 6 hours.

Mediterranean Spinach and Tomato Pasta

Preparation time: 3 minutes
Cooking time: 20 minutes
Servings: 6
Ingredients:

- 1 cup vegetable broth
- 12 dehydrated sun-dried tomatoes
- 1 (8 ounce) package uncooked penne pasta
- 2 tablespoons pine nuts
- 1 tablespoon olive oil
- 1/4 teaspoon crushed red pepper flakes
- 1 clove garlic, minced
- 1 bunch fresh spinach, rinsed and torn into bite-size pieces
- 1/4 cup grated Parmesan cheese

Directions:

1. In a small saucepan, bring the broth to a boil. Remove from heat. Place the sun-dried tomatoes in the broth 15 minutes, or until softened. Drain, reserving broth, and coarsely chop.

2. Bring a large pot of lightly salted water to a boil. Place penne pasta in the pot, cook 9 to 12 minutes, until al dente, and drain.

3. Place the pine nuts in a skillet over medium heat. Cook and stir until lightly toasted.

4. Heat the olive oil and red pepper flakes in a skillet over medium heat, and sauté the garlic 1 minute, until tender. Mix in the spinach, and cook until almost wilted. Pour in the reserved broth, and stir in the chopped sun-dried tomatoes. Continue cooking 2 minutes, or until heated through.

5. In a large bowl, toss the cooked pasta with the spinach and tomato mixture and pine nuts. Serve with Parmesan cheese.

Butternut Squash Stew

Preparation time: 15 minutes
Cooking time: 8-10 hours
Servings: 6
Ingredients:

- 1 butternut squash - peeled, seeded, and cubed
- 2 cups cubed eggplant, with peel
- 2 cups cubed zucchini
- 1 (10 ounce) package frozen okra, thawed
- 1 (8 ounce) can tomato sauce
- 1 cup chopped onion
- 1 ripe tomato, chopped
- 1 carrot, sliced thin
- 1/2 cup vegetable broth
- 1/3 cup raisins
- 1 clove garlic, chopped
- 1/2 teaspoon ground cumin
- 1/2 teaspoon ground turmeric
- 1/4 teaspoon crushed red pepper
- 1/4 teaspoon ground cinnamon
- 1/4 teaspoon paprika

Directions:

1. In a slow cooker, combine butternut squash, eggplant, zucchini, okra, tomato sauce, onion, tomato, carrot, broth,

raisins, and garlic. Season with cumin, turmeric, red pepper, cinnamon, and paprika.

2. Cover, and cook on Low for 8 to 10 hours, or until vegetables are tender.

Fish and Noodle Soup

Preparation Time: 30 minutes
Cooking time: 10 minutes
Servings: 4-5

Ingredients:

- 14 oz. firm white fish, cut into strips
- 2 carrots, cut into ribbons
- 1 zucchini, cut into thin ribbons
- 7 oz. white button mushrooms, sliced
- 1 celery rib, finely cut
- 1 cup baby spinach
- 7 oz. fresh noodles
- 3 cups chicken broth
- 2 cups water
- 2 tbsp. soy sauce
- 1/2 tsp ground ginger
- Black pepper, to taste

Directions:

1. Place chicken broth, water and soy sauce in a large saucepan. Bring to a boil and add in carrots, celery, zucchini, mushrooms, ginger and noodles.

2. Cook, partially covered, for 3-4 minutes then add in fish and simmer for 3 minutes or until the fish is cooked through. Add baby spinach and simmer, stirring, for 1 minute, or until it wilts. Season with black pepper and serve.

Lime Chicken Tortilla Soup

Preparation time: 10 minutes
Cooking time: 35 minutes
Servings: 4
Ingredients:

- 1 tablespoon extra-virgin olive oil
- 1 onion, thinly sliced
- 1 garlic clove, minced
- 1 jalapeño pepper, diced
- 2 boneless, skinless chicken breasts
- 4 cups low-sodium chicken broth
- 1 Roma tomato, diced
- ½ teaspoon salt
- 2 (6-inch) corn tortillas, cut into thin strips
- Nonstick cooking spray
- Juice of 1 lime
- Minced fresh cilantro, for garnish
- ¼ cup shredded Cheddar cheese, for garnish

Directions:

1. In a medium pot, heat the oil over medium-high heat. Add the onion and cook for 3 to 5 minutes until it begins to soften. Add the garlic and jalapeño, and cook until fragrant, about 1 minute more.

2. Add the chicken, chicken broth, tomato, and salt to the pot and bring to a boil. Reduce the heat to medium and simmer

gently for 20 to 25 minutes until the chicken breasts are cooked through. Remove the chicken from the pot and set aside.

3. Preheat a broiler to high.

4. Spray the tortilla strips with nonstick cooking spray and toss to coat. Spread in a single layer on a baking sheet and broil for 3 to 5 minutes, flipping once, until crisp.

5. When the chicken is cool enough to handle, shred it with two forks and return to the pot.

6. Season the soup with the lime juice. Serve hot, garnished with cilantro, cheese, and tortilla strips.

Beef Barley Mushroom Soup

Preparation time: 10 minutes
Cooking time: 1 hour 20 minutes
Servings: 6
Ingredients:

- 1-pound (454 g) beef stew meat, cubed
- ¼ teaspoon salt
- ¼ teaspoon freshly ground black pepper
- 1 tablespoon extra-virgin olive oil
- 8 ounces (227 g) sliced mushrooms
- 1 onion, chopped
- 2 carrots, chopped
- 3 celery stalks, chopped
- 6 garlic cloves, minced
- ½ teaspoon dried thyme
- 4 cups low-sodium beef broth
- 1 cup water
- ½ cup pearl barley

Directions:

1. Season the meat with the salt and pepper.

2. In an Instant Pot, heat the oil over high heat. Add the meat and brown on all sides. Remove the meat from the pot and set aside.

3. Add the mushrooms to the pot and cook for 1 to 2 minutes, until they begin to soften. Remove the mushrooms and set aside with the meat.

4. Add the onion, carrots, and celery to the pot. Sauté for 3 to 4 minutes until the vegetables begin to soften. Add the garlic and continue to cook until fragrant, about 30 seconds longer.

5. Return the meat and mushrooms to the pot, then add the thyme, beef broth, and water. Set the pressure to high and cook for 15 minutes. Let the pressure release naturally.

6. Open the Instant Pot and add the barley. Use the slow cooker function on the Instant Pot, affix the lid (vent open), and continue to cook for 1 hour until the barley is cooked through and tender. Serve.

Split Pea Soup with Carrots

Preparation time: 8 minutes
Cooking time: 15 minutes
Servings: 4
Ingredients:

- 1½ cups dried green split peas, rinsed and drained
- 4 cups vegetable broth or water
- 2 celery stalks, chopped
- 1 medium onion, chopped
- 2 carrots, chopped
- 3 garlic cloves, minced

- 1 teaspoon herbs de Provence
- 1 teaspoon liquid smoke
- Kosher salt and freshly ground black pepper, to taste
- Shredded carrot, for garnish (optional)

Directions:

1. In the electric pressure cooker, combine the peas, broth, celery, onion, carrots, garlic, herbs de Provence, and liquid smoke.
2. Close and lock the lid of the pressure cooker. Set the valve to sealing.
3. Cook on high pressure for 15 minutes.
4. When the cooking is complete, hit Cancel and allow the pressure to release naturally for 10 minutes, then quick release any remaining pressure.
5. Once the pin drops, unlock and remove the lid.
6. Stir the soup and season with salt and pepper.
7. Spoon into serving bowls and sprinkle shredded carrots on top (if using).

Buttercup Squash Soup

Preparation time: 15 minutes
Cooking time: 10 minutes
Servings: 6
Ingredients:

- 2 tablespoons extra-virgin olive oil
- 1 medium onion, chopped
- 4 to 5 cups vegetable broth or chicken bone broth
- 1½ pounds (680 g) buttercup squash, peeled, seeded, and cut into 1-inch chunks
- ½ teaspoon kosher salt
- ¼ teaspoon ground white pepper
- Whole nutmeg, for grating

Directions:

1. Set the electric pressure cooker to the Sauté setting. When the pot is hot, pour in the olive oil.
2. Add the onion and sauté for 3 to 5 minutes, until it begins to soften. Hit Cancel.
3. Add the broth, squash, salt, and pepper to the pot and stir. (If you want a thicker soup, use 4 cups of broth. If you want a thinner, drinkable soup, use 5 cups.)
4. Close and lock the lid of the pressure cooker. Set the valve to sealing.
5. Cook on high pressure for 10 minutes.
6. When the cooking is complete, hit Cancel and allow the pressure to release naturally.
7. Once the pin drops, unlock and remove the lid.
8. Use an immersion blender to purée the soup right in the pot. If you don't have an immersion blender, transfer the soup to a blender or food processor and purée. (Follow the instructions that came with your machine for blending hot foods.)
9. Pour the soup into serving bowls and grate nutmeg on top.

Creamy Sweet Potato Soup

Preparation time: 15 minutes
Cooking time: 10 minutes
Servings: 6
Ingredients:

- 2 tablespoons avocado oil
- 1 small onion, chopped

- 2 celery stalks, chopped
- 2 teaspoons minced garlic
- 1 teaspoon kosher salt
- ½ teaspoon freshly ground black pepper
- 1 teaspoon ground turmeric
- ½ teaspoon ground cinnamon
- 2 pounds (907 g) sweet potatoes, peeled and cut into 1-inch cubes
- 3 cups vegetable broth or chicken bone broth
- Plain Greek yogurt, to garnish (optional)
- Chopped fresh parsley, to garnish (optional)
- Pumpkin seeds (pepitas), to garnish (optional)

Directions:

1. Set the electric pressure cooker to the Sauté setting. When the pot is hot, pour in the avocado oil.
2. Sauté the onion and celery for 3 to 5 minutes or until the vegetables begin to soften.
3. Stir in the garlic, salt, pepper, turmeric, and cinnamon. Hit Cancel.
4. Stir in the sweet potatoes and broth.
5. Close and lock the lid of the pressure cooker. Set the valve to sealing.
6. Cook on high pressure for 10 minutes.
7. When the cooking is complete, hit Cancel and allow the pressure to release naturally.
8. Once the pin drops, unlock and remove the lid.
9. Use an immersion blender to purée the soup right in the pot. If you don't have an immersion blender, transfer the soup to a blender or food processor and purée. (Follow the instructions that came with your machine for blending hot foods.)
10. Spoon into bowls and serve topped with Greek yogurt, parsley, and/or pumpkin seeds (if using).

Bean Soup with Lime-Yogurt Drizzle

Preparation time: 10 minutes
Cooking time: 40 minutes
Servings: 8
Ingredients:

- 2 tablespoons avocado oil
- 1 medium onion, chopped
- 3 garlic cloves, minced
- 1 teaspoon ground cumin
- 1 (10-ounce / 283-g) can diced tomatoes and green chilies
- 6 cups chicken bone broth, vegetable broth, or water
- 1 pound (454 g) dried black beans, rinsed
- Kosher salt, to taste
- ¼ cup plain Greek yogurt or sour cream
- 1 tablespoon freshly squeezed lime juice

Directions:

1. Set the electric pressure cooker to the Sauté setting. When the pot is hot, pour in the avocado oil.
2. Sauté the onion for 3 to 5 minutes, until it begins to soften. Hit Cancel.
3. Stir in the garlic, cumin, tomatoes and their juices, broth, and beans.

4. Close and lock the lid of the pressure cooker. Set the valve to sealing.

5. Cook on high pressure for 40 minutes.

6. While the soup is cooking, combine the yogurt and lime juice in a small bowl.

7. When the cooking is complete, hit Cancel. Allow the pressure to release naturally for 15 minutes, then quick release any remaining pressure.

8. Once the pin drops, unlock and remove the lid.

9. (Optional) for a thicker soup, remove 1½ cups of beans from the pot using a slotted spoon. Use an immersion blender to blend the beans that remain in the pot. If you don't have an immersion blender, transfer the soup left in the pot to a blender or food processor and purée. (Follow the instructions that came with your machine for blending hot foods.) Stir in the reserved beans. Season with salt, if desired.

10. Spoon into serving bowls and drizzle with lime-yogurt sauce.

Chicken Noodle Soup

Preparation time: 15 minutes
Cooking time: 20 minutes
Servings: 12
Ingredients:

- 2 tablespoons avocado oil
- 1 medium onion, chopped
- 3 celery stalks, chopped
- 1 teaspoon kosher salt
- ¼ teaspoon freshly ground black pepper
- 2 teaspoons minced garlic
- 5 large carrots, peeled and cut into ¼-inch-thick rounds
- 3 pounds (1.4 kg) bone-in chicken breasts (about 3)
- 4 cups chicken bone broth
- 4 cups water
- 2 tablespoons soy sauce
- 6 ounces (170 g) whole grain wide egg noodles

Directions:

1. Set the electric pressure cooker to the Sauté setting. When the pot is hot, pour in the avocado oil.

2. Sauté the onion, celery, salt, and pepper for 3 to 5 minutes or until the vegetables begin to soften.

3. Add the garlic and carrots, and stir to mix well. Hit Cancel.

4. Add the chicken to the pot, meat-side down. Add the broth, water, and soy sauce. Close and lock the lid of the pressure cooker. Set the valve to sealing.

5. Cook on high pressure for 20 minutes.

6. When the cooking is complete, hit Cancel and quick release the pressure. Unlock and remove the lid.

7. Using tongs, remove the chicken breasts to a cutting board. Hit Sauté/More and bring the soup to a boil.

8. Add the noodles and cook for 4 to 5 minutes or until the noodles are al dente.

9. While the noodles are cooking, use two forks to shred the chicken. Add the meat back to the pot and save the bones to make more bone broth.

10. Season with additional pepper, if desired, and serve.

Roasted Brussels sprouts and Cauliflower Soup

Preparation Time: 25 minutes
Cooking time: 40 minutes
Servings: 4
Ingredients:

- 1 onion, finely chopped
- 2 garlic cloves, crushed
- 16 oz. cauliflower florets
- 16 oz. Brussels sprouts, halved
- 4 cups vegetable broth
- 6 tbsp. olive oil
- Salt and pepper, to taste
- Parmesan cheese, to serve

Directions:

1. Preheat oven to 450F.

2. Line a large baking sheet and place the cauliflower and Brussels sprouts on it. Drizzle with half the olive oil and roast on the bottom third of the oven for 30 minutes, or until slightly browned.

3. Heat the remaining oil in a saucepan over medium heat and sauté the onion and garlic, stirring, for 2-3 minutes or until soft.

4. Add in vegetable broth and bring to the boil then simmer 3-4 minutes. Stir in roasted vegetables and cook for 5 minutes more.

5. Set aside to cool then blend in batches and reheat. Serve sprinkled with Parmesan cheese.

Beetroot and Carrot Soup

Preparation Time: 20 minutes
Cooking time: 40 minutes
Servings: 6
Ingredients:

- 4 beets, washed and peeled
- 2 carrots, peeled, chopped
- 2 potatoes, peeled, chopped
- 1 medium onion, chopped
- 2 cups vegetable broth
- 3 cups water
- 2 tbsp. yogurt
- 2 tbsp. olive oil
- Salt and pepper, to taste
- A bunch or spring onions, finely cut, to serve

Directions:

1. Peel and chop the beets. Heat the olive oil in a saucepan over medium high heat and sauté the onion and carrot until tender.

2. Add in beets, potatoes, broth and water. Bring to the boil.

3. Reduce heat to medium and simmer, partially covered, for 30-40 minutes, or until the beets are tender.

4. set aside to cool slightly.

5. Blend the soup in batches until smooth. Return it to pan over low heat and cook, stirring, for 4-5 minutes or until heated through. Season with salt and pepper to taste. Serve topped with yogurt and sprinkled with spring onions.

Baked Beet and Apple Soup

Preparation Time: 10 minutes
Cooking time: 1-2 hours

Servings: 8
Ingredients:

- 1.5 lb. fresh beets, peeled and grated
- 2 carrots, chopped
- 1 onion, chopped
- 2 apples, peeled and chopped
- 1 tbsp. sugar
- 1 bay leaf
- 2 tbsp. lemon juice
- 3 cups vegetable broth
- 3 tbsp. olive oil
- 1 cup heavy cream
- A bunch of fresh parsley, chopped, to serve
- Salt and black pepper, to taste

Directions:

1. Preheat the oven to 350 F. Toss the beets, apples, onion and carrots in olive oil and arrange in a casserole dish.
2. Add in the bay leaf and vegetable broth. Season with salt and pepper, cover with foil and bake for 1-2 hours. Discard the bay leaf and set aside to cool.
3. Blend everything in a blender, in batches, until smooth, then transfer to a large saucepan.
4. Season with salt and pepper to taste, stir in the cream and reheat without boiling. Serve the soup with a dollop of extra cream and sprinkled with chopped parsley.

Vegetarian Borscht

Preparation Time: 45 minutes
Cooking time: 1hour 30 minutes
Servings: 6
Ingredients:

- 4 beets, peeled, quartered
- 1 carrot, peeled, chopped
- 1 parsnip, peeled, cut into chunks
- 1 leek, white part only, sliced
- 1 onion, chopped
- 1/3 cup lemon juice
- ½ tsp nutmeg
- 3 bay leaves
- 6 cups vegetable broth
- 1 cup sour cream
- 2-3 dill springs, chopped

Directions:

1. Place the beets, carrot, parsnip, leek, onion, lemon juice, spices and bay leaves in a large saucepan with the vegetable broth.
2. Bring to the boil, then reduce the heat to low and simmer, partially covered, for 1 ½ hours.
3. Cool slightly, then blend in batches and season well with salt and pepper. Return to the saucepan and gently heat through. Place in bowls and garnish with sour cream and dill.

Chapter 11

Poultry

Stuffed Chicken Breasts Greek-style

Preparation time: 10 minutes
Cooking Time: 20 Minutes
Servings: 4
Ingredients:

- 4 oz. chicken breasts, skinless and boneless
- ¼ cup onion, minced
- 4 artichoke hearts, minced
- 1 teaspoon oregano, crushed
- 4 lemon slices
- What you will need from the store cupboard:
- cup canned chicken broth, fat-free
- 1-1/2 lemon juice
- 2 tablespoon olive oil
- 2 teaspoons of cornstarch
- Ground pepper Salt, optional

Directions:

1. Take out all the fat from the chicken. Wash and pat dry. Season your chicken with pepper and salt.
2. Pound the chicken to make it flat and thin. Bring together the oregano, onion, and artichoke hearts.
3. Now spoon equal amounts of the mix at the center of your chicken.
4. Roll up the log and secure using a skewer or toothpick. Heat oil in your skillet over medium temperature.
5. Add the chicken. Brown all sides evenly.
6. Pour the lemon juice and broth.
7. Add lemon slices on top of the chicken.
8. Simmer covered for 10 minutes.
9. Transfer to a platter.
10. Remove the skewers or toothpick.
11. Mix cornstarch with a fork. Transfer to skillet and stir over high temperature. Put lemon sauce on the chicken.

Chicken & Tofu

Preparation Time: 1 hour and 15 minutes
Cooking Time: 25 minutes
Servings: 6
Ingredients:

- 2 tablespoons olive oil, divided
- 2 tablespoons orange juice
- 1 tablespoon Worcestershire sauce
- 1 tablespoon low-sodium soy sauce
- 1 teaspoon ground turmeric
- 1 teaspoon dry mustard
- 8 oz. chicken breast, cooked and sliced into cubes
- 8 oz. extra-firm tofu, drained and sliced into cubed
- 2 carrots, sliced into thin strips
- 1 cup mushroom, sliced
- 2 cups fresh bean sprouts
- 3 green onions, sliced
- Red sweet pepper, sliced into strips

Directions:

1. In a bowl, mix half of the oil with the orange juice, Worcestershire sauce, soy sauce, turmeric and mustard.
2. Coat all sides of chicken and tofu with the sauce.
3. Marinate for 1 hour. In a pan over medium heat, add 1 tablespoon oil.
4. Add carrot and cook for 2 minutes.
5. Add mushroom and cook for another 2 minutes.
6. Add bean sprouts, green onion and sweet pepper.
7. Cook for two to three minutes. Stir in the chicken and heat through.

Jerk Style Chicken Wings

Preparation time: 10 minutes
Cooking time: 30 minutes
Servings: 2-3
Ingredients:

- 1g ground thyme
- 1g dried rosemary
- 2g allspice
- 4g ground ginger
- 3 g garlic powder
- 2g onion powder
- 1g of cinnamon
- 2g of paprika
- 2g chili powder
- 1g nutmeg
- Salt to taste
- 30 ml of vegetable oil
- 0.5 - 1 kg of chicken wings
- 1 lime, juice

Directions:

1. Select Preheat, set the temperature to 200°C and press Start/Pause.
2. Combine all spices and oil in a bowl to create a marinade.
3. Mix the chicken wings in the marinade until they are well covered.
4. Place the chicken wings in the preheated air fryer.

5. Select Chicken and press Start/Pause. Be sure to shake the baskets in the middle of cooking.
6. Remove the wings and place them on a serving plate.
7. Squeeze fresh lemon juice over the wings and serve.

Italian Chicken

Preparation time: 10 minutes
Cooking time: 30 minutes
Servings: 4
Ingredients:

- 5 chicken thighs
- 1 tbsp. olive oil
- 1/4 cup parmesan; grated
- 1/2 cup sun dried tomatoes
- 2 garlic cloves; minced
- 1 tbsp. thyme; chopped.
- 1/2 cup heavy cream
- 3/4 cup chicken stock
- 1 tsp. red pepper flakes; crushed
- 2 tbsp. basil; chopped
- Salt and black pepper to the taste

Directions:

1. Season chicken with salt and pepper, rub with half of the oil, place in your preheated air fryer at 350 °F and cook for 4 minutes.
2. Meanwhile; heat up a pan with the rest of the oil over medium high heat, add thyme garlic, pepper flakes, sun dried tomatoes, heavy cream, stock, parmesan, salt and pepper; stir, bring to a simmer, take off heat and transfer to a dish that fits your air fryer.
3. Add chicken thighs on top, introduce in your air fryer and cook at 320 °F, for 12 minutes. Divide among plates and serve with basil sprinkled on top.

Coconut Chicken

Preparation time: 10 minutes
Cooking time: 30 minutes
Servings: 6
Ingredients:

- 2 garlic cloves, minced
- Fresh cilantro, minced
- 1/2 cup light coconut milk
- 6 tablespoons sweetened coconut, shredded and toasted
- 2 tablespoons brown sugar
- 6 (about 1-1/2 pounds) boneless skinless chicken thighs
- 2 tablespoons reduced-sodium soy sauce
- 1/8 teaspoon ground cloves

Directions:

1. Mix brown sugar, 1/2 cup light coconut milk, 2 tablespoons soy sauce, 1/8 teaspoon ground cloves and 2 minced cloves of garlic in a bowl.
2. Add 6 chicken boneless thighs into a Crockpot.
3. Now pour the mixture of coconut milk over chicken thighs. Cover the cooker and cook for about 4-5 hours on low.
4. Serve coconut chicken with cilantro and coconut; enjoy!

Spicy Lime Chicken

Preparation time: 10 minutes
Cooking time: 30 minutes
Servings: 6
Ingredients:

- 3 tablespoons lime juice
- Fresh cilantro leaves
- 1-1/2 pounds (about 4) boneless skinless chicken breast halves
- 1 teaspoon lime zest, grated
- 2 cups chicken broth
- 1 tablespoon chili powder

Directions:

1. Add chicken breast halves into a slow cooker.
2. Add 1 tablespoon chili powder, 3 tablespoons lime juice and 2 cups chicken broth in a small bowl; mix well and pour over chicken.
3. Cover the cooker and cook for about 3 hours on low. Once done, take chicken out from the cooker and let it cool.
4. Once cooled, shred chicken by using forks and transfer back to the Crockpot.
5. Stir in 1 teaspoon grated lime zest. Serve spicy lime chicken with cilantro and enjoy!

Chicken & Peanut Stir-Fry

Preparation Time: 15 minutes
Cooking Time: 15 minutes
Servings: 4
Ingredients:

- 3 tablespoons lime juice
- ½ teaspoon lime zest
- 4 cloves garlic, minced
- 2 teaspoons chili bean sauce
- ½ tablespoon fish sauce
- 1 tablespoon water
- 2 tablespoons peanut butter
- 3 teaspoons oil, divided
- 1 lb. chicken breast, sliced into strips
- Red sweet pepper, sliced into strips
- 3 green onions, sliced thinly
- 2 cups broccoli, shredded
- 2 tablespoons peanuts, chopped

Directions:

1. In a bowl, mix the lime juice, lime zest, garlic, chili bean sauce, fish sauce, water and peanut butter.
2. Mix well. In a pan over medium high heat, add 2 teaspoons of oil.
3. Cook the chicken until golden on both sides.
4. Pour in the remaining oil. Add the pepper and green onions.
5. Add the chicken, broccoli and sauce. Cook for 2 minutes. Top with peanuts before serving.

Honey Mustard Chicken

Preparation Time: 15 minutes
Cooking Time: 12 minutes
Servings: 4

Ingredients:
- 2 tablespoons honey mustard
- 2 teaspoons olive oil
- Salt to taste 1 lb. chicken tenders
- Baby carrots, steamed - Chopped parsley

Directions:
1. Preheat your oven to 450 degrees F.
2. Mix honey mustard, olive oil and salt.
3. Coat the chicken tenders with the mixture. Place the chicken on a single layer on the baking pan.
4. Bake for 10 to 12 minutes. Serve with steamed carrots and garnish with parsley.

Chicken Chili

Preparation Time: 15 minutes
Cooking Time: 40 minutes
Servings: 6
Ingredients:
- 4 cups low-sodium chicken broth, divided
- 3 cups boiled black beans, divided
- 1 tablespoon extra-virgin olive oil
- 1 large onion, chopped
- 1 jalapeño pepper, seeded and chopped
- 4 garlic cloves, minced
- 1 teaspoon dried thyme, crushed
- 1½ tablespoons ground coriander
- 1 tablespoon ground cumin
- ½ tablespoon red chili powder
- 4 cups cooked chicken, shredded
- ½ tablespoon fresh lime juice
- ¼ cup fresh cilantro, chopped

Directions:
1. In a food processor, add 1 cup of broth and 1 can of black beans and pulse until smooth. Transfer the beans puree into a bowl and set aside.
2. In a large pan, heat the oil over medium heat and sauté the onion and jalapeño for about 4-5 minutes.
3. Add the garlic, spices and sea salt and sauté for about 1 minute.
4. Add the beans puree and remaining broth and bring to a boil. Now, reduce the heat to low and simmer for about 20 minutes.
5. Stir in the remaining can of beans, chicken and lime juice and bring to a boil.
6. Now, reduce the heat to low and simmer for about 5-10 minutes.
7. Serve hot with the garnishing of cilantro.

Meal Prep Tip: Transfer the chili into a large bowl and set aside to cool.
Divide the chili into 6 containers evenly. Cover the containers and refrigerate for 1-2 days.
Reheat in the microwave before serving.

Chicken with Chickpeas

Preparation Time: 15 minutes
Cooking Time: 36 minutes
Servings: 4
Ingredients:
- 2 tablespoons olive oil

- 1 pound skinless, boneless chicken breast, cubed
- 2 carrots, peeled and sliced
- 1 onion, chopped
- 2 celery stalks, chopped 2 garlic cloves, chopped
- ½ tablespoon fresh ginger root, minced
- ½ teaspoon dried oregano, crushed
- ¾ teaspoon ground cumin
- ½ teaspoon paprika
- ¼-13 teaspoon cayenne pepper
- ¼ teaspoon ground turmeric
- 1 cup tomatoes, crushed
- 1½ cups low-sodium chicken broth
- Zucchini, sliced
- cup boiled chickpeas, drained
- 1 tablespoon fresh lemon juice

Directions:
1. In a large nonstick pan, heat the oil over medium heat and cook the chicken cubes for about 4-5 minutes.
2. With a slotted spoon, transfer the chicken cubes onto a plate.
3. In the same pan, add the carrot, onion, celery and garlic and sauté for about 4-5 minutes.
4. Add the ginger, oregano and spices and sauté for about 1 minute.
5. Add the chicken, tomato and broth and bring to a boil. Now, reduce the heat to low and simmer for about 10 minutes.
6. Add the zucchini and chickpeas and simmer, covered for about 15 minutes. Stir in the lemon juice and serve hot.

Meatballs Curry

Preparation Time: 20 minutes
Cooking Time: 25 minutes
Servings: 6
Ingredients:
- For Meatballs:
- 1 pound lean ground chicken
- ½ tablespoon onion paste
- 2 teaspoons fresh ginger paste
- 2 teaspoons garlic paste
- 1 green chili, chopped finely
- 1 tablespoon fresh cilantro leaves, chopped
- 1 teaspoon ground coriander
- ½ teaspoon cumin seeds
- ½ teaspoon red chili powder
- ½ teaspoon ground turmeric
- 1/8 teaspoon salt
- For Curry:
- 3 tablespoons olive oil
- ½ teaspoon cumin seeds
- (1-inch) cinnamon stick
- 2 onions, chopped
- 1 teaspoon fresh ginger, minced
- 2 teaspoons garlic, minced
- 4 tomatoes, chopped finely
- 2 teaspoons ground coriander

- ½ teaspoon garam masala powder
- ½ teaspoon ground nutmeg
- ½ teaspoon red chili powder
- ½ teaspoon ground turmeric
- Salt, as required
- 1 cup filtered water
- 3 tablespoons fresh cilantro, chopped

Directions:

For meatballs:

1. In a large bowl, add all Ingredients: and mix until well combined.
2. Make small equal-sized meatballs from mixture. In a large deep skillet, heat the oil over medium heat and cook the meatballs for about 3-5 minutes or until browned from all sides.
3. Transfer the meatballs into a bowl. In the same skillet, add the cumin seeds and cinnamon stick and sauté for about 1 minute.
4. Add the onions and sauté for about 4-5 minutes.
5. Add the ginger and garlic paste and sauté for about 1 minute.
6. Add the tomato and spices and cook, crushing with the back of spoon for about 2-3 minutes.
7. Add the water and meatballs and bring to a boil.
8. Now, reduce the heat to low and simmer for about 10 minutes.
9. Serve hot with the garnishing of cilantro.

Chicken, Oats & Chickpeas Meatloaf

Preparation Time: 20 minutes
Cooking Time: 1¼ hours
Servings: 4
Ingredients:

- ½ cup cooked chickpeas - 2 egg whites
- 2½ teaspoons poultry seasoning
- Ground black pepper, as required
- 10-ounce lean ground chicken
- 1 cup red bell pepper, seeded and minced
- 1 cup celery stalk, minced
- 1/3 cup steel-cut oats
- 1 cup tomato puree, divided
- 2 tablespoons dried onion flakes, crushed
- 1 tablespoon prepared mustard

Directions:

1. Preheat the oven to 350 degrees F. Grease a 9x5-inch loaf pan. In a food processor, add chickpeas, egg whites, poultry seasoning and black pepper and pulse until smooth.
2. Transfer the mixture into a large bowl. Add the chicken, veggies oats, ½ cup of tomato puree and onion flakes and mix until well combined. Transfer the mixture into prepared loaf pan evenly.
3. With your hands, press, down the mixture slightly. In another bowl mix together mustard and remaining tomato puree. Place the mustard mixture over loaf pan evenly.

4. Bake for about 1-1¼ hours or until desired doneness. Remove from the oven and set aside for about 5 minutes before slicing.
5. Cut into desired sized slices and serve.

Herbed Turkey Breast

Preparation Time: 15 minutes
Cooking Time: 1 hour 50 minutes
Servings: 6
Ingredients:

- ½ cup olive oil
- 2 tablespoons fresh lemon juice
- 1 tablespoon scallion, chopped
- ½ teaspoon dried marjoram, crushed
- ½ teaspoon dried sage, crushed
- ½ teaspoon dried thyme, crushed
- Salt and ground black pepper, as required
- (2-pound) boneless, skinless turkey breast half

Directions:

1. Preheat the oven to 325 degrees F. Arrange a rack into a greased shallow roasting pan. In a small pan, all the Ingredients: except turkey breast over medium heat and bring to a boil, stirring frequently.
2. Remove from the heat and set aside to cool. Place turkey breast into the prepared roasting pan. Place some of the herb mixture over the top of turkey breast.
3. Cover the roasting pan and bake for about 1¼-1¾ hours, basting with the remaining herb mixture occasionally.
4. Remove from the oven and set aside for about 10-15 minutes before slicing.
5. With a sharp knife, cut into desired slices and serve.

Turkey with Lentils

Preparation Time: 15 minutes
Cooking Time: 51 minutes
Servings: 7
Ingredients:

- 3 tablespoons olive oil, divided
- 1 onion, chopped
- 1 tablespoon fresh ginger, minced
- 4 garlic cloves, minced
- 3 plum tomatoes, chopped finely
- 2 cups dried red lentils, soaked for 30 minutes and drained
- 2 cups filtered water
- 2 teaspoons cumin seeds
- ½ teaspoon cayenne pepper
- 1 pound lean ground turkey
- Jalapeño pepper, seeded and chopped
- 2 scallions, chopped
- ¼ cup fresh cilantro, chopped

Directions:

1. In a Dutch oven, heat 1 tablespoon of oil over medium heat and sauté the onion, ginger and garlic for about 5 minutes.

2. Stir in tomatoes, lentils and water and bring to a boil now, reduce the heat to medium-low and simmer, covered for about 30 minutes.
3. Meanwhile, in a skillet, heat remaining oil over medium heat and sauté the cumin seeds and cayenne pepper for about 1 minute.
4. Transfer the mixture into a small bowl and set aside. In the same skillet, add turkey and cook for about 4-5 minutes
5. Add the jalapeño and scallion and cook for about 4-5 minutes. Add the spiced oil mixture and stir to combine well.
6. Transfer the turkey mixture in simmering lentils and simmer for about 10-15 minutes or until desired doneness. Serve hot.

Lemon Garlic Turkey

Preparation Time: 1 hour and 10 minutes
Cooking Time: 5 minutes
Servings: 4
Ingredients:
- 4 turkey breasts fillet - 2 cloves garlic, minced - 1 tablespoon olive oil
- 3 tablespoons lemon juice
- 1 oz. Parmesan cheese, shredded
- Pepper to taste
- 1 tablespoon fresh sage, snipped
- 1 teaspoon lemon zest

Directions:
1. Pound the turkey breast until flat. In a bowl, mix the olive oil, garlic and lemon juice.
2. Add the turkey to the bowl. Marinate for 1 hour.
3. Broil for 5 minutes until turkey is fully cooked. Sprinkle cheese on top on the last minute of cooking. In a bowl, mix the pepper, sage and lemon zest.
4. Sprinkle this mixture on top of the turkey before serving.

Crockpot Slow Cooker Ranch Chicken

Preparation time: 10 minutes
Cooking time: 30 minutes
Servings: 4
Ingredients:
- 1 cup chive and onion cream cheese spread
- ½ teaspoon freshly ground black pepper
- 4 boneless chicken breasts
- 1 1-oz package ranch dressing and seasoning mix
- ½ cup low sodium chicken stock

Directions:
1. Spray the Crock-Pot slow cooker with cooking spray and preheat it.
2. Dry chicken with paper towel and transfer it to the Crock-Pot slow cooker.
3. Cook each side, until chicken is browned, for about 4-5 minutes.
4. Add ½ cup low sodium chicken stock, 1 1-oz. package ranch dressing and seasoning mix, 1 cup chive and onion cream cheese spread and ½ teaspoon freshly

ground black pepper. Cover the Crock-Pot slow cooker and cook for about 4 hours on Low or until the internal temperature reaches 165 F. Once cooked, take it out from the Crock-Pot slow cooker.
5. Whisk the sauce present in the Crock-Pot slow cooker until smooth. If you need thick sauce, then cook for about 5-10 minutes, with frequent stirring.
6. Garnish chicken with sliced onions and bacon and serve.

Chicken Wings

Preparation time: 10 Minutes
Cooking time: 1 hour and 30 minutes
Servings: 4
Ingredients:
- 3 pounds chicken wing parts, pastured
- 1 tablespoon old bay seasoning
- 1 teaspoon lemon zest
- 3/4 cup potato starch
- 1/2 cup butter, unsalted, melted

Directions:
1. Switch on the air fryer, insert fryer basket, grease it with olive oil, then shut with its lid, set the fryer at 360 degrees F and preheat for 5 minutes.
2. Meanwhile, pat dry chicken wings and then place them in a bowl.
3. Stir together seasoning and starch, add to chicken wings and stir well until evenly coated.
4. Open the fryer, add chicken wings in it in a single layer, close with its lid and cook for 35 minutes, shaking every 10 minutes.
5. Then switch the temperature of air fryer to 400 degrees F and continue air frying the chicken wings for 10 minutes or until nicely golden brown and cooked, shaking every 3 minutes. When air fryer beeps, open its lid, transfer chicken wings onto a serving plate and cook the remaining wings in the same manner. Whisk together melted butter and lemon zest until blended and serve it with the chicken wings.

Chicken Tenders

Preparation time: 5 Minutes
Cooking time: 10 minutes
Servings: 2
Ingredients:
- 1/8 cup almond flour
- 12 ounces chicken breasts, pastured
- ½ teaspoon ground black pepper
- ¾ teaspoon salt
- 1.2 ounces panko bread crumbs
- 1 egg white, pastured

Directions:
1. Switch on the air fryer, insert fryer basket, grease it with olive oil, then shut with its lid, set the fryer at 350 degrees F and preheat for 5 minutes.
2. Meanwhile, season the chicken with salt and black pepper on both sides and then evenly coat with flour.
3. Crack the egg, whisk until blended, dip the coated chicken in it and then coat with bread crumbs. Open

the fryer, add chicken in it, close with its lid and cook for 10 minutes until nicely golden and cooked, turning the chicken halfway through the frying. When air fryer beeps, open its lid, transfer chicken onto a serving plate and serve.

Chicken Meatballs

Preparation time: 5 Minutes
Cooking time: 26 minutes
Servings: 4
Ingredients:

- 1-pound ground chicken
- 2 green onions, chopped
- ¾ teaspoon ground black pepper
- 1/4 cup shredded coconut, unsweetened
- 1 teaspoon salt
- 1 tablespoon hoisin sauce
- 1 tablespoon soy sauce
- 1/2 cup cilantro, chopped
- 1 teaspoon Sriracha sauce
- 1 teaspoon sesame oil

Directions:

1. Switch on the air fryer, insert fryer basket, grease it with olive oil, then shut with its lid, set the fryer at 350 degrees F and preheat for 5 minutes.
2. Meanwhile, place all the Ingredients: in a bowl, stir until well mixed and then shape the mixture into meatballs, 1 teaspoon of chicken mixture per meatball.
3. Open the fryer, add chicken meatballs in it in a single layer, close with its lid and then spray with oil.
4. Cook the chicken meatballs for 10 minutes, flipping the meatballs halfway through, and then continue cooking for 3 minutes until golden.
5. When air fryer beeps, open its lid, transfer chicken meatballs onto a serving plate and then cook the remaining meatballs in the same manner.
6. Serve straight away.

Chicken & Spinach

Preparation Time: 15 minutes
Cooking Time: 13 minutes
Servings: 4
Ingredients:

- 2 tablespoons olive oil
- 2 chicken breast fillets, sliced into small pieces
- Salt and pepper to taste
- 4 cloves garlic, minced
- 1 tablespoon lemon juice
- ½ cup dry white wine
- 1 teaspoon lemon zest
- 10 cups fresh spinach, chopped
- 4 tablespoons Parmesan cheese, grated

Directions:

1. Pour oil in a pan over medium heat. Season chicken with salt and pepper.
2. Cook in the pan for 7 minutes until golden on both sides.

3. Add the garlic and cook for 1 minute. Stir in the lemon juice and wine.
4. Sprinkle lemon zest on top. Simmer for 5 minutes.
5. Add the spinach and cook until wilted.
6. Serve with Parmesan cheese.

Balsamic Chicken

Preparation Time: 15 minutes
Cooking Time: 5 hours
Servings: 6
Ingredients:

- 6 chicken breast halves, skin removed
- 1 onion, sliced into wedges
- 1 tablespoon tapioca (quick cooking), crushed
- Salt and pepper to taste
- 1 teaspoon dried thyme, crushed
- 1 teaspoon dried rosemary, crushed
- ¼ cup balsamic vinegar
- 2 tablespoons chicken broth
- 9 oz. frozen Italian green beans
- Red sweet pepper, sliced into strips

Directions:

1. Put the chicken, onion and tapioca inside a slow cooker. Season with the salt, pepper, thyme and rosemary.
2. Seal the pot and cook on low setting for 4 hours and 30 minutes.
3. Add the sweet pepper and green beans.
4. Cook for 30 more minutes.
5. Pour sauce over the chicken and vegetables before serving.

Mustard Chicken with Basil

Preparation time: 10 minutes
Cooking time: 30 minutes
Servings: 4
Ingredients:

- 1 tsp Chicken stock
- 2 Chicken breasts; skinless and boneless chicken breasts: halved
- 1 tbsp. Chopped basil
- What you'll need from the store cupboard:
- Salt and black pepper
- 1 tbsp. Olive oil
- ½ tsp Garlic powder
- ½ tsp Onion powder
- 1 tsp Dijon mustard

Directions:

1. Press 'Sauté' on the instant pot and add the oil. When it is hot, brown the chicken in it for 2-3 minutes.
2. Mix in the remaining Ingredients: and seal the lid to cook for 12 minutes at high pressure. Natural release the pressure for 10 minutes, share into plates and serve.

Chicken with Cashew Nuts

Preparation time: 10 minutes
Cooking time: 30 minutes
Servings: 4

Ingredients:

- 1 lb. chicken cubes
- 2 tbsp. soy sauce
- 1 tbsp. corn flour
- 2 ½ onion cubes
- 1 carrot, chopped
- 1/3 cup cashew nuts, fried
- 1 capsicum, cut
- 2 tbsp. garlic, crushed
- Salt and white pepper

Directions:

1. Marinate the chicken cubes with ½ tbsp. of white pepper, ½ tsp salt, 2 tbsp. soya sauce, and add 1 tbsp. corn flour.
2. Set aside for 25 minutes. Preheat the Air Fryer to 380 F and transfer the marinated chicken. Add the garlic, the onion, the capsicum, and the carrot; fry for 5-6 minutes. Roll it in the cashew nuts before serving.

Chicken & Broccoli Bake

Preparation time: 10 minutes
Cooking time: 30 minutes
Servings: 6
Ingredients:

- 6 (6-ounce) boneless, skinless chicken breasts
- 3 broccoli heads, cut into florets
- 4 garlic cloves, minced
- ¼ cup olive oil
- 1 teaspoon dried oregano, crushed
- 1 teaspoon dried rosemary, crushed
- Sea Salt and ground black pepper, as required

Directions:

1. Preheat the oven to 375 degrees F. Grease a large baking dish.
2. In a large bowl, add all the Ingredients: and toss to coat well.
3. In the bottom of prepared baking dish, arrange the broccoli florets and top with chicken breasts in a single layer.
4. Bake for about 45 minutes.
5. Remove from the oven and set aside for about 5 minutes before serving.

Hoisin Chicken Lettuce Wraps

Preparation time: 10 minutes
Cooking time: 30 minutes
Servings: 4
Ingredients:
For the chicken

- 2 teaspoons peanut oil
- 1/3 cup low-sodium gluten-free tamari or soy sauce
- 1 tablespoon honey
- 2 tablespoons rice vinegar
- 2 teaspoons Sriracha sauce
- 1 tablespoon minced garlic
- 2 teaspoons peeled and minced fresh ginger
- 1/3 cup Chicken Bone Broth or water

- 2 scallions, both white and green parts, thinly sliced, divided
- 1 bone-in, skin-on chicken breast (about 1 pound)

For the lettuce wraps

- Large lettuce leaves (preferably Bibb)
- 1 cup broccoli slaw or shredded cabbage
- ¼ cup chopped cashews, toasted

Directions:
To make the chicken

1. In the electric pressure cooker, whisk together the peanut oil, tamari, honey, rice vinegar, Sriracha, garlic, ginger, and broth. Stir in the white parts of the scallions.
2. Place the chicken breast in the sauce, meat-side down.
3. Close and lock the lid of the pressure cooker. Set the valve to sealing.
4. Cook on high pressure for 20 minutes.
5. When the cooking is complete, hit Cancel and quick release the pressure.
6. Once the pin drops, unlock and remove the lid.
7. Using tongs, transfer the chicken breast to a cutting board. When the chicken is cool enough to handle, remove the skin, shred the chicken, and return it to the pot. Let the chicken soak in the sauce for at least 5 minutes.

To make the lettuce wraps

1. Spoon some of the chicken and sauce into the lettuce leaves.
2. Sprinkle with the broccoli slaw, the green parts of the scallions, and the cashews.
3. Serve immediately

Zucchini with Tomatoes

Preparation time: 10 minutes
Cooking time: 30 minutes
Servings: 8
Ingredients:

- 6 medium zucchinis, chopped roughly
- 1 pound cherry tomatoes
- 2 small onions, chopped roughly
- 2 tablespoons fresh basil, chopped
- 1 cup water
- 1 tablespoon olive oil
- 2 garlic cloves, minced
- Salt and ground black pepper, as required

Directions:

1. In the Instant Pot, place oil and press "Sauté". Now add the onion, garlic, ginger, and spices and cook for about 3-4 minutes.
2. Add the zucchinis and tomatoes and cook for about 1-2 minutes.
3. Press "Cancel" and stir in the remaining Ingredients: except basil.
4. Close the lid and place the pressure valve to "Seal" position.
5. Press "Manual" and cook under "High Pressure" for about 5 minutes.
6. Press "Cancel" and allow a "Natural" release.
7. Open the lid and transfer the vegetable mixture onto a serving platter.

8. Garnish with basil and serve.

Chicken Liver Curry

Preparation time: 10 minutes
Cooking time: 30 minutes
Servings: 2
Ingredients:

- 1lb diced chicken breast
- 0.5lb diced chicken liver
- 1lb chopped vegetables
- 1 cup broth
- 3tbsp curry paste

Directions:
1. Mix all the Ingredients: in your Instant Pot.
2. Cook on Stew for 35 minutes.
3. Release the pressure naturally.

Chicken Stuffed Potatoes

Preparation time: 10 minutes
Cooking time: 30 minutes
Servings: 4
Ingredients:

- 6-ounce chicken sausage links
- 4 medium potatoes, each about 8-ounce
- 1 medium zucchini, chopped
- 1 cup chopped green onion
- 1/8 teaspoon salt
- ¼ teaspoon ground black pepper
- ½ teaspoon dried oregano
- 1 teaspoon hot sauce
- 2 tablespoons olive oil, divided
- 2 cups water
- 2 tablespoons crumbled blue cheese, reduced fat

Directions:
1. Plugin instant pot, insert the inner pot, press sauté/simmer button, add 1 tablespoon oil and when hot, add chicken sausage and cook for 3 minutes or until edges are nicely golden brown.
2. Add zucchini and ¾ cup green onion, sprinkle with oregano, pour in 1/3 cup water and cook for 3 minutes or until tender-crisp.
3. Then transfer vegetables from the instant pot to a bowl, drizzle with remaining oil and hot sauce, toss until mixed and keep warm by covering the bowl.
4. Press the cancel button, pour in the remaining water, then insert steamer basket and place potatoes on it.
5. Shut the instant pot with its lid, turn the pressure knob to seal the pot, press the 'manual' button, then press the 'timer' to set the cooking time to 18 minutes and cook at high pressure, instant pot will take 5 minutes or more for building its inner pressure.
6. When the timer beeps, press 'cancel' button and do quick pressure release until pressure nob drops down.
7. Open the instant pot, transfer potatoes to a plate, let cool for 5 minutes, then cut each potato in half.
8. Use fork to fluff potatoes, then season with salt and black pepper and evenly top with prepared sausage and zucchini mixture.

9. Sprinkle remaining green onions and cheese on loaded potatoes and serve straight away.

Greek Chicken Lettuce Wraps

Preparation Time: 1 hour and 15 minutes
Cooking Time: 8 minutes
Servings: 4
Ingredients:

- 2 tablespoons freshly squeezed lemon juice
- 1 teaspoon lemon zest
- 5 teaspoons olive oil, divided
- 3 teaspoons garlic, minced and divided
- 1 teaspoon dried oregano
- ¼ teaspoon red pepper, crushed
- 1 lb. chicken tenders
- 1 cucumber, sliced in half and grated
- Salt and pepper to taste
- ¾ cup non-fat Greek yogurt
- 2 teaspoons fresh mint, chopped
- 2 teaspoons fresh dill, chopped
- 4 lettuce leaves
- ½ cup red onion, sliced
- 1 cup tomatoes, chopped

Directions:
1. In a bowl, mix the lemon juice, lemon zest, half of oil, half of garlic, and red pepper. Coat the chicken with the marinade.
2. Marinate it for 1 hour. Toss grated cucumber in salt. Squeeze to release liquid.
3. Add the yogurt, dill, salt, pepper, remaining garlic and remaining oil.
4. Grill the chicken for 4 minutes per side.
5. Shred the chicken and put on top of the lettuce leaves.
6. Top with the yogurt mixture, onion and tomatoes.
7. Wrap the lettuce leaves and secure with a toothpick.

Lemon Chicken with Kale

Preparation Time: 10 minutes
Cooking Time: 19 minutes
Servings: 4
Ingredients:

- ½ tablespoon olive oil
- 1 lb. chicken thighs, trimmed
- Salt and pepper to taste
- ½ cup low-sodium chicken stock
- 1 lemon, sliced
- 1 tablespoon fresh tarragon, chopped
- 4 cloves garlic, minced
- 6 cups baby kale

Directions:
1. Pour olive oil in a pan over medium heat. Season chicken with salt and pepper.
2. Cook until golden brown on both sides.
3. Pour in the stock. Add the lemon, tarragon and garlic. Simmer for 15 minutes.
4. Add the kale and cook for 4 minutes.

Chapter 12

Salads

Cabbage Slaw Salad

Preparation Time: 20 minutes
Cooking Time: 0 minutes
Servings: 6
Ingredients:

- 2 cups finely chopped green cabbage
- 2 cups finely chopped red cabbage
- 2 cups grated carrots
- 3 scallions, both white and green parts, sliced
- 2 tbsp. extra-virgin olive oil
- 2 tbsp. rice vinegar
- 1 tsp. honey
- 1 garlic clove, minced
- ¼ tsp. salt

Directions:
1. In a large bowl, toss together the green and red cabbage, carrots, and scallions.
2. In a small bowl, whisk together the oil, vinegar, honey, garlic, and salt.
3. Pour the dressing over the veggies and mix to thoroughly combine.
4. Serve immediately, or cover and chill for several hours before serving.

Green Salad with Blackberries, Goat Cheese, and Sweet Potatoes

Preparation Time: 20 minutes
Cooking Time: 15 minutes
Servings: 4
Ingredients:
For The Vinaigrette:

- 1-pint blackberries
- 2 tbsp. red wine vinegar
- 1 tbsp. honey
- 3 tbsp. extra-virgin olive oil
- ¼ tsp. salt
- Freshly ground black pepper

For The Salad:

- 1 sweet potato, cubed
- 1 tsp. extra-virgin olive oil
- 8 cups salad greens (baby spinach, spicy greens, romaine)
- ½ red onion, sliced
- ¼ cup crumbled goat cheese

Directions:
To Make the Vinaigrette:

1. In a blender jar, combine the blackberries, vinegar, honey, oil, salt, and pepper, and process until smooth. Set aside.
To Make the Salad:
2. Preheat the oven to 425°F.
3. Line a baking sheet with parchment paper.
4. In a medium mixing bowl, toss the sweet potato with the olive oil. Transfer to the prepared baking sheet and roast for 20 minutes, stirring once halfway through, until tender.
5. Remove and cool for a few minutes.
6. In a large bowl, toss the greens with the red onion and cooled sweet potato, and drizzle with the vinaigrette.
7. Serve topped with 1 tbsp. goat cheese per serving.

Pomegranate & Brussels Sprouts Salad

Preparation Time: 8 minutes
Cooking Time: 12 minutes
Servings: 6
Ingredients:

- 3 slices bacon, cooked crisp and crumbled
- 3 cup Brussels sprouts, shredded
- 3 cup kale, shredded
- 1 ½ cup pomegranate seeds
- ½ cup almonds, toasted and chopped
- ¼ cup reduced-fat parmesan cheese, grated
- Citrus Vinaigrette

Directions:
1. Combine all Ingredients: in a large bowl.
2. Drizzle vinaigrette over salad, and toss to coat well. Serve garnished with more cheese if desired.

Strawberry & Avocado Salad

Preparation Time: 6 minutes
Cooking Time: 9 minutes
Servings: 6
Ingredients:

- 6 oz. baby spinach
- 2 avocados, chopped
- 1 cup strawberries, sliced
- ¼ cup feta cheese, crumbled
- Creamy Poppy Seed Dressing

¼ cup almonds, sliced
Directions:
1. Add spinach, berries, avocado, nuts, and cheese to a large bowl and toss to combine.
2. Pour ½ recipe of Creamy Poppy Seed Dressing over salad and toss to coat. Add more dressing if desired. Serve.

Shrimp & Avocado Salad

Preparation Time: 11 minutes
Cooking Time: 5 minutes
Servings: 4
Ingredients:

- ½ lb. raw shrimp, peeled and deveined
- 3 cups romaine lettuce, chopped
- 1 cup Napa cabbage, chopped
- 1 avocado, pit removed, and sliced
- ¼ cup red cabbage, chopped
- ¼ cucumber, julienned
- 2 tbsp. green onions, diced fine
- 2 tbsp. fresh cilantro, diced
- 1 tsp. fresh ginger, diced fine
- 2 tbsp. coconut oil
- 1 tbsp. sesame seeds
- 1 tsp. Chinese 5 spice
- Fat-free Ranch dressing

Directions:
1. Toast sesame seeds in a medium skillet over medium heat. Shake the skillet to prevent them from burning. Cook until they start to brown, about 2 minutes. Set aside.
2. Add the coconut oil to the skillet. Pat the shrimp dry and sprinkle with the 5 spices. Add to hot oil. Cook 2 minutes per side, or until they turn pink. Set aside.
3. Arrange lettuce and cabbage on a serving platter. Top with green onions, cucumber, and cilantro. Add shrimp and avocado.
4. Drizzle with the desired amount of dressing and sprinkle sesame seeds over top. Serve.

Kale Salad with Avocado Dressing

Preparation Time: 10 minutes
Cooking Time: 0 minutes
Servings: 6
Ingredients:

- 6 cups chopped kale
- 1 cup finely chopped red bell pepper
- 1 bunch scallions, white and green parts, finely chopped
- 1 avocado, pitted and peeled
- ½ cup raw cashews
- 3 garlic cloves, peeled
- ½ lemon, juiced
- ¼ cup extra-virgin olive oil
- Salt
- Freshly ground black pepper

Directions:
1. In a large bowl, toss together the kale, red bell pepper, and scallions.
2. In a high-speed blender or food processor, combine the avocado, cashews, garlic, lemon juice, and olive oil, and process until smooth. Add up to ½ cup water as needed to create a pourable dressing. Season with salt and pepper. Pour the dressing over the kale, mix well, and serve.

Asian Noodle Salad

Preparation Time: 20 minutes

Cooking Time: 15 minutes
Servings: 4
Ingredients:

- 2 carrots, sliced thin
- 2 radishes, sliced thin
- 1 English cucumber, sliced thin
- 1 mango, julienned
- 1 bell pepper, julienned
- 1 small serrano pepper, seeded and sliced thin
- 1 bag tofu Shirataki Fettuccini noodles
- ¼ cup lime juice
- ¼ cup fresh basil, chopped
- ¼ cup fresh cilantro, chopped
- 2 tbsp. fresh mint, chopped
- 2 tbsp. rice vinegar
- 2 tbsp. sweet chili sauce
- 2 tbsp. roasted peanuts finely chopped
- 1 tbsp. Splenda
- ½ tsp. sesame oil

Directions:
1. Pickle the vegetables: In a large bowl, place radish, cucumbers, and carrots.
2. Add vinegar, coconut sugar, and lime juice and stir to coat the vegetables. Cover and chill for 15–20 minutes.
3. Prep the noodles: remove the noodles from the package and rinse under cold water.
4. Cut into smaller pieces. Pat dry with paper towels.
5. To assemble the salad. Remove the vegetables from the marinade, reserving marinade, and place them in a large mixing bowl.
6. Add noodles, mango, bell pepper, chili, and herbs.
7. In a small bowl, combine 2 tbsp. marinade with the chili sauce and sesame oil.
8. Pour over salad and toss to coat.
9. Top with peanuts and serve.

Avocado & Citrus Shrimp Salad

Preparation Time: 11 minutes
Cooking Time: 5 minutes
Servings: 4
Ingredients:

- 1 lb. medium shrimp, peeled and deveined, remove tails
- 8 cup salad greens
- 1 lemon
- 1 avocado, diced
- 1 shallot, diced fine
- ½ cup almonds, sliced and toasted
- 1 tbsp. olive oil
- Salt and freshly ground black pepper

Directions:
1. Cut the lemon in half and squeeze the juice, from both halves, into a small bowl, set aside. Slice the lemon into thin wedges.
2. Heat the oil in a skillet over medium heat. Add lemon wedges and let cook, about 1 minute, to infuse the oil with the lemons.
3. Add the shrimp and cook, stirring frequently, until shrimp turn pink. Discard the lemon wedges and let cool.

4. Place the salad greens in a large bowl. Add the shrimp, with the juices from the pan, and toss to coat. Add remaining Ingredients: and toss to combine. Serve.

Healthy Taco Salad

Preparation Time: 20 minutes
Cooking Time: 9 minutes
Servings: 4
Ingredients:

- 2 whole Romaine hearts, chopped
- 1 lb. lean ground beef
- 1 whole avocado, cubed
- 3 oz. grape tomatoes, halved
- ½ cup cheddar cheese, cubed
- 2 tbsp. sliced red onion
- ½ batch Tangy Mexican Salad Dressing
- 1 tsp. ground cumin
- Salt and pepper to taste

Directions:
1. Cook ground beef in a skillet over medium heat. Break the beef up into little pieces as it cooks. Add seasonings and stir to combine. Drain grease and let cool for about 5 minutes.
2. To assemble the salad, place all Ingredients: into a large bowl. Toss to mix then add dressing and toss. Top with reduced-fat sour cream and/or salsa if desired.

Chicken Guacamole Salad

Preparation Time: 6 minutes
Cooking Time: 25 minutes
Servings: 6
Ingredients:

- 1 lb. chicken breast, boneless and skinless
- 2 avocados
- 1–2 jalapeno peppers, seeded and diced
- 1/3 cup onion, diced
- 3 tbsp. cilantro, diced
- 2 tbsp. fresh lime juice
- 2 garlic cloves, diced
- 1 tbsp. olive oil
- Salt and pepper, to taste

Directions:
1. Heat oven to 400°F. Line a baking sheet with foil.
2. Season chicken with salt and pepper and place on prepared pan. Bake 20 minutes, or until chicken is cooked through. Let cool completely.
3. Once the chicken has cooled, shred or dice and add to a large bowl. Add the remaining Ingredients: and mix well, mashing the avocado as you mix it in. Taste and season with salt and pepper as desired. Serve immediately.

Warm Portobello Salad

Preparation Time: 20 minutes
Cooking Time: 9 minutes
Servings: 4
Ingredients:

- 6 cup mixed salad greens
- 1 cup Portobello mushrooms, sliced
- 1 green onion, sliced

- Walnut or Warm Bacon Vinaigrette
- 1 tbsp. olive oil
- 1/8 tsp. ground black pepper

Directions:
1. Heat oil in a nonstick skillet over med-high heat. Add mushrooms and cook, stirring occasionally, 10 minutes, or until they are tender. Stir in onions and reduce heat to low.
2. Place salad greens on serving plates, top with mushrooms, and sprinkle with pepper. Drizzle lightly with your choice of vinaigrette.

Cucumber Salad

Preparation Time: 10 minutes
Cooking Time: 0 minutes
Servings: 4
Ingredients:

- 2 medium cucumbers, peeled and chopped
- 1 cup cherry tomatoes, halved
- ½ red onion, thinly sliced
- 2 tbsp. red wine vinegar
- 2 tbsp. extra-virgin olive oil
- ¼ tsp. dried oregano
- ¼ tsp. salt, plus more as needed
- Freshly ground black pepper

Directions:
1. In a medium bowl, combine the cucumbers, tomatoes, and red onion.
2. In a small bowl, whisk the vinegar, olive oil, oregano, salt, and some pepper. Pour the vinaigrette over the vegetables, and toss to coat. Taste and season with more salt and pepper, if desired. Serve immediately, or refrigerate in an airtight container for 2 to 3 days.

Green Power Salad

Preparation time: 5 minutes
Cooking time: 10 minutes
Servings: 3-4
Ingredients:

- 2 cups mixed green salad leaves
- 1 cup broccoli or sunflower sprouts
- 1 small cucumber, chopped
- 1 avocado, peeled and cubed
- 5-6 radishes, sliced
- 1 tbsp. chia seeds
- 1 tbsp. pumpkin seeds

For the dressing:

- 1 tbsp. lemon juice
- 1 tbsp. red wine vinegar
- 2 tbsp. extra virgin olive oil
- 1 tbsp. Dijon mustard
- Salt and pepper, to taste

Directions:
1. Place all Ingredients: in a large salad bowl and toss until combined.
2. In a medium bowl, whisk Ingredients: for the dressing until smooth. Pour over salad, toss thoroughly and serve.

Spinach and Green Bean Salad

Preparation time: 7 minutes
Cooking time: 20-30 minutes
Servings: 4-5
Ingredients:

- 12 oz. green beans, halved diagonally
- 1 bag baby spinach leaves
- 1 cup walnuts, halved and toasted
- 1 cup sun-dried tomatoes
- 2 tbsp. pumpkin seeds

For the dressing:

- 3 tbsp. extra virgin olive oil
- 2 tbsp. red wine vinegar
- 2 garlic cloves, crushed

Directions:
1. Cook beans in a large saucepan of boiling salted water for one minute or until bright green. Rinse under cold running water, drain, pat dry and set aside.
2. Whisk oil, vinegar, garlic, salt and pepper in a small glass bowl until well combined.
3. Place spinach, walnuts, cooked beans and sun-dried tomatoes in a salad bowl and toss to combine. Drizzle with dressing and serve.

Mediterranean Spinach Salad

Preparation time: 15 minutes
Cooking time: 20 minutes
Servings: 4
Ingredients:

- 1 bag baby spinach, washed and dried
- 4-5 spring onions, finely chopped
- 1 cucumber, peeled and cut
- 1/2 cup walnuts, halved and roasted
- 1/3 cup yogurt
- 2 tbsp. red wine vinegar
- 3 tbsp. extra virgin olive oil
- Salt and black pepper, to taste

Directions:
1. Whisk yogurt, olive oil and vinegar in a small bowl. Place the baby spinach leaves in a large salad bowl.
2. Add the onions, cucumber and walnuts. Season with black pepper and salt, stir, and toss with the dressing.

Arugula and Avocado Salad

Preparation time: 5 minutes
Cooking time: 15-20 minutes
Servings: 4
Ingredients:

- 1 bunch arugula leaves
- 2 avocados, peeled and sliced
- 1 cup strawberries, halved
- 1/2 cup corn kernels, cooked
- 1 tbsp. poppy seeds
- 1 tbsp. lemon juice
- 2 tbsp. extra virgin olive oil

Directions:
1. Combine all Ingredients: in a salad bowl and gently toss. Sprinkle with lemon juice and olive oil, stir, top with poppy seeds and serve.

Arugula, Radicchio and Pomegranate Salad

Preparation time: 5 minutes
Cooking time: 10 minutes
Servings: 4
Ingredients:

- 1 bunch arugula leaves
- 1 small head radicchio, chopped
- 1 avocado, peeled and cubed
- 1/2 cup pomegranate seeds, from 1 medium pomegranate
- 1/3 cup hazelnuts

For the dressing:

- 1 tbsp. honey
- 1 tbsp. balsamic vinegar
- 2 tbsp. extra virgin olive oil
- 1/2 tsp salt

Directions:
1. Place arugula, radicchio, avocado, hazelnuts and pomegranate seeds in a large salad bowl and gently toss to combine.
2. Whisk dressing Ingredients: until smooth, pour over the salad, serve and enjoy!

Roasted Beet Salad

Preparation Time: 20 minutes
Cooking Time: 70 minutes
Servings: 4
Ingredients:

- 6 medium beets, scrubbed, tops removed
- ¼ cup balsamic vinegar
- ¼ cup extra-virgin olive oil
- 1 tsp. Dijon mustard
- Salt
- Freshly ground black pepper
- ¼ cup walnuts
- 6 oz. baby arugula
- 2 oz. feta cheese, crumbled

Directions:
1. Preheat the oven to 400°F.
2. Wrap each beet tightly in aluminum foil, and arrange it on a baking sheet. Roast for 45 to 60 minutes, depending on their size, until tender when pierced with a knife. Remove from the oven, carefully unwrap each beet, and let cool for 10 minutes.
3. Reduce the oven temperature to 350°F. Meanwhile, in a medium bowl, whisk the vinegar, olive oil, and mustard. Season with salt and pepper.
4. On the same baking sheet, spread the walnuts in a single layer. Toast for 5 to 7 minutes, until lightly browned.
5. Using a small knife, peel and slice the beets, and place them in another medium bowl. Add half of the vinaigrette, and toss to coat. Add the arugula to the remaining vinaigrette, and toss to coat. On a serving platter, arrange the arugula and top with the beets.
6. Sprinkle the toasted walnuts and feta cheese over the top and serve.

Black Bean and Corn Salad

Preparation Time: 20 minutes
Cooking Time: 0 minutes
Servings: 5
Ingredients:

- 2 (15 oz.) cans reduced-sodium black beans, rinsed and drained
- 1 red bell pepper, chopped
- 1 cucumber, chopped
- 1 avocado, peeled, seeded, and chopped
- 1 cup fresh, frozen and thawed, or canned and drained corn
- ½ cup minced red onion
- 1 jalapeño pepper, seeded and minced
- ¼ cup chopped fresh cilantro
- ¼ cup extra-virgin olive oil
- 3 tbsp. freshly squeezed lime juice
- 1 tsp. honey
- 1 tsp. ground cumin
- Salt
- Freshly ground black pepper

Directions:
1. In a large bowl, stir together the black beans, red bell pepper, cucumber, avocado, corn, red onion, jalapeño, and cilantro.
2. In a small bowl, whisk the olive oil, lime juice, honey, and cumin. Season with salt and pepper. Pour the dressing over the salad, mix well to coat, and serve.

Perfect Quinoa Salad

Preparation Time: 16 minutes
Cooking Time: 14 minutes
Servings: 6
Ingredients:

- 1 cup quinoa, rinsed
- 1½ cups water
- 1 cucumber, finely chopped
- 1 red bell pepper, finely chopped
- ½ red onion, chopped
- ½ cup fresh flat-leaf parsley
- ¼ cup extra-virgin olive oil
- 2 lemons, juiced
- 3 garlic cloves, minced
- ½ tsp. salt
- ¼ tsp. freshly ground black pepper

Directions:
1. In a small saucepan over high heat, combine the quinoa and water. Bring to a boil, reduce the heat to low, cover the pot, and cook for 10 to 15 minutes, until the water is absorbed. Turn off the heat, fluff with a fork, re-cover, and let rest for about 5 minutes.
2. Meanwhile, in a large bowl, toss the cucumber, red bell pepper, red onion, and parsley.
3. In a small bowl, whisk the olive oil, lemon juice, garlic, salt, and pepper. Pour the dressing over the vegetables, and toss well to coat. Fold in the quinoa and serve.

Tropical Fruit Salad with Coconut Milk

Preparation Time: 10 minutes
Cooking Time: 0 minutes
Servings: 8
Ingredients:

- 2 cups pineapple chunks
- 2 kiwi fruits, peeled and sliced
- 1 mango, peeled and chopped
- ¼ cup canned light coconut milk
- 1 tbsp. freshly squeezed lime juice
- 1 tbsp. honey

Directions:
1. In a medium bowl, toss together the pineapple, kiwi, and mango.
2. In a small bowl, combine the coconut milk, lime juice, and honey, stirring until the honey dissolves. Pour the mixture over the fruits, and toss to coat. Serve immediately or refrigerate in an airtight container for up to 3 days.

Cucumber, Tomato, and Avocado Salad

Preparation Time: 10 minutes
Cooking Time: 0 minutes
Servings: 4
Ingredients:

- 1 cup cherry tomatoes, halved
- 1 large cucumber, chopped
- 1 small red onion, thinly sliced
- 1 avocado, diced
- 2 tbsp. chopped fresh dill
- 2 tbsp. extra-virgin olive oil
- 1 lemon, juiced
- ¼ tsp. salt

¼ tsp. freshly ground black pepper
Directions:
1. In a large mixing bowl, combine the tomatoes, cucumber, onion, avocado, and dill.
2. In a small bowl, combine the oil, lemon juice, salt, and pepper, and mix well.
3. Drizzle the dressing over the vegetables and toss to combine. Serve.

Layered Salad

Preparation Time: 9 minutes
Cooking Time: 15 minutes
Servings: 10
Ingredients:

- 6 slices bacon, chopped and cooked crisp
- 2 tomatoes, diced
- 2 stalks celery, sliced
- 1 head romaine lettuce, diced
- 1 red bell pepper, diced
- 1 cup frozen peas, thawed
- 1 cup sharp cheddar cheese, grated
- ¼ cup red onion, fine diced
- What you'll need from the store cupboard
- 1 cup fat-free ranch dressing

Directions:

1. Use a 9x13-inch glass baking dish and layer half the lettuce, pepper, celery, tomatoes, peas, onion, cheese, bacon, and dressing. Repeat. Serve or cover and chill until ready to serve.

Baked "Potato" Salad

Preparation Time: 6 minutes
Cooking Time: 15 minutes
Servings: 8
Ingredients:

- 2 lb. cauliflower, separated into small florets
- 6-8 slices bacon, chopped and fried crisp
- 6 boiled eggs, cooled, peeled, and chopped
- 1 cup sharp cheddar cheese, grated
- ½ cup green onion, sliced
- 1 cup reduced-fat mayonnaise
- 2 tsp. yellow mustard
- 1 ½ tsp. onion powder, divided
- Salt and fresh-ground black pepper to taste

Directions:
1. Place cauliflower in a vegetable steamer, or a pot with a steamer insert, and steam for 5–6 minutes.
2. Drain the cauliflower and set it aside.
3. In a small bowl, whisk together mayonnaise, mustard, 1 tsp. onion powder, salt, and pepper.
4. Pat cauliflower dries with paper towels and place in a large mixing bowl. Add eggs, salt, pepper, remaining ½ tsp. onion powder, then dressing. Mix gently to combine Ingredients: together.
5. Fold in the bacon, cheese, and green onion. Serve warm or cover and chill before serving.

Caprese Salad

Preparation Time: 6 minutes
Cooking Time: 15 minutes
Servings: 4
Ingredients:

- 3 medium tomatoes, cut into 8 slices
- 2 (1 oz.) slices mozzarella cheese, cut into strips
- ¼ cup fresh basil, sliced thin
- 2 tsp. extra-virgin olive oil
- 1/8 tsp. salt
- Pinch black pepper

Directions:
1. Place tomatoes and cheese on serving plates. Sprinkle with salt and pepper. Drizzle oil over and top with basil. Serve.

Chopped Veggie Salad

Preparation Time: 4 minutes
Cooking Time: 15 minutes
Servings: 4
Ingredients:

- 1 cucumber, chopped
- 1-pint cherry tomatoes, cut in half
- 3 radishes, chopped
- 1 yellow bell pepper chopped
- ½ cup fresh parsley, chopped

What you'll need from the store cupboard:

- 3 tbsp. lemon juice

- 1 tbsp. olive oil
- Salt to taste

Directions:
1. Place all Ingredients: in a large bowl and toss to combine. Serve immediately, or cover and chill until ready to serve.

Tofu Salad Sandwiches

Preparation Time: 9 minutes
Cooking Time: 16 minutes
Servings: 4
Ingredients:

- 1 pkg. silken firm tofu, pressed
- 4 lettuce leaves
- 2 green onions, diced
- ¼ cup celery, diced
- 8 slices bread
- ¼ cup lite mayonnaise
- 2 tbsp. sweet pickle relish
- 1 tbsp. Dijon mustard
- ¼ tsp. turmeric - ¼ tsp. salt
- 1/8 tsp. cayenne pepper

Directions:
1. Press tofu between layers of paper towels for 15 minutes to remove excess moisture. Cut into small cubes.
2. In a medium bowl, stir together the remaining Ingredients. Fold in tofu. Spread over 4 slices of bread. Top with a lettuce leaf and another slice of bread. Serve.

Lobster Roll Salad with Bacon Vinaigrette

Preparation Time: 20 minutes
Cooking Time: 15 minutes
Servings: 6
Ingredients:

- 6 slices bacon
- 2 whole-grain ciabatta rolls, halved horizontally
- 3 medium tomatoes, cut into wedges
- 2 (8 oz.) spiny lobster tails, fresh or frozen (thawed)
- 2 cups fresh baby spinach
- 2 cups romaine lettuce, torn
- 1 cup seeded cucumber, diced
- 1 cup red sweet peppers, diced
- 2 tbsp. shallot, diced fine
- 2 tbsp. fresh chives, diced fine

What you'll need from the store cupboard:

- 2 garlic cloves, diced fine
- 3 tbsp. white wine vinegar
- 3 tbsp. olive oil, divided

Directions:
1. Heat a grill to medium heat, or medium heat charcoals.
2. Rinse lobster and pat dry. Butterfly lobster tails. Place on the grill, cover, and cook 25–30 minutes, or until meat is opaque.
3. Remove lobster and let cool.
4. In a small bowl, whisk together 2 tbsp. olive oil and garlic. Brush the cut sides of the rolls with the oil mixture. Place on grill, cut side down, and cook until crisp, about 2 minutes. Transfer to cutting board.

5. While lobster is cooking, chop bacon and cook in a medium skillet until crisp. Transfer to paper towels. Reserve 1 tbsp. bacon grease.

6. To make the vinaigrette: combine reserved bacon grease, vinegar, shallot, remaining 1 tbsp. oil and chives in a glass jar with an air-tight lid. Screw on the lid and shake to combine.

7. Remove the lobster from the shells and cut it into 1 ½-inch pieces. Cut rolls into 1-inch cubes.

8. To assemble salad: In a large bowl, combine spinach, romaine, tomatoes, cucumber, peppers, lobster, and bread cubes. Toss to combine. Transfer to serving platter and drizzle with vinaigrette. Sprinkle bacon over top and serve.

Bean and Basil Salad

Preparation Time: 20 minutes
Cooking Time: 0 minutes
Servings: 8
Ingredients:

- 1 (15 oz.) can low-sodium chickpeas, drained and rinsed
- 1 (15 oz.) can low-sodium kidney beans, drained and rinsed
- 1 (15 oz.) can low-sodium white beans, drained and rinsed
- 1 red bell pepper, seeded and finely chopped
- ¼ cup chopped scallions, both white and green parts
- ¼ cup finely chopped fresh basil
- 3 garlic cloves, minced
- 2 tbsp. extra-virgin olive oil
- 1 tbsp. red wine vinegar
- 1 tsp. Dijon mustard
- ¼ tsp. freshly ground black pepper

Directions:

1. In a large mixing bowl, combine the chickpeas, kidney beans, white beans, bell pepper, scallions, basil, and garlic. Toss gently to combine.

2. In a small bowl, combine the olive oil, vinegar, mustard, and pepper. Toss with the salad.

3. Cover and refrigerate for an hour before serving, to allow the flavors to mix.

4. Substitution tip: Feel free to substitute home-cooked beans in place of canned, using about 1½ cups per variety.

Tenderloin Grilled Salad

Preparation Time: 10 minutes
Cooking Time: 20 minutes
Servings: 5
Ingredients:

- 1 lb. pork tenderloin
- 10 cups mixed salad greens
- 2 oranges, seedless, cut into bite-sized pieces
- 1 tbsp. orange zest, grated
- 2 tbsp. cider vinegar
- 2 tbsp. olive oil
- 2 tsp. Dijon mustard

- ½ cup orange juice
- 2 tsp. honey

- ½ tsp. ground pepper

Directions:

1. Bring together all the dressing Ingredients: in a bowl.

2. Grill each side of the pork covered over medium heat for 9 minutes.

3. Slice after 5 minutes.

4. Slice the tenderloin thinly.

5. Keep the greens on your serving plate.

6. Top with the pork and oranges.

7. Sprinkle nuts (optional).

Barley Veggie Salad

Preparation Time: 10 minutes
Cooking Time: 20 minutes
Servings: 6
Ingredients:

- 1 tomato, seeded and chopped
- 2 tbsp. parsley, minced
- 1 yellow pepper, chopped
- 1 tbsp. basil, minced
- ¼ cup almonds, toasted
- 1-¼ cups vegetable broth
- 1 cup barley
- 1 tbsp. lemon juice
-
-
- 2 tbsp. white wine vinegar
- 3 tbsp. olive oil
- ¼ tsp. pepper
- ½ tsp. salt
- 1 cup water

Directions:

1. Boil the broth, barley, and water in a saucepan.

2. Reduce heat. Cover and let it simmer for 10 minutes.

3. Take out from the heat.

4. In the meantime, bring together the parsley, yellow pepper, and tomato in a bowl.

5. Stir the barley in.

6. Whisk the vinegar, oil, basil, lemon juice, water, pepper, and salt in a bowl.

7. Pour this over your barley mix. Toss to coat well.

8. Stir the almonds in before serving.

Spinach Shrimp Salad

Preparation Time: 10 minutes
Cooking Time: 10 minutes
Servings: 4
Ingredients:

- 1 lb. uncooked shrimp, peeled and deveined
- 2 tbsp. parsley, minced
- ¾ cup halved cherry tomatoes
- 1 medium lemon
- 4 cups baby spinach
- 2 tbsp. butter
- 3 minced garlic cloves
- ¼ tsp. pepper
- ¼ tsp. salt

Directions:

1. Melt the butter over a medium temperature in a nonstick skillet.
2. Add the shrimp.
3. Now cook the shrimp for 3 minutes until your shrimp becomes pink.
4. Add the parsley and garlic.
5. Cook for another minute. Take out from the heat.
6. Keep the spinach in your salad bowl.
7. Top with the shrimp mix and tomatoes.
8. Drizzle lemon juice on the salad.
9. Sprinkle pepper and salt.

Sweet Potato and Roasted Beet Salad

Preparation Time: 10 minutes
Cooking Time: 10 minutes
Servings: 4
Ingredients:

- 2 beets
- 1 sweet potato, peeled and cubed
- 1 garlic clove, minced
- 2 tbsp. walnuts, chopped and toasted
- 1 cup fennel bulb, sliced
- 3 tbsp. balsamic vinegar
- 1 tsp. Dijon mustard
- 1 tbsp. honey
- 3 tbsp. olive oil
- ¼ tsp. pepper
- ¼ tsp. salt
- 3 tbsp. water

Directions:
1. Scrub the beets. Trim the tops to 1 inch.
2. Wrap in foil and keep on a baking sheet.
3. Bake until tender. Take off the foil. Combine water and sweet potato in a bowl.
4. Cover. Microwave for 5 minutes. Drain off.
5. Now peel the beets. Cut into small wedges.
6. Arrange the fennel, sweet potato, and beets on 4 salad plates.
7. Sprinkle nuts.
8. Whisk the honey, mustard, vinegar, water, garlic, pepper, and salt.
9. Whisk in oil gradually. Drizzle over the salad.

Harvest Salad

Preparation Time: 9 minutes
Cooking Time: 25 minutes
Servings: 6
Ingredients:

- 10 oz. kale, deboned and chopped
- 1 ½ cup blackberries
- ½ butternut squash, cubed
- ¼ cup goat cheese, crumbled

What you'll need from the store cupboard:
- Maple Mustard Salad Dressing
- 1 cup raw pecans
- 1/3 cup raw pumpkin seeds
- ¼ cup dried cranberries

- 3 ½ tbsp. olive oil
- 1 ½ tbsp. sugar-free maple syrup
- 3/8 tsp. salt, divided
- Pepper, to taste
- Nonstick cooking spray

Directions:
1. Heat oven to 400°F.
2. Spray a baking sheet with cooking spray.
3. Spread squash on the prepared pan, add 1 ½ tbsp. oil, 1/8 tsp. salt, and pepper to squash, and stir to coat the squash evenly. Bake 20–25 minutes.
4. Place kale in a large bowl. Add 2 tbsp. oil and ½ tsp. salt and massage it into the kale with your hands for 3–4 minutes.
5. Spray a clean baking sheet with cooking spray.
6. In a medium bowl, stir together pecans, pumpkin seeds, and maple syrup until nuts are coated. Pour onto prepared pan and bake 8–10 minutes, these can be baked at the same time as the squash.
7. To assemble the salad: place all of the Ingredients: in a large bowl. Pour dressing over and toss to coat.
8. Serve.

Rainbow Black Bean Salad

Preparation Time: 16 minutes
Cooking Time: 0 minutes
Servings: 5
Ingredients:

- 1 (15 oz.) can low-sodium black beans, drained and rinsed
- 1 avocado, diced
- 1 cup cherry tomatoes, halved
- 1 cup chopped baby spinach
- ½ cup finely chopped red bell pepper
- ¼ cup finely chopped jicama
- ½ cup chopped scallions, both white and green parts
- ¼ cup chopped fresh cilantro
- 2 tbsp. freshly squeezed lime juice
- 1 tbsp. extra-virgin olive oil
- 2 garlic cloves, minced
- 1 tsp. honey
- ¼ tsp. salt
- ¼ tsp. freshly ground black pepper

Directions:
1. In a large bowl, combine the black beans, avocado, tomatoes, spinach, bell pepper, jicama, scallions, and cilantro.
2. In a small bowl, mix the lime juice, oil, garlic, honey, salt, and pepper. Add to the salad and toss.
3. Chill for 1 hour before serving.

Warm Barley and Squash Salad with Balsamic Vinaigrette

Preparation Time: 20 minutes
Cooking Time: 41 minutes
Servings: 8
Ingredients:

- 1 small butternut squash
- 3 tsp. plus 2 tbsp. extra-virgin olive oil, divided
- 2 cups broccoli florets

- 1 cup pearl barley
- 1 cup toasted chopped walnuts
- 2 cups baby kale
- ½ red onion, sliced
- 2 tbsp. balsamic vinegar
- 2 garlic cloves, minced
- ½ tsp. salt
- ¼ tsp. freshly ground black pepper

Directions:

1. Preheat the oven to 400°F.

2. Line a baking sheet with parchment paper.

3. Peel and seed the squash, and cut it into dice. In a large bowl, toss the squash with 2 tsp. of olive oil.

4. Transfer to the prepared baking sheet and roast for 20 minutes.

5. While the squash is roasting, toss the broccoli in the same bowl with 1 tsp. of olive oil. After 20 minutes, flip the squash and push it to one side of the baking sheet.

6. Add the broccoli to the other side and continue to roast for 20 more minutes until tender.

7. While the veggies are roasting, in a medium pot, cover the barley with several inches of water.

8. Bring to a boil, then reduce the heat, cover, and simmer for 30 minutes until tender. Drain and rinse.

9. Transfer the barley to a large bowl, and toss with the cooked squash and broccoli, walnuts, kale, and onion.

10. In a small bowl, mix the remaining 2 tbsp. olive oil, balsamic vinegar, garlic, salt, and pepper. Toss the salad with the dressing and serve.

Winter Chicken and Citrus Salad

Preparation Time: 20 minutes

Cooking Time: 0 minutes

Servings: 4

Ingredients:

- 4 cups baby spinach
- 2 tbsp. extra-virgin olive oil
- 1 tbsp. freshly squeezed lemon juice
- 1/8 tsp. salt
- Freshly ground black pepper
- 2 cups chopped cooked chicken
- 2 mandarin oranges, peeled and sectioned
- ½ peeled grapefruit, sectioned
- ¼ cup sliced almonds

Directions:

1. In a large mixing bowl, toss the spinach with the olive oil, lemon juice, salt, and pepper.

2. Add the chicken, oranges, grapefruit, and almonds to the bowl. Toss gently.

3. Arrange on 4 plates and serve.

Chapter 13

Dinner

Cauliflower Mash

Preparation time: 30 minutes
Cooking time: 5 minutes
Servings: 4
Ingredients:
- 2 tbsp. butter
- 1/4 c. milk
- 10 oz. cauliflower florets
- 3/4 tsp. salt

Directions:
1. Add water to the saucepan and bring to boil.
2. Reduce the heat and simmer for 10 minutes.
3. Drain the vegetables well. Transfer vegetables, butter, milk, and salt to a blender and blend until smooth.
4. Serve and enjoy.

French toast in Sticks

Preparation time: 5 minutes
Cooking time: 10 minutes
Servings: 4
Ingredients:
- 4 slices of white bread, 38 mm. thick, preferably hard
- 2 eggs
- 60 ml of milk
- 15 ml maple sauce
- 2 ml vanilla extract
- Nonstick spray oil
- 38 g of sugar
- 3 g. ground cinnamon
- Maple syrup, to serve
- Powdered sugar to sprinkle

Directions:
1. Cut each slice of bread into thirds making 12 pieces. Place sideways
2. Beat the eggs, milk, maple syrup, and vanilla.
3. Preheat the air fryer, set it to 175 °C.
4. Dip the sliced bread into the egg mixture and place it in the preheated air fryer. Sprinkle French toast generously with oil spray.
5. Cook French toast for 10 minutes at 175 °C. Turn the toast halfway through cooking.
6. Mix the sugar and cinnamon in a bowl.
7. Cover the French toast with the sugar and cinnamon mixture when you have finished cooking.
8. Serve with maple syrup and sprinkle with powdered sugar

Misto Quente

Preparation time: 5 minutes
Cooking time: 10 minutes
Servings: 4
Ingredients:
- 4 slices of bread without shell
- 4 slices of turkey breast
- 4 slices of cheese
- 2 tbsp. cream cheese
- 2 spoons of butter

Directions:
1. Preheat the air fryer. Set the timer of 5 minutes and the temperature to 200 °C.
2. Pass the butter on one side of the slice of bread, and on the other side of the slice, the cream cheese.
3. Mount the sandwiches placing 2 slices of turkey breast and 2 slices of cheese between the bread, with the cream cheese inside and the side with butter.
4. Place the sandwiches in the basket of the air fryer. Set the timer of the air fryer for 5 minutes and press the power button.

Seared Tuna Steak

Preparation time: 10 minutes
Cooking time: 10 minutes
Servings: 2
Ingredients:
- 1 tsp. sesame seeds
- 1 tbsp. sesame oil
- 2 tbsp. soya sauce
- Salt and pepper, to taste
- 2 (6 oz.) ahi tuna steaks

Directions:
1. Seasoning the tuna steaks with salt and pepper. Keep it aside on a shallow bowl.
2. In another bowl, mix soya sauce and sesame oil.
3. Pour the sauce over the salmon and coat them generously with the sauce.
4. Keep it aside for 10–15 minutes and then heat a large skillet over medium heat.
5. Once hot, keep the tuna steaks and cook them for 3 minutes or until seared underneath.
6. Flip the fillets and cook them for a further 3 minutes.
7. Transfer the seared tuna steaks to the serving plate and slice them into 1/2-in. slices. Top with sesame seeds.

Vegetable Soup

Preparation time: 10 minutes
Cooking time: 30 minutes
Servings: 5

Ingredients:

- 8 c. vegetable broth
- 2 tbsp. olive oil
- 1 tbsp. Italian seasoning
- 1 onion, large and diced
- 2 bay leaves, dried
- 2 bell peppers, large and diced
- Sea salt and black pepper, as needed
- 4 cloves of garlic, minced
- 28 oz. tomatoes, diced
- 1 cauliflower head, medium and torn into florets
- 2 c. green beans, trimmed and chopped

Directions:

1. Heat oil in a Dutch oven over medium heat.
2. Once the oil becomes hot, stir in the onions and pepper.
3. Cook for 10 minutes or until the onion is softened and browned.
4. Spoon in the garlic and sauté for a minute or until fragrant.
5. Add all the remaining Ingredients: to it. Mix until everything comes together.
6. Bring the mixture to a boil. Lower the heat and cook for further 20 minutes or until the vegetables have softened.
7. Serve hot.

Pork Chop Diane

Preparation time: 10 minutes
Cooking time: 20 minutes
Servings: 4
Ingredients:

- 1/4 c. low-sodium chicken broth
- 1 tbsp. freshly squeezed lemon juice
- 2 tsps. Worcestershire sauce
- 2 tsps. Dijon mustard
- 4 (5-oz.) boneless pork top loin chops
- 1 tsp. extra-virgin olive oil
- 1 tsp. lemon zest
- 1 tsp. butter
- 2 tsps. Chopped fresh chives

Directions:

1. Blend together the chicken broth, lemon juice, Worcestershire sauce, and Dijon mustard and set it aside.
2. Season the pork chops lightly.
3. Situate a large skillet over medium-high heat and add the olive oil.
4. Cook the pork chops, turning once, until they are no longer pink, about 8 minutes per side.
5. Put aside the chops.
6. Pour the broth mixture into the skillet and cook until warmed through and thickened, about 2 minutes. Blend lemon zest, butter, and chives.
7. Garnish with a generous spoonful of sauce.

Autumn Pork Chops with Red Cabbage and Apples

Preparation time: 15 minutes
Cooking time: 30 minutes
Servings: 4
Ingredients:

- 1/4 c. apple cider vinegar
- 2 tbsps. Granulated sweetener
- 4 (4-oz.) pork chops, about 1 in. thick
- 1 tbsp. extra-virgin olive oil
- 1/2 red cabbage, finely shredded
- 1 sweet onion, thinly sliced
- 1 apple, peeled, cored, and sliced
- 1 tsp. chopped fresh thyme
- Salt and pepper, to taste

Directions:

1. Mix vinegar and sweetener. Set it aside.
2. Season the pork with salt and pepper.
3. Position a big skillet over medium-high heat and add the olive oil.
4. Cook the pork chops until no longer pink, turning once, about 8 minutes per side.
5. Put chops aside.
6. Add the cabbage and onion to the skillet and sauté until the vegetables have softened, for about 5 minutes.
7. Add the vinegar mixture and the apple slices to the skillet and bring the mixture to a boil.
8. Adjust heat to low and simmer, covered, for 5 additional minutes.
9. Return the pork chops to the skillet, along with any accumulated juices and thyme, cover, and cook for 5 more minutes.

Chipotle Chili Pork Chops

Preparation time: 4 hours
Cooking time: 20 minutes
Servings: 4
Ingredients:

- Juice and zest of 1 lime
- 1 tbsp. extra-virgin olive oil
- 1 tbsp. chipotle chili powder
- 2 tsps. Minced garlic
- 1 tsp. ground cinnamon
- Pinch sea salt
- 4 (5-oz.) pork chops
- Lime wedges

Directions:

1. Combine the lime juice and zest, oil, chipotle chili powder, garlic, cinnamon, and salt in a resealable plastic bag. Add the pork chops. Remove as much air as possible and seal the bag.
2. Marinate the chops in the refrigerator for at least 4 hours, and up to 24 hours, turning them several times.
3. Ready the oven to 400 °F and set a rack on a baking sheet. Let the chops rest at room temperature for 15 minutes, then arrange them on the rack and discard the remaining marinade.
4. Roast the chops until cooked through, turning once, about 10 minutes per side.
5. Serve with lime wedges.

Orange-Marinated Pork Tenderloin

Preparation time: 2 hours
Cooking time: 30 minutes
Servings: 4
Ingredients:

- 1/4 c. freshly squeezed orange juice

- 2 tsps. Orange zest
- 2 tsps. Minced garlic
- 1 tsp. low-sodium soy sauce
- 1 tsp. grated fresh ginger
- 1 tsp. honey
- 1 1/2 lbs. pork tenderloin roast
- 1 tbsp. extra-virgin olive oil

Directions:

1. Blend together the orange juice, zest, garlic, soy sauce, ginger, and honey.
2. Pour the marinade into a resealable plastic bag and add the pork tenderloin.
3. Remove as much air as possible and seal the bag. Marinate the pork in the refrigerator, turning the bag a few times, for 2 hours.
4. Preheat the oven to 400 °F.
5. Pull out tenderloin from the marinade and discard the marinade.
6. Position big ovenproof skillet over medium-high heat and add the oil.
7. Sear the pork tenderloin on all sides, about 5 minutes in total.
8. Position skillet to the oven and roast for 25 minutes.
9. Put aside for 10 minutes before serving.

Homestyle Herb Meatballs

Preparation time: 10 minutes
Cooking time: 15 minutes
Servings: 4
Ingredients:

- 1/2-lb. lean ground pork
- 1/2-lb. lean ground beef
- 1 sweet onion, finely chopped
- 1/4 c. bread crumbs
- 2 tbsps. Chopped fresh basil
- 2 tsps. Minced garlic
- 1 egg
- Salt and pepper, to taste

Directions:

1. Preheat the oven to 350 °F.
2. Prepare a baking tray with parchment paper and set it aside.
3. In a large bowl, mix together the pork, beef, onion, bread crumbs, basil, garlic, egg, salt, and pepper until very well mixed.
4. Roll the meat mixture into 2-in. meatballs.
5. Transfer the meatballs to the baking sheet and bake until they are browned and cooked through, about 15 minutes.
6. Serve the meatballs with your favorite marinara sauce and some steamed green beans.

Lime-Parsley Lamb Cutlets

Preparation time: 4 hours
Cooking time: 10 minutes
Servings: 4
Ingredients:

- 1/4 c. extra-virgin olive oil
- 1/4 c. freshly squeezed lime juice
- 2 tbsps. Lime zest
- 2 tbsps. Chopped fresh parsley
- 12 lamb cutlets (about 1 1/2 lbs. total)

- Salt and pepper, to taste

Directions:

1. Scourge the oil, lime juice, zest, parsley, salt, and pepper.
2. Pour the marinade into a resealable plastic bag.
3. Add the cutlets to the bag and remove as much air as possible before sealing.
4. Marinate the lamb in the refrigerator for about 4 hours, turning the bag several times.
5. Preheat the oven to broil.
6. Remove the chops from the bag and arrange them on an aluminum foil-lined baking sheet. Discard the marinade.
7. Broil the chops for 4 minutes per side for medium doneness. Let the chops rest for 5 minutes before serving.

Beef Chili

Preparation time: 10 minutes
Cooking time: 20 minutes
Servings: 4
Ingredients:

- 1/2 tsp. garlic powder
- 1 tsp. coriander, grounded
- 1 lb. beef, grounded
- 1/2 tsp. sea salt
- 1/2 tsp. cayenne pepper
- 1 tsp. cumin, grounded
- 1/2 tsp. pepper, grounded
- 1/2 c. salsa, low-carb and no-sugar

Directions:

1. Heat a large-sized pan over medium-high heat and cook the beef in it until browned.
2. Stir in all the spices and cook them for 7 minutes or until everything is combined.
3. When the beef gets cooked, spoon in the salsa.
4. Bring the mixture to a simmer and cook for another 8 minutes or until everything comes together.
5. Take it from heat and transfer it to a serving bowl.

Greek Broccoli Salad

Preparation time: 10 minutes
Cooking time: 15 minutes
Servings: 4
Ingredients:

- 1 1/4 lb. broccoli, sliced into small bites
- 1/4 c. almonds, sliced
- 1/3 c. sun-dried tomatoes
- 1/4 c. feta cheese, crumbled
- 1/4 c. red onion, sliced

For the Dressing

- 1/4 c. olive oil
- Dash of red pepper flakes
- 1 garlic clove, minced
- 1/4 tsp. salt
- 2 tbsp. lemon juice
- 1/2 tsp. Dijon mustard
- 1 tsp. low carb sweetener syrup
- 1/2 tsp. oregano, dried

Directions:

1. Mix broccoli, onion, cheese, almonds, and sun-dried tomatoes in a large mixing bowl.
2. In another small-sized bowl, combine all the dressing Ingredients: until emulsified.
3. Spoon the dressing over the broccoli salad.
4. Allow the salad to rest for half an hour before serving.

Mediterranean Steak Sandwiches

Preparation time: 1 hour
Cooking time: 10 minutes
Servings: 4
Ingredients:

- 2 tbsps. Extra-virgin olive oil
- 2 tbsps. Balsamic vinegar
- 2 tsps. Garlic
- 2 tsps. Lemon juice
- 2 tsps. Fresh oregano
- 1 tsp. fresh parsley
- 1-pound flank steak
- 4 whole-wheat pitas
- 2 c. shredded lettuce
- 1 red onion, thinly sliced
- 1 tomato, chopped
- 1 oz. low-sodium feta cheese

Directions:
1. Scourge olive oil, balsamic vinegar, garlic, lemon juice, oregano, and parsley.
2. Add the steak to the bowl, turning to coat it completely.
3. Marinate the steak for 1 hour in the refrigerator, turning it over several times.
4. Preheat the broiler. Line a baking sheet with aluminum foil.
5. Put the steak out of the bowl and discard the marinade. . Situate the steak on the baking sheet and broil for 5 minutes per side for medium. Set aside for 10 minutes before slicing. Stuff the pitas with the sliced steak, lettuce, onion, tomato, and feta.

Roasted Beef with Peppercorn Sauce

Preparation time: 10 minutes
Cooking time: 90 minutes
Servings: 4
Ingredients:

- 1 1/2 lbs. top rump beef roast
- 3 tsps. Extra-virgin olive oil
- 3 shallots, minced
- 2 tsps. Minced garlic
- 1 tbsp. green peppercorns
- 2 tbsps. Dry sherry
- 2 tbsps. All-purpose flour
- 1 c. sodium-free beef broth
- Salt and pepper, to taste

Directions:
1. Heat the oven to 300 °F.
2. Season the roast with salt and pepper.
3. Position a big skillet over medium-high heat and add 2 tsps. Of olive oil.
4. Brown the beef on all sides, about 10 minutes in total, and transfer the roast to a baking dish.

5. Roast until desired doneness, about 1 1/2 hours for medium. When the roast has been in the oven for 1 hour, start the sauce.
6. In a medium saucepan over medium-high heat, sauté the shallots in the remaining 1 tsp of olive oil until translucent, about 4 minutes.
7. Stir in the garlic and peppercorns, and cook for another minute. Whisk in the sherry to deglaze the pan.
8. Whisk in the flour to form a thick paste, cooking for 1 minute and stirring constantly.
9. Fill in the beef broth and whisk for 4 minutes. Season the sauce.
10. Serve the beef with a generous spoonful of sauce.

Coffee-and-Herb-Marinated Steak

Preparation time: 2 hours
Cooking time: 10 minutes
Servings: 3
Ingredients:

- 1/4 c. whole coffee beans
- 2 tsps. Garlic
- 2 tsps. Rosemary
- 2 tsps. Thyme
- 1 tsp. black pepper
- 2 tbsps. Apple cider vinegar
- 2 tbsps. Extra-virgin olive oil
- 1-pound flank steak, trimmed of visible fat

Directions:
1. Place the coffee beans, garlic, rosemary, thyme, and black pepper in a coffee grinder or food processor and pulse until coarsely ground.
2. Transfer the coffee mixture to a resealable plastic bag and add the vinegar and oil. Shake to combine.
3. Add the flank steak and squeeze the excess air out of the bag. Seal it. Marinate the steak in the refrigerator for at least 2 hours, occasionally turning the bag over.
4. Preheat the broiler. Line a baking sheet with aluminum foil.
5. Pull the steak out and discard the marinade.
6. Position steak on the baking sheet and broil until it is done to your liking.
7. Put aside for 10 minutes before cutting it.
8. Serve with your favorite side dish. .

Traditional Beef Stroganoff

Preparation time: 10 minutes
Cooking time: 30 minutes
Servings: 4
Ingredients:

- 1 tsp. extra-virgin olive oil
- 1-lb. top sirloin, cut into thin strips
- 1 c. sliced button mushrooms
- 1/2 sweet onion, finely chopped
- 1 tsp. minced garlic
- 1 tbsp. whole-wheat flour
- 1/2 c. low-sodium beef broth
- 1/4 c. dry sherry
- 1/2 c. fat-free sour cream
- 1 tbsp. chopped fresh parsley
- Salt and pepper, to taste

Directions:

1. Position the skillet over medium-high heat and add the oil.
2. Sauté the beef until browned, about 10 minutes, then remove the beef with a slotted spoon to a plate and set it aside.
3. Add the mushrooms, onion, and garlic to the skillet and sauté until lightly browned, for about 5 minutes.
4. Whisk in the flour and then whisk in the beef broth and sherry.
5. Return the sirloin to the skillet and bring the mixture to a boil.
6. Reduce the heat to low and simmer until the beef is tender, about 10 minutes.
7. Stir in the sour cream and parsley. Season with salt and pepper.

Chicken and Roasted Vegetable Wraps

Preparation time: 10 minutes
Cooking time: 20 minutes
Servings: 4
Ingredients:
- 1/2 small eggplant
- 1 red bell pepper
- 1 medium zucchini
- 1/2 small red onion, sliced
- 1 tbsp. extra-virgin olive oil
- 2 (8-oz.) cooked chicken breasts, sliced
- 4 whole-wheat tortilla wraps
- Salt and pepper, to taste

Directions:
1. Preheat the oven to 400 °F.
2. Wrap a baking sheet with foil and set it aside.
3. In a large bowl, toss the eggplant, bell pepper, zucchini, and red onion with olive oil.
4. Transfer the vegetables to the baking sheet and lightly season with salt and pepper.
5. Roast the vegetables until soft and slightly charred, about 20 minutes.
6. Divide the vegetables and chicken into four portions.
7. Wrap 1 tortilla around each portion of chicken and grilled vegetables, and serve.

Spicy Chicken Cacciatore

Preparation time: 20 minutes
Cooking time: 1 hour
Servings: 6
Ingredients:
- 1 (2-lb.) chicken
- 1/4 c. all-purpose flour
- 2 tbsps. Extra-virgin olive oil
- 3 slices bacon
- 1 sweet onion
- 2 tsps. Minced garlic
- 4 oz. button mushrooms, halved
- 1 (28-oz.) can of low-sodium stewed tomatoes
- 1/2 c. red wine
- 2 tsps. Chopped fresh oregano
- 2 tsps. Red pepper flakes
- Salt and pepper, to taste

Directions:
1. Cut the chicken into pieces 2 drumsticks, 2 thighs, 2 wings, and 4 breast pieces.
2. Dredge the chicken pieces in the flour and season each piece with salt and pepper.
3. Place a large skillet over medium-high heat and add the olive oil.
4. Brown the chicken pieces on all sides, about 20 minutes in total. Transfer the chicken to a plate.
5. Cook the chopped bacon in the skillet for 5 minutes. With a slotted spoon, transfer the cooked bacon to the same plate as the chicken.
6. Pour off most of the oil from the skillet, leaving just a light coating. Sauté the onion, garlic, and mushrooms in the skillet until tender, about 4 minutes.
7. Stir in the tomatoes, wine, oregano, and red pepper flakes.
8. Bring the sauce to a boil. Return the chicken and bacon, plus any accumulated juices from the plate, to the skillet.
9. Reduce the heat to low and simmer until the chicken is tender, about 30 minutes.

Scallion Sandwich

Preparation time: 10 minutes
Cooking time: 10 minutes
Servings: 1
Ingredients:
- 2 slices wheat bread
- 2 tsps. Butter, low-fat
- 2 scallions, sliced thinly
- 1 tbsp. of parmesan cheese, grated
- 3/4 c of cheddar cheese, reduced-fat, grated

Directions:
1. Preheat the Air fryer to 356 °F.
2. Spread butter on a slice of bread. Place inside the cooking basket with the butter side facing down.
3. Place cheese and scallions on top. Spread the rest of the butter on the other slice of bread Put it on top of the sandwich and sprinkle it with parmesan cheese.
4. Cook for 10 minutes.

Cheesy Cauliflower Gratin

Preparation time: 5 minutes
Cooking time: 25 minutes
Servings: 6
Ingredients:
- 6 deli slices pepper jack cheese
- 4 c. cauliflower florets
- Salt and pepper, as needed
- 4 tbsp. butter
- 1/3 c. heavy whipping cream

Directions:
1. Mix the cauliflower, cream, butter, salt, and pepper in a safe microwave bowl and combine well.
2. Microwave the cauliflower mixture for 25 minutes on high until it becomes soft and tender.
3. Remove the Ingredients: from the bowl and mash with the help of a fork.
4. Taste for seasonings and spoon in salt and pepper as required.

5. Arrange the slices of Pepper Jack cheese on top of the cauliflower mixture and microwave for 3 minutes until the cheese starts melting.
6. Serve warm.
Nutrition: Calories 421 Carbohydrates 3 g. Proteins 19 g. Fat 37 g. Sodium 111 mg.

Strawberry Spinach Salad

Preparation time: 5 minutes
Cooking time: 10 minutes
Servings: 4
Ingredients:

- 4 oz. feta cheese, crumbled
- 8 strawberries, sliced
- 2 oz. almonds
- 6 slices bacon, thick-cut, crispy, and crumbled
- 10 oz. spinach leaves, fresh
- 2 Roma tomatoes, diced
- 2 oz. red onion, sliced thinly

Directions:
1. For making this healthy salad, mix all the Ingredients: needed to make the salad in a large-sized bowl and toss them well.

Garlic Bread

Preparation time: 10 minutes
Cooking time: 15 minutes
Servings: 4–5
Ingredients:

- 2 stale French rolls
- 4 tbsp. crushed or crumpled garlic
- 1 c of mayonnaise
- Powdered grated Parmesan
- 1 tbsp. olive oil

Directions:
1. Preheat the air fryer. Set the time of 5 minutes and the temperature to 200 °C.
2. Mix mayonnaise with garlic and set aside.
3. Cut the French rolls into slices, but without separating them completely.
4. Fill the cavities of equals. Brush with olive oil and sprinkle with grated cheese.
5. Place in the basket of the air fryer. Set the timer to 10 minutes, adjust the temperature to 180 °C, and press the power button.

Bruschetta

Preparation time: 5 minutes
Cooking time: 10 minutes
Servings: 2
Ingredients:

- 4 slices of Italian bread
- 1 c. chopped tomato tea
- 1 c. grated mozzarella tea
- Olive oil
- Oregano, salt, and pepper
- 4 fresh basil leaves

Directions:
1. Preheat the air fryer. Set the timer of 5 minutes and the temperature to 200 °C.

2. Sprinkle the slices of Italian bread with olive oil. Divide the chopped tomatoes and mozzarella between the slices. Season with salt, pepper, and oregano.
3. Put oil in the filling. Place a basil leaf on top of each slice.
4. Put the bruschetta in the basket of the air fryer being careful not to spill the filling. Set the timer of 5 minutes, set the temperature to 180 °C, and press the power button.
5. Transfer the bruschetta to a plate and serve.

Cream Buns with Strawberries

Preparation time: 10 minutes
Cooking time: 12 minutes
Servings: 6
Ingredients:

- 240 g. all-purpose flour
- 50 g. granulated sugar
- 8 g. baking powder
- 1 g of salt
- 85 g. chopped cold butter
- 84 g. chopped fresh strawberries
- 120 ml whipping cream
- 2 large eggs
- 10 ml vanilla extract
- 5 ml of water

Directions:
1. Sift flour, sugar, baking powder, and salt in a large bowl. Put the butter with the flour with the use of a blender or your hands until the mixture resembles thick crumbs.
2. Mix the strawberries in the flour mixture. Set aside for the mixture to stand. Beat the whipping cream, 1 egg, and the vanilla extract in a separate bowl.
3. Put the cream mixture in the flour mixture until they are homogeneous, and then spread the mixture to a thickness of 38 mm.
4. Use a round cookie cutter to cut the buns. Spread the buns with a combination of egg and water. Set aside
5. Preheat the air fryer, set it to 180 °C.
6. Place baking paper in the preheated inner basket.
7. Place the buns on top of the baking paper and cook for 12 minutes at 180 °C, until golden brown.

Blueberry Buns

Preparation time: 10 minutes
Cooking time: 12 minutes
Servings: 6
Ingredients:

- 240 g. all-purpose flour
- 50 g. granulated sugar
- 8 g. baking powder
- 2 g of salt
- 85 g. chopped cold butter
- 85 g of fresh blueberries
- 3 g. grated fresh ginger
- 113 ml whipping cream
- 2 large eggs
- 4 ml vanilla extract
- 5 ml of water

Directions:
1. Put sugar, flour, baking powder, and salt in a large bowl.

2. Put the butter with the flour using a blender or your hands until the mixture resembles thick crumbs.

3. Mix the blueberries and ginger in the flour mixture and set aside

4. Mix the whipping cream, 1 egg, and the vanilla extract in a different container.

5. Put the cream mixture with the flour mixture until combined.

6. Shape the dough until it reaches a thickness of approximately 38 mm and cut it into eighths.

7. Spread the buns with a combination of egg and water. Set aside.

8. Preheat the air fryer to 180 °C.

9. Place baking paper in the preheated inner basket and place the buns on top of the paper. Cook for 12 minutes at 180 °C, until golden brown

Lean Lamb and Turkey Meatballs with Yogurt

Preparation time: 10 minutes
Servings: 4
Cooking time: 8 minutes
Ingredients:
For the Meatballs
- 1 egg white
- 4 oz. ground lean turkey
- 1 lb. of ground lean lamb
- 1 tsp. each of cayenne pepper, ground coriander, red chili pastes, salt, and ground cumin
- 2 garlic cloves, minced
- 1 1/2 tbsps. Parsley, chopped
- 1 tbsp. mint, chopped
- 1/4 c of olive oil

For the Yogurt
- 2 tbsps. Of buttermilk
- 1 garlic clove, minced
- 1/4 c. mint, chopped
- 1/2 c of Greek yogurt, non-fat
- Salt to taste

Directions:

1. Set the air fryer to 390 °F.

2. Mix all the Ingredients: for the meatballs in a bowl. Roll and mold them into golf-size round pieces. Arrange in the cooking basket. Cook for 8 minutes.

3. While waiting, combine all the ingredients: for the mint yogurt in a bowl. Mix well.

4. Serve the meatballs with mint yogurt. Top with olives and fresh mint.

Air Fried Section and Tomato

Preparation time: 10 minutes
Cooking time: 5 minutes
Servings: 2
Ingredients:
- 1 aubergine, sliced thickly into 4 disks
- 1 tomato, sliced into 2 thick disks
- 2 tsp. feta cheese, reduced fat
- 2 fresh basil leaves, minced
- 2 balls, small buffalo mozzarella, reduced fat, torn
- Pinch of salt
- Pinch of black pepper

Directions:

1. Preheat air fryer to 330 °F.

2. Spray a small amount of oil into the air fryer basket. Fry the aubergine slices for 5 minutes or until golden brown on both sides. Transfer to a plate.

3. Fry tomato slices in batches for 5 minutes or until seared on both sides.

4. To serve, stack salad starting with an aborigine base, buffalo mozzarella, basil leaves, tomato slice, and 1/2-teaspoon feta cheese.

5. Top of with another slice of aborigine and 1/2 tsp. feta cheese. Serve.

Cheesy Salmon Fillets

Preparation time: 15 minutes
Cooking time: 20 minutes
Servings: 2–3
Ingredients:
For the Salmon Fillets
- 2 pieces, 4 oz. each salmon fillets, choose even cuts
- 1/2 c. sour cream, reduced fat
- 1/4 c. cottage cheese, reduced fat
- 1/4 c. Parmigiano-Reggiano cheese, freshly grated

For the Garnish
- Spanish paprika
- 1/2-piece lemon, cut into wedges

Directions:

1. Preheat the air fryer to 330 °F.

2. To make the salmon fillets, mix sour cream, cottage cheese, and Parmigiano-Reggiano cheese in a bowl.

3. Layer salmon fillets in the Air fryer basket. Fry for 20 minutes or until cheese turns golden brown.

4. To assemble, place a salmon fillet and sprinkle paprika. Garnish with lemon wedges and squeeze lemon juice on top. Serve.

Salmon with Asparagus

Preparation time: 5 minutes
Cooking time: 10 minutes
Servings: 3
Ingredients:
- 1 lb. salmon, sliced into fillets
- 1 tbsp. olive oil
- Salt and pepper, as needed
- 2 cloves of garlic, minced
- Zest and juice of 1/2 lemon
- 1 tbsp. butter, salted

Directions:

1. Spoon in the butter and olive oil into a large pan and heat it over medium-high heat.

2. Once it becomes hot, place the salmon and season it with salt and pepper.

3. Cook for 4 minutes per side and then cook the other side.

4. Stir in the garlic and lemon zest to it.

5. Cook for further 2 minutes or until slightly browned.

6. Off the heat and squeeze the lemon juice over it.

7. Serve it hot.

Shrimp in Garlic Butter

Preparation time: 5 minutes
Cooking time: 20 minutes
Servings: 4
Ingredients:

- 1 lb. shrimp, peeled and deveined
- 1/4 tsp. red pepper flakes
- 6 tbsp. butter, divided
- 1/2 c. chicken stock
- Salt and pepper, as needed
- 2 tbsp. parsley, minced
- 5 cloves of garlic, minced
- 2 tbsp. lemon juice

Directions:
1. Heat a large, bottomed skillet over medium-high heat.
2. Spoon in 2 tbsps. Of the butter and melt it. Add the shrimp.
3. Season it with salt and pepper. Sear for 4 minutes or until shrimp gets cooked.
4. Transfer the shrimp to a plate and stir in the garlic.
5. Sauté for 30 seconds or until aromatic.
6. Pour the chicken stock and whisk it well. Allow it to simmer for 5–10 minutes or until it has reduced to half.
7. Spoon the remaining butter, red pepper, and lemon juice into the sauce. Mix.
8. Continue cooking for another 2 minutes.
9. Take off the pan from the heat and add the cooked shrimp to it.
10. Garnish with parsley and transfer to the serving bowl.
11. Enjoy.

Cauliflower Mac and Cheese

Preparation time: 5 minutes
Cooking time: 25 minutes
Servings: 4
Ingredients:

- 1 cauliflower head, torn into florets
- Salt and black pepper, as needed
- 1/4 c. almond milk, unsweetened
- 1/4 c. heavy cream
- 3 tbsp. butter, preferably grass-fed
- 1 c. cheddar cheese, shredded

Directions:
1. Preheat the oven to 450 °F.
2. Melt the butter in a small microwave-safe bowl and heat it for 30 seconds.
3. Pour the melted butter over the cauliflower florets along with salt and pepper. Toss them well.
4. Place the cauliflower florets in a parchment paper-covered large baking sheet.
5. Bake them for 15 minutes or until the cauliflower is crisp-tender.
6. Once baked, mix the heavy cream, cheddar cheese, almond milk, and the remaining butter in a large microwave-safe bowl and heat it on high heat for 2 minutes or until the cheese mixture is smooth. Repeat the procedure until the cheese has melted.
7. Finally, stir in the cauliflower to the sauce mixture and coat well.

Easy Egg Salad

Preparation time: 5 minutes
Cooking time: 15–20 minutes
Servings: 4
Ingredients:

- 6 eggs, preferably free-range
- 1/4 tsp. salt
- 2 tbsp. mayonnaise
- 1 tsp. lemon juice
- 1 tsp. Dijon mustard
- Pepper, to taste
- Lettuce leaves, to serve

Directions:
1. Keep the eggs in a saucepan of water and pour cold water until it covers the egg by another 1 in.
2. Bring to a boil and then remove the eggs from heat.
3. Peel the eggs under cold running water.
4. Transfer the cooked eggs into a food processor and pulse them until chopped.
5. Stir in the mayonnaise, lemon juice, salt, Dijon mustard, pepper and mix them well.
6. Taste for seasoning and add more if required.
7. Serve in the lettuce leaves.

Baked Chicken Legs

Preparation time: 10 minutes
Cooking time: 40 minutes
Servings: 6
Ingredients:

- 6 chicken legs
- 1/4 tsp. black pepper
- 1/4 c. butter
- 1/2 tsp. sea salt
- 1/2 tsp. smoked paprika
- 1/2 tsp. garlic powder

Directions:
1. Preheat the oven to 425 °F.
2. Pat the chicken legs with a paper towel to absorb any excess moisture.
3. Marinate the chicken pieces by first applying the butter over them and then with the seasoning. Set it aside for a few minutes.
4. Bake them for 25 minutes. Turnover and bake for further 10 minutes or until the internal temperature reaches 165 °F.
5. Serve them hot.

Creamed Spinach

Preparation time: 5 minutes
Cooking time: 10 minutes
Servings: 4
Ingredients:

- 3 tbsp. butter
- 1/4 tsp. black pepper
- 4 cloves of garlic, minced
- 1/4 tsp. sea salt
- 10 oz. baby spinach, chopped
- 1 tsp. Italian seasoning
- 1/2 c. heavy cream
- 3 oz. cream cheese

Directions:
1. Melt butter in a large sauté pan over medium heat.
2. Once the butter has melted, spoon in the garlic and sauté for 30 seconds or until aromatic.
3. Spoon in the spinach and cook for 3–4 minutes or until wilted.
4. Add all the remaining Ingredients: to it and continuously stir until the cream cheese melts and the mixture gets thickened. Serve hot.

Stuffed Mushrooms

Preparation time: 10 minutes
Cooking time: 20 minutes
Servings: 4
Ingredients:

- 4 portobello mushrooms, large
- 1/2 c. mozzarella cheese, shredded
- 1/2 c. marinara, low sugar
- Olive oil spray

Directions:
1. Preheat the oven to 375 °F.
2. Take out the dark gills from the mushrooms with the help of a spoon.
3. Keep the mushroom stem upside down and spoon it with 2 tbsps. Of marinara sauce and mozzarella cheese.
4. Bake for 18 minutes or until the cheese is bubbly.

Cobb Salad

Preparation time: 5 minutes
Cooking time: 5 minutes
Servings: 1
Ingredients:

- 4 cherry tomatoes, chopped
- 1/4 c. bacon, cooked and crumbled
- 1/2 of 1 avocado, chopped
- 2 oz. chicken breast, shredded
- 1 egg, hardboiled
- 2 c. mixed green salad
- 1 oz. feta cheese, crumbled

Directions:
1. Toss all the Ingredients: for the cobb salad in a large mixing bowl and toss well.
2. Serve and enjoy it.

Muffins Sandwich

Preparation time: 2 minutes
Cooking time: 10 minutes
Servings: 1
Ingredients:

- Nonstick spray oil
- 1 slice of white cheddar cheese
- 1 slice of Canadian bacon
- 1 English muffin, divided
- 15 ml. hot water
- 1 large egg
- Salt and pepper to taste

Directions:
1. Spray the inside of an 85 g. mold with oil spray and place it in the air fryer.

2. Preheat the air fryer, set it to 160 °C.
3. Add the cheese and Canadian bacon to the preheated air fryer.
4. Pour the hot water and the egg into the hot pan and season with salt and pepper.
5. Select Bread, set to 10 minutes.
6. Take out the English muffins after 7 minutes, leaving the egg for the full time.
7. Build your sandwich by placing the cooked egg on top of the English muffing and serve

Bacon BBQ

Preparation time: 2 minutes
Cooking time: 8 minutes
Servings: 2
Ingredients:

- 13 g. dark brown sugar
- 5 g. chili powder
- 1 g. ground cumin
- 1 g. cayenne pepper
- 4 slices of bacon, cut in half

Directions:
1. Mix seasonings until well combined.
2. Dip the bacon in the dressing until it is completely covered. Leave aside.
3. Preheat the air fryer, set it to 160 °C.
4. Place the bacon in the preheated air fryer
5. Select Bacon and press Start/Pause.

Stuffed French toast

Preparation time: 4 minutes
Cooking time: 10 minutes
Servings: 1
Ingredients:

- 1 slice of brioche bread, 64 mm. thick, preferably rancid
- 113 g. cream cheese
- 2 eggs
- 15 ml of milk
- 30 ml whipping cream
- 38 g of sugar
- 3 g. cinnamon
- 2 ml vanilla extract
- Nonstick spray oil
- Pistachios chopped to cover
- Maple syrup, to serve

Directions:
1. Preheat the air fryer, set it to 175 °C.
2. Cut a slit in the middle of the bread.
3. Fill the inside of the slit with cream cheese. Leave aside.
4. Mix the eggs, milk, whipping cream, sugar, cinnamon, and vanilla extract.
5. Moisten the stuffed bread in the egg mixture for 10 seconds on each side.
6. Sprinkle each side of the bread with oil spray.
7. Place the French toast in the preheated air fryer and cook for 10 minutes at 175 °C
8. Stir the French toast carefully with a spatula when you finish cooking.

9. Serve topped with chopped pistachios and maple syrup.

Chapter 14

Snacks and Appetizers

Crispy Parmesan Cauliflower

Preparation Time: 12 minutes
Cooking Time: 14 to 17 minutes
Servings: 20 cauliflower bites
Ingredients:

- 4 cups of cauliflower florets
- 1 cup of whole-wheat breadcrumbs
- 1 teaspoon of coarse sea salt or kosher salt
- 1/4 cup of grated Parmesan cheese
- 1/4 cup of butter
- 1/4 cup of mild hot sauce
- Olive oil spray

Directions:

1. Place a parchment liner in the Air Fryer basket.
2. Cut the cauliflower florets in half and set aside.
3. In a small bowl, mix the breadcrumbs, salt, and Parmesan; set aside.
4. In a small microwave-safe bowl, combine the butter and hot sauce. Heat in the microwave until the butter is melted, about 15 seconds. Whisk.
5. Holding the stems of the cauliflower florets, dip them in the butter mixture to coat. Shake off any excess mixture.
6. Dredge the dipped florets with the bread crumb mixture, then put them in the Air Fryer basket. There's no need for a single layer; just toss them all in there.
7. Spray the cauliflower lightly with olive oil and air fry at 350 °F (177 °C) for 14 to 17 minutes, shaking the basket a few times throughout the cooking process. The florets are done when they are lightly browned and crispy. Serve warm.

Cream Cheese Stuffed Jalapeños

Preparation Time: 12 minutes
Cooking Time: 6-8 minutes
Servings: 10 poppers
Ingredients:

- 8 ounces (227 g) of cream cheese, at room temperature
- 1 cup of whole-wheat breadcrumbs, divided
- 2 tablespoons of fresh parsley, minced
- 1 teaspoon of chili powder
- 10 jalapeño peppers, halved and seeded

Directions:

1. In a small bowl, combine the cream cheese, 1/2 cup of breadcrumbs, the parsley, and the chili powder. Whisk to combine.
2. Stuff the cheese mixture into the jalapeños.
3. Sprinkle the tops of the stuffed jalapeños with the remaining 1/2 cup of breadcrumbs.
4. Place in the Air Fryer basket and air fry at 360 °F (182 °C) for 6 to 8 minutes, until the peppers are softened, and the cheese is melted. Serve warm.

Honeydew & Ginger Smoothies

Preparation Time: 10 minutes
Cooking Time: 3 Minutes
Servings: 3
Ingredients:

- 1 1/2 cup honeydew melon, cubed
- 1/2 cup banana
- 1/2 cup nonfat vanilla yogurt
- 1/4 tsp fresh ginger, grated

What you'll need from store cupboard:

- 1/2 cup ice cubes

Directions:

1. Place all Ingredients: in a blender and pulse until smooth. Pour into glasses and serve immediately.

Pea Soup

Preparation time: 10 minutes
Cooking Time: 20 minutes
Servings: 2
Ingredients:

- 1 1/2 spring onions
- 250 g potatoes - 375 g peas (frozen)
- 1/2 vegetable broth
- 1 tbsp. rapeseed oil
- 1 tbsp. sour cream

Directions:

1. Clean the spring onions and cut into rings.
2. Peel the potatoes and cut into cubes.
3. Fill 1 cup with peas and arrange.
4. Heat a saucepan with the rapeseed oil and fry the onions until golden.
5. Put the potatoes and peas in the pot and sauté. Stir well every now and then.
6. Deglaze with the broth and cook everything for about 20 minutes over a low flame.
7. Puree the soup. Add sour cream. Stir. Season with salt and pepper. Bring everything to the boil briefly and then serve.

Potato Curry Soup

Preparation time: 10 minutes
Cooking Time: 20 minutes
Servings: 2
Ingredients:

- 400 g potatoes
- 2 onions
- 1 teaspoon butter
- 400 ml vegetable broth
- 3 tbsp. heavy cream
- Coriander

Directions:

1. Wash, peel and cut the potatoes into small cubes. Peel the onion and cut it into small cubes.
2. Heat the butter in a saucepan. Add onion and sauté until translucent. Add the potatoes, season with curry, and sweat.
3. Prepare the vegetable stock and use it to deglaze the potatoes. Stir and cook for about 15 minutes.
4. Take out some potato pieces and set them aside. Puree the soup. Add the cream. Season with salt and pepper. Add the potato pieces again. The soup can now be served on a plate.

Asparagus Salad

Preparation time: 15 minutes
Cooking Time: 10 minutes
Servings: 2
Ingredients:

- 2 potatoes (50 g)
- 200 g frisée salad
- 200 g carrots
- 250 g carrots
- 250 g asparagus
- 2 tbsp. vinegar
- 2 tablespoons oil
- 1 teaspoon pink berries

Directions:

1. Peel the potatoes, cook them in salted boiling water and drain them. Then place in a bowl and mash with a fork.
2. Wash the frisée salad, spin dry.
3. Cook the asparagus in salted water for about 8 minutes, remove, and drain and set aside.
4. Peel the carrots, cut into small pieces, and cook in the asparagus water for about 2 minutes.
5. Add asparagus and carrots to the potatoes, let cool down a bit and add the salad.
6. Mix vinegar with salt, pepper, sugar, and asparagus water. Add oil. Put everything in the bowl and mix well.
7. Sprinkle the lettuce with the pink berries.

Zucchini Salmon Salad

Preparation time: 15 minutes
Cooking Time: 0 minutes
Servings: 2
Ingredients:

- 400 g zucchini
- 100 g smoked salmon
- 2 tbsp. olive oil
- 2 tbsp. lemon juice

Directions:

1. Wash and peel the zucchini and cut thin strips. If you have one, use a spiral cutter to do this. Lightly fry the zucchini strips with a little olive oil, allow to cool and pat dry with kitchen paper. Then put the strips in a salad bowl.
2. Cut the smoked salmon into slices (or you can use cut salmon or have it cut at a specialist store).
3. Wash, drain and finely chop the basil. Add the basil and salmon to the zucchini. Add lemon juice, salt, and pepper. Stir the salad well. Season a little if necessary.

Cheesy Onion Dip

Preparation Time: 10 minutes
Cooking Time: 5 Minutes
Servings: 8
Ingredients:

- 8 oz. low fat cream cheese, soft
- 1 cup onions, grated
- 1 cup low fat Swiss cheese, grated
- What you'll need from store cupboard:
- 1 cup lite mayonnaise

Directions:

1. Heat oven to broil.
2. Combine all Ingredients: in a small casserole dish. Microwave on high, stirring every 30 seconds, until cheese is melted and Ingredients: are combined.
3. Place under the broiler for 1-2 minutes until the top is nicely browned. Serve warm with vegetables for dipping.

Almond Coconut Biscotti

Preparation Time: 10 minutes
Cooking Time: 50 Minutes
Servings: 16
Ingredients:

- 1 egg, room temperature
- 1 egg white, room temperature
- 1/2 cup margarine, melted

What you'll need from store cupboard:

- 2 1/2 cup flour
- 1 1/3 cup unsweetened coconut, grated
- 3/4 cup almonds, sliced
- 2/3 cup Splenda
- 2 tsp. baking powder
- 1 tsp. vanilla
- 1/2 tsp. salt

Directions:

1. Heat oven to 350 °F. Line a baking sheet with parchment paper.
2. In a large bowl, combine dry Ingredients.
3. In a separate mixing bowl, beat other Ingredients: together. Add to dry Ingredients: and mix until thoroughly combined.

4. Divide dough in half. Shape each half into a loaf measuring 8x2 3/4-inches. Place loaves on pan 3 inches apart.
5. Bake 25-30 minutes or until set and golden brown. Cool on wire rack 10 minutes.
6. With a serrated knife, cut loaf diagonally into 1/2-inch slices. Place the cookies, cut side down, back on the pan and bake another 20 minutes, or until firm and nicely browned. Store in airtight container

Margarita Chicken Dip

Preparation Time: 10 minutes
Cooking Time: 1 Hour
Servings: 12
Ingredients:
- 2 1/2 cup Monterrey jack cheese, grated
- 1 1/2 cup chicken, cooked and shredded
- 1 1/2 blocks cream cheese, soft, cut into cubes
- 1/4 cup fresh lime juice
- 2 tbsp. fresh orange juice
- 2 tbsp. Pico de Gallo
- 1 tbsp. lime zest

What you'll need from store cupboard:
- 1/4 cup tequila
- 2 cloves garlic, diced fine
- 1 tsp cumin
- 1 tsp salt

Directions:
1. Place the cream cheese on bottom of crock pot. Top with chicken, then grated cheese. Add remaining Ingredients, except the Pico de Gallo.
2. Cover and cook on low 60 minutes. Stir the dip occasionally to combine Ingredients.
3. When dip is done transfer to serving bowl. Top with Pico de Gallo and serve with tortilla chips.

Parmesan Truffle Chips

Preparation Time: 10 minutes
Cooking Time: 20 Minutes
Servings: 4
Ingredients:
- 4 egg whites
- 1/2 tsp fresh parsley, diced fine
- What you'll need from store cupboard:
- 3 tbsp. reduced fat parmesan cheese, divided
- 2 tsp water
- 1/2 tsp salt
- Truffle oil to taste
- Nonstick cooking spray

Directions:
1. Heat oven to 400 °F. Spray two muffin pans with cooking spray.
2. In a small bowl, whisk together egg whites, water, and salt until combined.
3. Spoon just enough egg white mixture into each muffin cup to barely cover the bottom. Sprinkle a small pinch of parmesan on each egg white.
4. Bake 10-15 minutes or until the edges are dark brown, be careful not to burn them.

5. Let cool in the pans 3-4 minutes then transfer to a small bowl and drizzle lightly with truffle oil. Add parsley and 1/2 tablespoon parmesan and toss to coat. Serve.

Filled Mushrooms

Preparation time: 30 minutes
Cooking Time: 20 minutes
Servings: 2
Ingredients:
- 6 mushrooms
- 1 small onion
- 1 clove of garlic
- 1 piece of ginger
- 1 small zucchini
- 2 tomatoes
- 1 tbsp. rapeseed oil
- Coriander

Directions:
1. Clean the mushrooms. Peel the garlic, onion, ginger and cut everything into small pieces.
2. Peel the zucchini. Remove the case and cut them into small pieces.
3. Wash the tomatoes. Remove the stem and pulp. Cut the tomato into small pieces.
4. Heat the pan with canola oil. Add the mushroom stalks, zucchini, onion, ginger, and garlic and braise everything. Add the tomato pieces. Add salt and pepper.
5. Grease a baking dish. Put in the mushroom heads. Add the fried vegetables. Sprinkle cheese on top. Cook everything in the oven for 20 minutes.

Mango and Avocado Salad

Preparation time: 10 min
Cooking Time: 0 minutes
Servings: 2
Ingredients:
- 1/2 mango
- 1 avocado
- 2 tbsp. lemon juice
- 175 g tomatoes
- 125 g rocket
- 2 tbsp. orange juice
- 1 tbsp. mustard
- 2 tbsp. olive oil

Directions:
1. Peel the mango. Cut the pulp into small cubes.
2. Cut the avocado open. Remove the core, cut the meat into pieces and sprinkle with 1 tablespoon of lemon.
3. Wash the tomatoes and cut them in half.
4. Wash the rocket, shake dry and cut into small pieces.
5. Mix all Ingredients: in a bowl.
6. Mix lemon and orange juice with mustard in a small bowl or cup. Add pepper and stir in the olive oil.
7. Serve the salad on plates. Add the dressing.

Salad with Strips of Ham

Preparation time: 15 min

Cooking Time: 0 minutes
Servings: 2
Ingredients:

- 150 g cooked ham
- 1 yellow and 1 red pepper each
- 40 g peas (frozen)
- 1/4 bunch of spring onions
- 1 clove of garlic
- 3 pickles
- 1/2 tbsp. mustard
- 3 tbsp. mayonnaise

Directions:
1. Wash the peppers, cut into small strips and place in a bowl.
2. Cut the ham and the pickles into small cubes and add to the pepper.
3. Finely chop the spring onions and garlic and place in the bowl. Add the peas.
4. Add mayonnaise, some cucumber water, and the mustard. Stir everything well. Season with salt, pepper, and season to taste.

Pointed Cabbage Pot

Preparation time: 10 minutes
Cooking Time: 1 hour 5 minutes
Servings: 2
Ingredients:

- 300 g potatoes
- 240 g carrots
- 400 g pointed cabbage
- 1cl. onion
- 500 ml vegetable broth
- 20 g sour cream
- 2 bunches of chives

Directions:
1. Peel the potatoes and cut into small cubes.
2. Peel the carrots. Wash the cabbage and shake dry. Cut both into small pieces.
3. Peel the onion and cut into small cubes.
4. Skip the bacon. In the interim fry EBELN. Add potatoes and carrots and fry briefly. Deglaze with the vegetable stock. Put a lid on the pot and cook everything for a quarter of an hour. After about 5 minutes, add the cabbage. Mix well.
5. Pour the cream into the stew and stir in
6. Season with salt and pepper.
7. Cut the chives into small pieces.
8. Serve on a deep plate. Sprinkle the chives.

Rustic Pear Pie with Nuts

Preparation Time: 10 minutes
Cooking Time: 45 Minutes
Servings: 4
Ingredients:

- Cake
- 100g all-purpose flour
- 1g of salt
- 12g granulated sugar
- 84g unsalted butter, cold, cut into 13 mm pieces

- 30 ml of water, frozen
- 1 egg, beaten
- 12g turbinated sugar
- Nonstick Spray Oil
- 20g of honey
- 5 ml of water
- Roasted nuts, chopped, to decorate

Filling:

- 1 large pear, peeled, finely sliced
- 5g cornstarch
- 24g brown sugar
- 1g ground cinnamon
- A pinch salt

Directions:
1. Mix 90 g of flour, salt, and granulated sugar in a large bowl until well combined. Join the butter in the mixture using a pastry mixer or food processor until thick crumbs form. Add cold water and mix until it joins. Shape the dough into a bowl, cover with plastic and let cool in the refrigerator for 1 hour.
2. Mix the stuffing Ingredients: in a bowl until they are combined. Roll a roll through your cooled dough until it is 216 mm in diameter. Add 10 g of flour on top of the dough leaving 38 mm without flour. Place the pear slices in decorative circles superimposed on the floured part of the crust. Remove any remaining pear juice on the slices. Fold the edge over the filling.
3. Cover the edges with beaten eggs and sprinkle the sugar over the whole cake. Set aside
4. Preheat the air fryer set the temperature to 320 °F (160 °C). Spray the preheated air fryer with oil spray and place the cake inside. Set the time to 45 minutes at 320 °F (160 °C). Mix the honey and water and pass the mixture through the cake when you finish cooking.
5. Garnish with toasted chopped nuts.

Apricot Soufflé

Preparation Time: 10 minutes
Cooking Time: 30 Minutes
Servings: 6
Ingredients:

- 4 egg whites
- 3 egg yolks, beaten
- 3 tbsp. margarine

What you'll need from store cupboard

- 3/4 cup sugar free apricot fruit spread
- 1/3 cup dried apricots, diced fine
- 1/4 cup warm water
- 2 tbsp. flour
- 1/4 tsp. cream of tartar
- 1/8 tsp. salt

Directions:
1. Heat oven to 325 °F.
2. In a medium saucepan, over medium heat, melt margarine. Stir in flour and cook, stirring, until bubbly.
3. Stir together the fruit spread and water in a small bowl and add it to the saucepan with the apricots. Cook, stirring, 3 minutes or until mixture thickens.

4. Remove from heat and whisk in egg yolks. Let cool to room temperature, stirring occasionally.
5. In a medium bowl, beat egg whites, salt, and cream of tartar on high speed until stiff peaks form. Gently fold into cooled apricot mixture.
6. Spoon into a 1 1/2-quart soufflé dish. Bake 30 minutes, or until puffed and golden brown. Serve immediately.

Cinnamon Apple Popcorn

Preparation Time: 10 minutes
Cooking Time: 50 Minutes
Servings: 11
Ingredients:
- 4 tbsp. margarine, melted
- What you'll need from store cupboard
- 10 cup plain popcorn
- 2 cup dried apple rings, unsweetened and chopped
- 1/2 cup walnuts, chopped
- 2 tbsp. Splenda brown sugar
- 1 tsp. cinnamon
- 1/2 tsp. vanilla

Directions:
1. Heat oven to 250 °F.
2. Place chopped apples in a 9x13-inch baking dish and bake 20 minutes. Remove from oven and stir in popcorn and nuts.
3. In a small bowl, whisk together margarine, vanilla, Splenda, and cinnamon. Drizzle evenly over popcorn and toss to coat.
4. Bake 30 minutes, stirring quickly every 10 minutes. If apples start to turn a dark brown, remove immediately.
5. Pout onto waxed paper to cool at least 30 minutes. Store in an airtight container. Servings is 1 cup.

Blackberry Crostata

Preparation Time: 10 minutes
Cooking Time: 20 Minutes
Servings: 6
Ingredients:
- 1 9-inch pie crust, unbaked
- 2 cup fresh blackberries
- Juice and zest of 1 lemon
- 2 tbsp. butter, soft
- What you'll need from store cupboard:
- 3 tbsp. Splenda, divided
- 2 tbsp. cornstarch

Directions:
1. Heat oven to 425 °F. Line a large baking sheet with parchment paper and unroll pie crust in pan.
2. In a medium bowl, combine blackberries, 2 tablespoons Splenda, lemon juice and zest, and cornstarch. Spoon onto crust leaving a 2-inch edge. Fold and crimp the edges.
3. Dot the berries with 1 tablespoon butter. Brush the crust edge with remaining butter and sprinkle crust and fruit with remaining Splenda.

4. Bake 20-22 minutes or until golden brown. Cool before cutting and serving.

Ratatouille Salat

Preparation time: 10 minutes
Cooking Time: 15 minutes
Servings: 2
Ingredients:
- 2 peppers
- 1 small zucchini
- 1 onion & 1 clove of garlic
- 1 sprig of rosemary
- 10 g parmesan cheese
- 150 g tomatoes
- 2 sprigs of basil
- 2 tbsp. balsamic vinegar

Directions:
1. Heat the oven to 200 °F. Wash the vegetables and herbs. Cut the peppers into strips.
2. Peel the zucchini and cut into large pieces.
3. Peel and slice the onion. Put everything in an oven-safe bowl. Cut the tomatoes into small pieces.
4. Peel and squeeze the garlic with a press and add it to the vegetables.
5. Chop the rosemary and add to the vegetables. Add salt, pepper, and olive oil. Mix everything well and then cooks in the oven for about a quarter of an hour.
6. Chop the basil.
7. Put the oven vegetables in a bowl. Add tomatoes, basil, and vinegar. Mix everything well. Slice the parmesan on top of the salad.

Brussels sprouts

Preparation Time: 5 minutes
Cooking Time: 3 minutes
Servings: 5
Ingredients:
- 1 tsp. extra-virgin olive oil
- 1 lb. halved Brussels sprouts
- 3 tbsps. Apple cider vinegar
- 3 tbsps. Gluten-free tamari soy sauce
- 3 tbsps. Chopped sun-dried tomatoes

Directions:
1. Select the "Sauté" function on your Instant Pot, add oil and allow the pot to get hot.
2. Cancel the "Sauté" function and add the Brussels sprouts.
3. Stir well and allow the sprouts to cook in the residual heat for 2-3 minutes.
4. Add the tamari soy sauce and vinegar, and then stir.
5. Cover the Instant Pot, sealing the pressure valve by pointing it to "Sealing."
6. Select the "Manual, High Pressure" setting and cook for 3 minutes.
7. Once the cook cycle is done, do a quick pressure release, and then stir in the chopped sun-dried tomatoes.
8. Serve immediately.

Garlic and Herb Carrots

Preparation Time: 2 minutes
Cooking Time: 18 minutes
Servings: 3
Ingredients:

- 2 tbsps. Butter
- 1 lb. baby carrots
- 1 cup water
- 1 tsp. fresh thyme or oregano
- 1 tsp. minced garlic
- Black pepper
- Coarse sea salt

Directions:

1. Add water to the inner pot of the Instant Pot, and then put in a steamer basket.
2. Layer the carrots into the steamer basket.
3. Close and seal the lid, with the pressure vent in the "Sealing" position.
4. Select the "Steam" setting and cook for 2 minutes on high pressure.
5. Quick release the pressure and then carefully remove the steamer basket with the steamed carrots, discarding the water.
6. Add butter to the inner pot of the Instant Pot and allow it to melt on the "Sauté" function.
7. Add garlic and sauté for 30 seconds, and then add the carrots. Mix well.
8. Stir in the fresh herbs and cook for 2-3 minutes.
9. Season with salt and black pepper, and the transfer to a serving bowl.
10. Serve warm and enjoy!

Mushroom and Leek Soup

Preparation time: 5 min
Cooking Time: 15 minutes
Servings: 2
Ingredients:

- 1 leek
- 1/2 tbsp. rapeseed oil
- 400 ml vegetable stock
- 150g mushrooms
- 100 ml of milk
- Parsley

Directions:

1. Wash the leek sticks and cut them into small strips. Put the leek in a saucepan and sauté lightly over a low heat while adding the rapeseed oil.
2. Add vegetable stock
3. Clean the mushrooms and cut them into small pieces. Put a few mushrooms aside. Add the rest of the leek and let everything stand for about 12 minutes.
4. Now add the milk. Puree everything now.
5. Clean and chop the parsley. Add the parsley to the soup. Add salt, pepper, and the remaining mushrooms.

Pistachio Cookies

Preparation Time: 5 minutes
Cooking Time: 15 Minutes
Servings: 13-14
Ingredients:

- 2 eggs, beaten
- What you'll need from store cupboard:
- 1 2/3 cup almond flour
- 1 cup + 2 tbsp. Splenda
- 3/4 cup + 50 pistachio nuts, shelled

Directions:

1. Add the 3/4 cup nuts and 2 tablespoons Splenda to a food processor. Process until nuts are ground fine.
2. Pour the ground nuts into a large bowl and stir in flour and remaining Splenda until combined.
3. Add eggs and mix Ingredients: thoroughly. Wrap dough with plastic wrap and chill at least 8 hours or overnight.
4. Heat oven 325 °F. Line a cookie sheet with parchment paper.
5. Roll teaspoonful of dough into small balls, about 1-inch in diameter. Place on prepared sheet.
6. Smash cookie slightly then presses a pistachio in the center. Bake 12-15 minutes or until the edges are lightly browned.
7. Transfer to wire rack to cool completely. Store in airtight container. Servings is 3 cookies.

Crispy Apple Chips

Preparation Time: 3 minutes
Cooking Time: 2 Hours
Servings: 4
Ingredients:

- 2 medium apples, sliced
- 1 teaspoon ground cinnamon

Directions:

1. Preheat the oven to 200 °F (93 °C). Line a baking sheet with parchment paper.
2. Arrange the apple slices on the prepared baking sheet, then sprinkle with cinnamon.
3. Bake in the preheated oven for 2 hours or until crispy. Flip the apple chips halfway through the cooking time.
4. Allow to cool for 10 minutes and serve warm.

Chili Lime Tortilla Chips

Preparation Time: 5 minutes
Cooking Time: 15 Minutes
Servings: 10
Ingredients:

- 12 6-inch corn tortillas cut into 8 triangles
- 3 tbsp. lime juice

What you'll need from store cupboard:

- 1 tsp. cumin
- 1 tsp. chili powder

Directions:

1. Heat oven to 350 °F.
2. Place tortilla triangles in a single layer on a large baking sheet.
3. In a small bowl stir together spices.
4. Sprinkle half the lime juice over tortillas, followed by 1/2 the spice mixture. Bake 7 minutes.
5. Remove from oven and turn tortillas over. Sprinkle with remaining lime juice and spices. Bake another 8 minutes or until crisp, but not brown. Serve with your favorite salsa, Servings is 10 chips.

Palm Trees Holder

Preparation Time: 3 minutes
Cooking Time: 15 Minutes
Servings: 2
Ingredients:

- 1 Sheet of puff pastry
- Sugar

Directions:

1. Stretch the puff pastry sheet.
2. Pour the sugar over and fold the puff pastry sheet in half.
3. Put a thin layer of sugar on top and fold the puff pastry in half again.
4. Roll the puff pastry sheet from both ends towards the center (creating the shape of the palm tree).
5. Cut into sheets 5-8 mm thick.
6. Preheat the air fryer to 356 °F (180 °C) and put the palm trees in the basket.
7. Set the timer about 10 minutes at 356 °F (180 °C).

Homemade Cheetos

Preparation Time: 10 minutes
Cooking Time: 30 Minutes
Servings: 6
Ingredients:

- 3 egg whites
- 1/2 cup cheddar cheese, grated and frozen
- What you'll need from store cupboard:
- 1/4 cup reduced fat parmesan cheese
- 1/8 tsp cream of tartar

Directions:

1. Heat oven to 300 °F. Line a baking sheet with parchment paper.
2. Put the frozen cheese in a food processor/blender and pulse, until it's in tiny little pieces.
3. In a large mixing bowl, beat egg whites and cream of tartar until very stiff peaks from. Gently fold in chopped cheese. Spoon mixture into a piping bag with 1/2-inch hole. Gently pipe "cheeto" shapes onto prepared pan. Sprinkle with parmesan cheese.
4. Bake 20-30 minutes. Turn off oven and leave the puffs inside another 30 minutes. Let cool completely and store in an airtight container.

Butternut Cream Soup

Preparation time: 10 min
Cooking Time: 36 minutes
Servings: 2

Ingredients:

- 1 small Butternut squash
- 2 tbsp. rapeseed oil
- 1 onion
- 1 piece of ginger (the size of a thumb)
- 1-2 cloves - 600 ml vegetable stock
- 100 g sour cream

Directions:

1. Peel the pumpkin. Remove the cores. Cut 3 cm pieces from the pumpkin flesh.
2. Peel the onion. Cut them up small. Stew them with the rapeseed oil.
3. Put the pumpkin pieces in the pot and sauté them for about 6 minutes.
4. Peel the ginger. Cut it up.
5. Prepare the vegetable stock. Add these, the ginger, and the cloves to the pumpkin. Bring the mixture to the boil briefly and then cook over a low heat for half an hour.
6. Take out the cloves. Add the cream and puree the mixture. Serve with pumpkin seed oil.

Pea Soup with Avocado

Preparation time: 5 min
Cooking Time: 10 minutes
Servings: 2
Ingredients:

- 1 onion
- 1 clove of garlic
- 225 g peas (frozen or fresh)
- 1 bunch of mint
- 1 lime
- 1/2 avocado

Directions:

1. Peel the onion and garlic and cut into small pieces.
2. Briefly sear the onion and garlic in oil.
3. Add about 140 g of the peas, sauté and deglaze with vegetable stock. Pepper and cook gently about 6-10 minutes.
4. Wash the mint, shake dry and finely chop.
5. The washing lime. Grate the peel and squeeze out the juice.
6. Peel and cut the avocado. Add the lime juice, salt, and a little mint.
7. Blanch the remaining peas.
8. Add the lime zest and the mint to the soup and puree.
9. Place the avocado on two preheated plates. Add the soup and the blanched peas. Scatter mint on top.

Chapter 15

Dessert

Sticky Ginger Cake

Preparation Time: 10 minutes
Cooking Time: 30 minutes
Servings: 16
Ingredients:

- 2 eggs, beaten
- 1 cup buttermilk
- 2 tbsps. butter
- 2 tsps. fresh ginger, grated
- 1 cup flour
- ¼ cup + 1 tbsp. honey
- ¼ cup + 1 tbsp. molasses
- ¼ cup Splenda brown sugar
- 1 tbsp. water
- 1 tsp. baking soda
- 1 tsp. ginger
- 1 tsp. cinnamon
- ½ tsp. allspice
- ¼ tsp. salt
- Nonstick cooking spray
- Swerve confections sugar, for dusting

Directions:
1. Heat the oven to 400°F. Spray an 8-inch square pan with cooking spray.
2. In a saucepan over medium heat, stir together ¼ of honey, ¼ cup of molasses, Splenda, butter, and grated ginger until the butter is melted. Remove from heat and let cool for 5 minutes.
3. In a medium bowl, stir together the dry Ingredients:.
4. In a small bowl, beat the eggs and buttermilk together. Whisk into the molasses mixture until combined. Add to the dry Ingredients: and mix well. Pour into the prepared pan.
5. Bake for 25 minutes. Use a skewer to poke holes every inch across the top of the cake.
6. In a small bowl, mix the remaining honey, molasses, and water together. Brush over the hot cake. Cool completely and dust lightly with the confectioner's sugar before serving.

Tiramisu

Preparation Time: 20 minutes
Cooking Time: 4 Hours
Servings: 15
Ingredients:

- 2 (8 oz.) pkgs. reduced-fat cream cheese, soft
- 2 cups fat-free sour cream
- 2 (3 oz.) pkgs. ladyfingers, split
- ¼ cup skim milk
- 2 tbsps. Coffee liqueur
- 2/3 cup Splenda
- ½ cup strong brewed coffee
- 2 tbsps. Unsweetened cocoa powder, sifted
- ½ tsp. vanilla

Directions:
1. In a large bowl, combine the sour cream, cream cheese, sugar substitute, milk, and vanilla. Beat on high until smooth.
2. In a small bowl, stir together the coffee and liqueur.
3. Place one package of ladyfingers, cut side up, in a 2-quart baking dish. Brush with ½ of the coffee mixture. Spread ½ of the cheese mixture over the top. Repeat the layers.
4. Sprinkle the cocoa powder over top. Cover and chill for 4 hours or overnight. Cut into squares to serve.

Toffee Apple Mini Pies

Preparation Time: 20 minutes
Cooking Time: 25 minutes
Servings: 12
Ingredients:

- 2 9-inch pie crusts, soft
- 2 cups Gala apples, diced fine
- 1 egg, beaten
- 1 tbsp. butter, cut in 12 cubes
- 1½ tsp. fresh lemon juice
- 2 tbsps. Toffee bits
- 1 tbsp. Splenda
- ½ tsp. cinnamon
- Nonstick cooking spray

Directions:
1. Heat the oven to 375°F. Spray a cookie sheet with cooking spray.
2. In a medium bowl, stir together the apples, toffee, Splenda, lemon juice, and cinnamon.
3. Roll pie crusts, one at a time, out on a lightly floured surface. Use a 3-inch round cookie cutter to cut 12 circles from each crust. Place 12 on the prepared pan.
4. Brush the dough with half the egg. Spoon 1 tbsp. of the apple mixture on each round, leaving ½-inch edge. Top with a pat of butter. Place the second dough round on top and seal edges closed with a fork. Brush with the remaining egg.
5. Bake for 25 minutes, or until golden brown. Serve warm.

Pineapple Frozen Yogurt

Preparation Time: 5 minutes
Cooking Time: 1 Hour
Servings: 4
Ingredients:

- ½ cup half-and-half
- ½ cup plain reduced-fat yogurt
- ¼ cup egg substitute
- ¾ cup crushed pineapple, in juice
- ¼ cup Splenda

Directions:

1. In a medium bowl, beat the egg substitute until thick and cream-colored. Add the remaining Ingredients: and mix to thoroughly combine. Cover and chill completely, if using an ice cream maker. Once chilled, add to the ice cream maker and freeze according to the manufacturer's directions.

2. Or, you can pour the mixture into a shallow glass baking dish and freeze. Stir and scrape the mixture, every 10 minutes, with a rubber spatula until it reaches the desired consistency, about 1 hour.

Pomegranate Panna Cotta

Preparation Time: 15 minutes
Cooking Time: 4 Hours
Servings: 8
Ingredients:

- 2 ½ cup heavy cream
- ½ cup skim milk
- 8 tbsps. Pomegranate seeds
- ½ vanilla pod
- 1 envelope plain gelatin
- ¼ cup Splenda

Directions:

1. Pour the milk in a small, wide bowl and sprinkle gelatin over. Let it sit for 10 minutes.

2. Scrape the seeds from the vanilla pod into a heavy-bottomed saucepan, add the pod, too. Add the cream and Splenda and bring to a simmer over medium heat, stirring frequently. Remove from heat and stir in the gelatin mixture.

3. Pour the mixture through a fine-mesh sieve, then divide evenly between 8 4 oz. ramekins or jars. Cover and refrigerate it for at least 4 hours or overnight.

4. Serve it topped with 1 tbsp. of pomegranate seeds.

Coconutty Pudding Clouds

Preparation Time: 5 minutes
Cooking Time: 10 minutes
Servings: 4
Ingredients:

- 2 cups of heavy whipping cream
- ½ cup of reduced-fat cream cheese, soft
- ½ cup hazelnuts, ground
- 4 tbsps. Unsweetened coconut flakes, toasted
- 2 tbsps. Stevia, divided
- ½ tsp. of vanilla
- ½ tsp. of hazelnut extract
- ½ tsp. of cacao powder, unsweetened

Directions:

1. In a medium bowl, beat the cream, vanilla, and 1 tbsp. of stevia until soft peaks form.

2. In another mixing bowl, beat the cream cheese, cocoa, remaining stevia, and hazelnut extract until smooth.

3. In 4 glasses, place the ground nuts on the bottom, add a layer of the cream cheese mixture, then the whip cream, and top with toasted coconut.

Cream Cheese Pound Cake

Preparation Time: 10 minutes
Cooking Time: 35 minutes
Servings: 14
Ingredients:

- 4 eggs
- 3 ½ oz. cream cheese, soft
- 4 tbsps. Butter, soft
- 1¼ cup almond flour
- ¾ cup Splenda
- 1 tsp. baking powder
- 1 tsp. of vanilla
- ¼ tsp. of salt
- Butter flavored cooking spray

Directions:

1. Heat the oven to 350°F. Spray an 8-inch loaf pan with cooking spray.

2. In a medium bowl, combine flour, baking powder, and salt.

3. In a large bowl, beat the butter and Splenda until light and fluffy. And the cream cheese and vanilla and beat well.

4. Add the eggs, one at a time, beating after each one. Stir in the dry the ingredients: until thoroughly combined.

5. Pour it into the prepared pan and bake for 30-40 minutes or until the cake passes the toothpick test. Let it cool for 10 minutes in the pan, then invert it onto a serving plate. Slice and serve.

Dark Chocolate Coffee Cupcakes

Preparation Time: 10 minutes
Cooking Time: 20 minutes
Servings: 24
Ingredients:

- 2 eggs
- ½ cup fat-free sour cream
- ½ cup butter, melted
- 2 cups Splenda
- 1 cup almond flour, sifted
- 1 cup strong coffee, room temperature
- 4 oz. unsweetened chocolate
- ½ cup coconut flour
- 3 tsps. Of baking powder
- ½ tsp salt

Directions:

1. Heat the oven to 350°F. Line two 12-cups muffin tins with cupcake liners.

2. Melt the chocolate in a double broiler, set it aside, and allow it to cool.

3. Combine the Splenda, almond, and coconut flours, baking powder, and sea salt.

4. In a small bowl, combine the coffee, sour cream, and butter.

5. Add the butter mixture to the dry Ingredients: and beat on low speed until thoroughly combined.

6. Add the eggs, one at a time, beating after each one. Fold in the chocolate until well blended.

7. Spoon into the prepared pans and bake for 20-25 minutes or until they pass the toothpick test. Cool completely before serving.

German Chocolate Cake Bars

Preparation Time: 10 minutes
Cooking Time: 5 minutes
Servings: 20
Ingredients:

- 2 cups unsweetened coconut flakes
- 1 cup coconut milk, divided
- ¾ cup chopped pecans
- ¾ cup dark baking chocolate, chopped
- 1½ cup almond flour cracker crumbs
- ½ cup + 2 tbsps. Powdered sugar substitute
- ½ cup coconut oil
- Nonstick cooking spray

Directions:
1. Spray an 8x8-inch baking dish with cooking spray.
2. In a large bowl, combine the coconut, ½ cup sugar substitute, cracker crumbs, and pecan, stir to combine.
3. In a medium saucepan, combine ½ cup of milk and oil, cook over medium heat until the oil is melted, and the mixture is heated through. Pour over the coconut mixture and stir to combine. Press evenly in the prepared baking dish and chill for 1-2 hours.
4. In a clean saucepan, place the chocolate and remaining milk over med-low heat. Cook, stirring constantly until chocolate is melted and the mixture is smooth. Add the 2 tbsps. Of sugar substitute and stir to combine.
5. Pour the chocolate over the coconut layer and chill for 1 hour, or until set. Cut into squares to serve.

Gingerbread Soufflés

Preparation Time: 15 minutes
Cooking Time: 25 minutes
Servings: 10
Ingredients:

- 6 eggs, separated
- 1 cup skim milk
- 1 cup fat-free whipped topping
- 2 tbsps. Butter, soft
- ½ cup Splenda
- 1/3 cup molasses
- ¼ cup flour
- 2 tsps. Pumpkin pie spice
- 2 tsps. Vanilla
- 1 tsp. ginger
- ¼ tsp. salt
- 1/8 tsp. cream of tartar
- Butter flavored cooking spray

Directions:
1. Heat the oven to 350°F. Spray 10 ramekins with cooking spray and sprinkle with Splenda to coat, shaking out excess. Place on a large baking sheet.
2. In a large saucepan, over medium heat, whisk together the milk, Splenda, flour, and salt until smooth. Bring to a boil, whisking constantly. Pour it into a large bowl and whisk in molasses, butter, vanilla, and spices. Let it cool for 15 minutes.

3. Once the spiced mixture has cooled, whisk in the egg yolks.
4. In a large bowl, beat the egg whites and cream of tartar on high speed until stiff peaks form. Fold into the spiced mixture, a third at a time, until blended completely. Spoon into ramekins.
5. Bake for 25 minutes until puffed and set. Serve immediately with a dollop of whipped topping.

Lemon Meringue Ice Cream

Preparation Time: 5 minutes
Cooking Time: 15 minutes
Servings: 8
Ingredients:

- 4 eggs, separated
- 2 cans coconut milk, refrigerated for 24 hours
- 6 tbsps. Fresh lemon juice
- Zest of 2 lemons
- 2 ½ tbsp. Liquid stevia
- 1 tbsp. Vanilla
- 1 tsp. Cream of tartar

Directions:
1. Heat the oven to 325°F.
2. In a medium bowl, beat the egg whites and cream of tartar on high speed until soft peaks form. Add 1½ tbsps. Of stevia and continue beating on high until stiff peaks form.
3. Spread the meringue in a small baking dish and bake for 15 minutes, or until the top is golden brown. Remove it from the oven and let it cool completely.
4. Turn the canned coconut milk upside down and open. Drain off the water, save it for another use later. Scoop the cream into a large bowl. Add the egg yolks, juice, zest, remaining tablespoon of stevia, and vanilla and beat until the Ingredients: are thoroughly combined.
5. Pour into an ice cream maker and freeze according to directions.
6. In a liter-sized plastic container, spread a layer of ice cream to cover the bottom. Top with a layer of meringue. Repeat layers. Place an airtight cover on the container and freeze at least 3 hours before serving.

Mini Bread Puddings

Preparation Time: 5 minutes
Cooking Time: 35 minutes
Servings: 12
Ingredients:

- 6 slices cinnamon bread, cut into cubes
- 1¼ cup skim milk
- ½ cup egg substitute
- 1 tbsp. margarine, melted
- 1/3 cup Splenda
- 1 tsp. vanilla
- 1/8 tsp. salt
- 1/8 tsp. nutmeg

Directions:
1. Heat the oven to 350°F. Line 12 medium-size muffin cups with paper baking cups.
2. In a large bowl, stir together milk, egg substitute, Splenda, vanilla, salt, and nutmeg until combined. Add bread cubes and stir until moistened. Let it rest for 15 minutes.

3. Spoon evenly into the prepared baking cups. Drizzle margarine evenly over the tops. Bake for 30-35 minutes or until puffed and golden brown. Remove it from the oven and let cool completely.

Pumpkin Ice Cream with Candied Pecans

Preparation Time: 20 minutes
Cooking Time: 1 Hour
Servings: 8
Ingredients:

- 2 eggs
- 2 cups almond milk, unsweetened, divided
- 1 cup half-n-half
- 1 cup pumpkin
- 1 envelope unflavored gelatin
- ¾ cup Splenda
- ¾ cup Candied Pecans
- 2 tsps. Pumpkin pie spice

Directions:
1. Pour 1 cup of almond milk into a small bowl. Sprinkle the gelatin on top. Allow sitting for about 5 minutes.
2. In a medium saucepan, whisk together the Splenda and the eggs. Whisk in the pumpkin and pumpkin spice. Whisk in the gelatin.
3. Bring the mixture just to a simmer, then remove it from the heat. Allow it to cool for about 5 minutes at room temperature, then refrigerate, uncovered for 45 minutes, stirring occasionally. Do not cool too long or the mixture will set.
4. Remove the pumpkin mixture from the refrigerator and whisk in half-n-half and the remaining cup of almond milk. Pour into an ice-cream freezer and freeze according to the manufacturer's instructions.
5. When the ice cream reaches the desired consistency, transfer to a freezer-safe container with a lid. Stir in the candied pecans, cover, and place the container in the freezer to further harden the ice cream.

Raspberry Almond Clafoutis

Preparation Time: 10 minutes
Cooking Time: 1 Hour
Servings: 8
Ingredients:

- 1-pint raspberries, rinse, and pat dry
- 3 eggs
- ¾ cup almond milk, unsweetened
- ¼ cup half-n-half
- 4 tbsps. Margarine
- ½ cup almond flour
- 1/3 cup Splenda
- ¼ cup almonds, sliced
- 1 tbsp. coconut flour
- 1½ tsp. vanilla
- ½ tsp. baking powder
- ¼ tsp. allspice
- ¼ tsp. almond extract
- Nonstick cooking spray

Directions:

1. Heat the oven to 350°F. Spray a 9-inch pie dish with cooking spray and place it on a baking sheet.
2. Place the berries, in a single layer, in the pie dish.
3. In a medium bowl, stir together the flours, baking powder, and allspice.
4. Add the margarine to a small saucepan and melt over low heat. Once melted, remove from heat and whisk in Splenda until smooth.
5. Pour the margarine into a large bowl and whisk in eggs, one at a time. Add the extracts and dry Ingredients. Stir in the almond milk and half-n-half, the batter will be thin.
6. Pour over the raspberries and top with almonds. Bake for 50-60 minutes, or until the center is set and the top is lightly browned. Cool to room temperature before serving.

Blackberry Soufflés

Preparation Time: 15 minutes
Cooking Time: 30 minutes
Servings: 4
Ingredients:

- 12 oz. blackberries
- 4 egg whites
- 1/3 cup Splenda
- 1 tbsp. water
- 1 tbsp. Swerve powdered sugar
- Nonstick cooking spray

Directions:
1. Heat the oven to 375°F. Spray 4 1-cup ramekins with cooking spray.
2. In a small saucepan, over med-high heat, combine the blackberries and 1 tbsp. of water, bring to a boil. Reduce the heat and simmer until the berries are soft. Add the Splenda and stir it over medium heat until it dissolves, without boiling.
3. Bring back to boiling, reduce the heat and simmer for 5 minutes. Remove from the heat and cool for 5 minutes.
4. Place a fine-meshed sieve over a small bowl and push the berry mixture through it using the back of a spoon. Discard the seeds. Cover and chill for 15 minutes.
5. In a large bowl, beat the egg whites until soft peaks form. Gently fold in the berry mixture. Spoon evenly into the prepared ramekins and place them on a baking sheet.
6. Bake for 12 minutes, or until puffed and light brown. Dust with the powdered Swerve and serve immediately.

Blueberry Lemon "Cup" Cakes

Preparation Time: 5 minutes
Cooking Time: 10 minutes
Servings: 5
Ingredients:

- 4 eggs
- ½ cup coconut milk
- ½ cup blueberries
- 2 tbsps. Lemon zest
- ½ cup + 1 tsp. coconut flour
- ¼ cup Splenda
- ¼ cup coconut oil, melted
- 1 tsp. baking soda
- ½ tsp. lemon extract
- ¼ tsp. stevia extract

- Pinch salt

Directions:
1. In a small bowl, toss berries in the 1 tsp. of flour.
2. In a large bowl, stir together remaining flour, Splenda, baking soda, salt, and zest.
3. Add the remaining Ingredients: and mix well. Fold in the blueberries.
4. Divide batter evenly into 5 coffee cups. Microwave, one at a time, for 90 seconds, or until they pass the toothpick test.

Blueberry No-Bake Cheesecake

Preparation Time: 5 minutes
Cooking Time: 3 Hours
Servings: 8
Ingredients:

- 16 oz. fat-free cream cheese, softened
- 1 cup sugar-free frozen whipped topping, thawed
- ¾ cup blueberries
- 1 tbsp. margarine, melted
- 8 zwieback toasts
- 1 cup boiling water
- 1/3 cup Splenda
- 1 envelope unflavored gelatin
- 1 tsp. vanilla

Directions:
1. Place the toasts and margarine in a food processor. Pulse until the mixture resembles coarse crumbs. Press on the bottom of a 9-inch springform pan.
2. Place the gelatin in a medium bowl and add the boiling water. Stir until gelatin dissolved completely.
3. In a large bowl, beat cream cheese, Splenda, and vanilla on medium speed until well blended. Beat in whipped topping. Add gelatin, in a steady stream, while beating at low speed. Increase the speed to medium and beat for 4 minutes or until smooth and creamy.
   1. Add the chicken, tomato and broth and bring to a boil. Now, reduce the heat to low and simmer for about 10 minutes.
   2. Add the zucchini and chickpeas and simmer, covered for about 15 minutes. Stir in the lemon juice and serve hot.

Broiled Stone Fruit

Preparation Time: 5 minutes
Cooking Time: 5 minutes
Servings: 2
Ingredients:

- 1 peach
- 1 nectarine
- 2 tbsps. Sugar-free whipped topping
- 1 tbsp. Splenda brown sugar
- Nonstick cooking spray

Directions:
1. Heat the oven to broil. Line a shallow baking dish with foil and spray with cooking spray.
2. Cut the peach and nectarine in half and remove pits. Place cut side down in prepared dish. Broil for 3 minutes.
3. Turn the fruit over and sprinkle with the Splenda brown sugar. Broil for another 2-3 minutes.

4. Transfer 1 of each fruit to a dessert bowl and top with 1 tbsp. of whipped topping.

Café Mocha Torte

Preparation Time: 15 minutes
Cooking Time: 25 minutes
Servings: 14
Ingredients:

- 8 eggs
- 1 cup margarine, cut into cubes
- 1 pound Bittersweet chocolate, chopped
- ¼ cup brewed coffee, room temperature
- Nonstick cooking spray

Directions:
1. Heat the oven to 325°F. Spray an 8-inch springform pan with cooking spray. Line the bottom of the sides with parchment paper and spray again. Wrap the outside with a double layer of foil and place in a 9x13-inch baking dish. Put a small saucepan of water on to boil.
2. In a large bowl, beat the eggs on med speed until doubled in volume, about 5 minutes.
3. Place the chocolate, margarine, and coffee into a microwave-safe bowl and microwave on high, until chocolate is melted and mixture is smooth, stir every 30 seconds.
4. Fold 1/3 of the eggs into the chocolate mixture until almost combined. Add the remaining eggs, 1/3 at a time, and fold until combined.
5. Pour into the prepared pan. Pour the boiling water around the springform pan until it reaches halfway up the sides. Bake 22-25 minutes, or until the cake has risen slightly and edges are just beginning to set.
6. Remove it from the water bath and let it cool completely. Cover with plastic wrap and chill for 6 hours or overnight. About 30 minutes before serving, run a knife around the edges and remove the side of the pan. Slice and serve.

Cappuccino Mousse

Preparation Time: 5 minutes
Cooking Time: 1 Hour
Servings: 8
Ingredients:

- 2 cups low fat cream cheese, soft
- 1 cup half-n-half
- ½ cup almond milk, unsweetened
- ¼ cup strong brewed coffee, cooled completely
- 1-2 tsps. Coffee extract
- 1 tsp. Vanilla liquid sweetener
- Whole coffee beans for garnish

Directions:
1. In a large bowl, beat the cream cheese and coffee on high speed until smooth. Add milk, 1 tsp. coffee extract and liquid sweetener. Beat until smooth and thoroughly combined.
2. Pour in half-n-half and continue beating until the mixture resembles the texture of mousse.
3. Spoon into dessert glasses or ramekins, cover, and chill at least 1 hour before serving. Garnish with a coffee bean and serve.

Caramel Pecan Pie

Preparation Time: 5 minutes

Cooking Time: 35 minutes
Servings: 8
Ingredients:

- 1 cup pecans, chopped
- ¾ cup almond milk, unsweetened
- 1/3 cup margarine, melted
- 1 tbsp. margarine, cold
- 2 cups almond flour
- ½ cup + 2 tbsps. Splenda for baking
- 1 tsp. vanilla
- 1 tsp. Arrowroot powder
- ¾ tsp. sea salt
- ½ tsp. vanilla
- ½ tsp. maple syrup, sugar-free
- Nonstick cooking spray

Directions:
1. Heat the oven to 350°F. Spray a 9-inch pie pan with cooking spray.
2. In a medium bowl, combine the flour, melted margarine, 2 tbsps. Of Splenda, and vanilla. Mix to thoroughly combine the ingredients. Press on the bottom and sides of a prepared pie pan. Bake for 12-15 minutes, or until the edges start to brown. Set it aside.
3. In a small saucepan, combine the milk, remaining Splenda, arrowroot, salt, ½ tsp. vanilla and syrup. Cook over medium heat until it starts to boil, stirring constantly. Keep cooking until it turns a gold color and starts to thicken for about 2-3 minutes. Remove it from the heat and let it cool. Stir in ½ the pecans.
4. Pour the filling in the crust and top with the remaining pecans. Bake for about 15 minutes, or until the filling starts to bubble. Cool completely before serving.

Carrot Cupcakes

Preparation Time: 10 minutes
Cooking Time: 35 minutes
Servings: 12
Ingredients:

- 2 cups carrots, grated
- 1 cup low fat cream cheese, soft
- 2 eggs
- 1-2 tsps. Skim milk
- ½ cup coconut oil, melted
- ¼ cup coconut flour
- ¼ cup Splenda
- ¼ cup honey
- 2 tsps. Vanilla, divided
- 1 tsp. baking powder
- 1 tsp. cinnamon
- Nonstick cooking spray

Directions:
1. Heat the oven to 350°F. Lightly spray a muffin pan with cooking spray, or use paper liners.
2. In a large bowl, stir together the flour, baking powder, and cinnamon.
3. Add the carrots, eggs, oil, Splenda, and vanilla to a food processor. Process until the Ingredients are combined but carrots still have some large chunks remaining. Add the dry Ingredients and stir them to combine.

4. Pour evenly into the prepared pan, filling cups 2/3 full. Bake for 30-35 minutes, or until cupcakes pass the toothpick test. Remove it from the oven and let it cool.
5. In a medium bowl, beat the cream cheese, honey, and vanilla on high speed until smooth. Add milk, 1 tsp. at a time, beating after each addition, until frosting is creamy enough to spread easily.
6. Once cupcakes have cooled, spread each one with about 2 tbsps. Of frosting. Chill until ready to serve.

Raspberry and Dark Chocolate Mini Soufflés

Preparation Time: 10 minutes
Cooking Time: 10 minutes
Servings: 6
Ingredients:

- 1 cup fresh raspberries
- 4 egg whites
- ½ oz. dark chocolate, chopped
- 6 tsps. Splenda
- 1 tsp. margarine, soft

Directions:
1. Heat the oven to 400°F. Use the margarine to grease 6 small ramekins.
2. Puree the raspberries in a blender or food processor and press through a fine sieve to get all of the seeds out. Add 1 tbsp. of the Splenda and set it aside.
3. Beat the egg whites until thickened and start adding the remaining Splenda, gradually, until the mixture forms stiff glossy peaks.
4. Gently fold 1/3 of the egg whites into the raspberry puree. Once mixed, fold the raspberry puree mixture into the remaining egg whites and fold gently until there are no streaks of pink left.
5. Spoon the raspberry mixture into the ramekins filling them half full. Divide the chocolate between the ramekins and then fill to the top with soufflé mixture. Place the ramekins on a baking sheet. Bake it for 9 minutes until golden brown and puffed up. Serve immediately.

Tropical Fruit Tart

Preparation Time: 10 minutes
Cooking Time: 10 minutes
Servings: 8
Ingredients:

- 1 mango, peeled, pitted, and sliced thin
- 1 banana, sliced thin
- 2 egg whites
- 15 ¼ oz. can pineapple chunks in juice, undrained
- 3 ½ oz. can sweetened flaked coconut
- 1 cup cornflakes, crushed
- 3 tsps. Splenda
- 2 tsps. Cornstarch
- 1 tsp. coconut extract
- Nonstick cooking spray

Directions:
1. Heat the oven to 425°F. Spray a 9-inch springform pan with cooking spray.

2. In a medium bowl, combine the cornflakes, coconut, and egg whites. Toss until blended. Press firmly over the bottom and ½-inch up the sides of the prepared pan. Bake for 8 minutes or until the edges start to brown. Cool completely.

3. Drain the juice from the pineapple into a small saucepan. Add the cornstarch and stir until smooth. Bring to a boil over high heat and let it cook for 1 minute, stirring constantly. Remove from heat and cool completely. Once cooled, stir in the Splenda and coconut extract.

4. In a medium bowl, combine the pineapple, mango, and banana. Spoon over the crust and drizzle with the pineapple juice mixture. Cover and chill at least for 2 hours before serving.

Sweet Potato Crème Brule

Preparation Time: 10 minutes
Cooking Time: 1 hour 5 minutes
Servings: 12
Ingredients:

- 7 egg yolks
- 1¼ cup sweet potato, baked, peeled, and mashed
- 2 cups half-n-half
- 1 tbsp. fresh lemon juice
- ¾ cup Splenda
- ¼ cup + 1/3 cup Splenda brown sugar
- 3 tsps. Vanilla
- Butter flavored cooking spray

Directions:
1. Heat the oven to 325°F. Spray a 10-inch metal quiche dish with cooking spray.
2. In a medium bowl, combine sweet potato, ¼ cup the Splenda brown sugar, and lemon juice. Spoon into the prepared dish.
3. In a 2-quart saucepan, whisk together the half-n-half, Splenda, egg yolks, and vanilla. Cook over med-low heat for 15 minutes, stirring frequently until hot, do not boil. Pour over the sweet potato mixture.
4. Place the dish in a shallow pan and put it in the oven. Pour enough boiling water to cover halfway up the sides of the dish. Bake for 1 hour or until a knife inserted in the center comes out clean. Cool it on a rack. Cover and refrigerate for 8 hours or overnight.
5. Heat the oven to broil. Sprinkle the custard with 1/3 cup of Splenda brown sugar and place the dish on a baking sheet. Broil for 3-5 minutes or until the sugar has melted. Cool for 5 minutes before serving.

Raspberry Lemon Cheesecake Squares

Preparation Time: 5 minutes
Cooking Time: 40 minutes
Servings: 12
Ingredients:

- 2 cups raspberries
- 1 cup fat-free sour cream
- ¾ cup fat-free cream cheese, softened
- ½ cup egg substitute
- 2 tbsps. Lemon juice
- 2 tsps. Lemon zest, divided
- ½ cup + 3 tbsps. Splenda
- 1 tsp. vanilla

- Nonstick cooking spray

Directions:
1. Heat the oven to 350°F. Spray 8-inch square baking pan with cooking spray.
2. In a large bowl, beat the cream cheese, ½ cup of Splenda, and vanilla on high speed until smooth. Add juice, 1 tsp. zest and egg substitute. Beat until thoroughly combined. Pour into the prepared pan.
3. Bake for 40 minutes or until firm to the touch. Remove it from the oven and cool completely.
4. In a small bowl, stir together the sour cream and 1 tbsp. of Splenda until smooth. Spoon evenly over cooled cheesecake. Cover and refrigerate overnight.
5. 30 minutes before serving, toss the berries and the remaining 2 tbsps. Of Splenda in a small bowl. Let it sit. Just before serving, stir in the remaining zest and spoon the berry mixture over the top of the cheesecake.

Mini Key Lime Tarts

Preparation Time: 5 minutes
Cooking Time: 10 minutes
Servings: 8
Ingredients:

- 4 sheets phyllo dough*
- ¾ cup skim milk
- ¾ cup fat-free whipped topping, thawed
- ½ cup egg substitute
- ½ cup fat-free sour cream
- 6 tbsps. Fresh lime juice
- 2 tbsps. Cornstarch
- ½ cup Splenda
- Butter-flavored cooking spray

Directions:
1. In a medium saucepan, combine milk, juice, and cornstarch. Cook, stirring, over medium heat for 2-3 minutes or until thickened. Remove from heat.
2. Add the egg substitute and whisk for 30 seconds to allow it to cook. Stir in the sour cream and Splenda. Cover and chill until completely cool.
3. Heat the oven to 350°F. Spray 8 muffin cups with cooking spray.
4. Lay 1 sheet of the phyllo on a cutting board and lightly spray it with cooking spray. Repeat this with the remaining sheets so they are stacked on top of each other.
5. Cut the phyllo into 8 squares and gently place them in the prepared muffin cups, pressing firmly on the bottom and sides. Bake for 8-10 minutes or until golden brown. Remove them from the pan and let them cool.
6. To serve: spoon the lime mixture evenly into the 8 cups and top with whipped topping. Garnish with the fresh lime slices if desired.

Moist Butter Cake

Preparation Time: 15 minutes
Cooking Time: 30 minutes
Servings: 14
Ingredients:

- 3 eggs
- ¾ cup margarine, divided
- ½ cup fat-free sour cream

- 2 cups almond flour, packed
- 1 cup Splenda, divided
- 1 tsp. baking powder
- 2 tbsps. Water
- 1 tbsp. + 1 tsp. vanilla, divided
- Butter flavored cooking spray

Directions:

1. Heat the oven to 350°F. Spray a Bundt cake pan generously with cooking spray.

2. In a large bowl, whisk together the flour, sour cream, ½ cup of margarine, 3 eggs, 2/3 cup of Splenda, baking powder, and 1 tsp. vanilla until thoroughly combined.

3. Pour into the prepared pan and bake for 30-35 minutes, or until it passes the toothpick test. Remove it from the oven.

4. Melt ¼ cup of margarine in a small saucepan over medium heat. Whisk in 1/3 cup of Splenda, tablespoon vanilla, and water. Continue to stir until the Splenda is completely dissolved.

5. Use a skewer to poke several small holes on top of the cake. Pour the syrup mixture evenly over the cake making sure all the holes are filled. Swirl the pan for a couple of minutes until the syrup is absorbed into the cake.

No-Bake Chocolate Swirl Cheesecake

Preparation Time: 25 minutes
Cooking Time: 10 minutes
Servings: 16
Ingredients:

- 3 (8 oz.) pkgs. fat-free cream cheese, soft
- 1 cup fat-free sour cream
- ¾ cup skim milk
- ½ cup semisweet chocolate, melted and cooled
- 2 tbsps. Margarine, melted
- ½ cup graham crackers, finely crushed
- 1/3 cup Splenda
- 1 envelope unflavored gelatin
- 2 tsps. Vanilla

Directions:

1. In a medium bowl, stir together the cracker crumbs and margarine until moistened. Press evenly on the bottom of an 8-inch springform pan. Cover and chill.

2. In a small saucepot, add the milk and sprinkle gelatin over the top, let stand for 5 minutes. Heat to low heat, and stir until the gelatin dissolves. Remove from the heat and let it cool for 15 minutes.

3. In a large bowl, beat the cream cheese until smooth. Beat in the sour cream, sugar, and vanilla. Slowly beat in the gelatin mixture.

4. Divide the cheese mixture in half. Slowly stir the melted chocolate into one half.

5. Spread half the chocolate mixture evenly over chilled crust. Spoon half the white cheese mix over the chocolate in small dollops. Using a butter knife, swirl the two layers together. Repeat with the remaining fillings. Cover and chill for 6 hours, or until set.

No-Bake Lemon Tart

Preparation Time: 10 minutes
Cooking Time: 2 Hours

Servings: 8
Ingredients:

- ½ cup margarine, soft
- 1/3 cup + 3 tbsps. Fresh lemon juice, divided
- 1/3 cup almond milk, unsweetened
- 4 ½ tbsp. margarine, melted
- 3-4 tbsps. Lemon zest, grated fine
- 1 cup almond flour
- ¾ cup coconut, grated fine
- ¼ cup + 3 tbsps. Splenda
- 2 ½ tsp. vanilla, divided
- 2 tsps. Lemon extract
- ¼ tsp. salt

Directions:

1. Spray a 9-inch tart pan with cooking spray.

2. In a medium bowl, combine the flour, coconut, 3 tbsps. Of lemon juice, 2 tbsps. Of Splenda, melted margarine, 1½ tsps. Of vanilla, and a pinch of salt until thoroughly combined. Dump into the prepared pan and press evenly on the bottom and halfway up the sides. Cover and chill until ready to use.

3. In a medium bowl, beat the soft margarine until fluffy. Add the remaining Ingredients: and beat until the mixture is smooth. Taste and add more lemon juice or Splenda if desired.

4. Pour the filling into the crust. Cover and chill until the filling are set, about 2 hours.

Chocolate Cherry Cake Roll

Preparation Time: 10 minutes
Cooking Time: 15 minutes
Servings: 10
Ingredients:

- 10 maraschino cherries, drained and patted dry
- 4 eggs, room temperature
- 1 cup sugar-free Cool Whip, thawed
- 2/3 cup maraschino cherries, chop, drain and pat dry
- ½ cup cream cheese, soft
- 1/3 cup flour
- ½ cup Splenda for baking
- ¼ cup unsweetened cocoa powder
- 1 tbsp. sugar-free hot fudge ice cream topping
- ¼ tsp. baking soda
- ¼ tsp. salt
- Unsweetened cocoa powder
- Nonstick cooking spray

Directions:

1. Heat the oven to 375°F. Spray a large sheet baking pan with cooking spray. Line bottom with parchment paper, spray and flour the paper.

2. In a small bowl, stir together the flour, ¼ cup cocoa, baking soda, and salt.

3. In a large bowl, beat the eggs at high speed for 5 minutes.

4. Gradually add the sweetener and continue beating until the mixture is thick and lemon-colored.

5. Fold in the dry Ingredients. Spread evenly into the prepared pan. Bake for 15 minutes or top springs back when touched lightly.
6. Place a clean towel on a cutting board and sprinkle with cocoa powder. Turn the cake onto a towel and carefully remove parchment paper.
7. Starting at a short end, roll up the towel. Cool on a wire rack for 1 hour.
8. Prepare the filling: In a small bowl, beat the cream cheese until smooth. Add ½ cup whipped topping, beat on low until combined. Fold in another ½ cup whipped topping. Fold in the chopped cherries.
9. Unroll the cake and remove the towel. Spread the filling to within 1 inch of the edges. Reroll the cake and trim the ends. Cover and chill for at least 2 hours or overnight.
10. To serve, warm up the fudge topping and drizzle it over the cake, garnish with whole cherries, then slice and serve.

Chocolate Orange Bread Pudding

Preparation Time: 10 minutes
Cooking Time: 35 minutes
Servings: 8
Ingredients:

- 4 cups French baguette cubes
- 1½ cups skim milk
- 3 eggs, lightly beaten
- 1-2 tsps. Orange zest, grated
- ¼ cup Splenda
- ¼ cup sugar-free chocolate ice cream topping
- 3 tbsps. Unsweetened cocoa powder
- 1 tsp. vanilla
- ¾ tsp. cinnamon

Directions:
1. Heat the oven to 350°F.
2. In a medium bowl, stir together the Splenda and cocoa. Stir in milk, eggs, zest, vanilla, and cinnamon until well blended.
3. Place bread cubes in an 8-inch square baking dish. Pour the milk mixture evenly over the top.
4. Bake for 35 minutes or until a knife inserted in the center comes out clean. Cool for 5-10 minutes.
5. Spoon into dessert dishes and drizzle lightly with ice cream topping.

Chocolate Torte

Preparation Time: 15 minutes
Cooking Time: 35 minutes
Servings: 12
Ingredients:

- 5 eggs, separated, room temperature
- ¾ cup margarine, sliced
- 1 pkg. semisweet chocolate chips
- ½ cup Splenda
- ¼ tsp. cream of tartar
- Nonstick cooking spray

Directions:
1. Heat the oven to 350°F. Spray a 6-7-inch springform pan with cooking spray.

2. In a microwave-safe bowl, melt chocolate chips and margarine, in 30-second intervals.
3. In a large bowl, beat the egg yolks till thick and lemon-colored. Beat in the chocolate.
4. In a separate large bowl, with clean beaters, beat egg whites and cream of tartar till foamy. Beat in the Splenda, 1 tbsp. at a time, till sugar is dissolved, continue beating till stiff glossy peaks form.
5. Fold ¼ of the egg whites into the chocolate mixture, then fold in the rest. Transfer to the prepared pan. Bake for 30-35 minutes, or until the center is set. Let it cool completely before removing the side of the pan and serving.

Cinnamon Bread Pudding

Preparation Time: 10 minutes
Cooking Time: 45 minutes
Servings: 6
Ingredients:

- 4 cups day-old French or Italian bread, cut into ¾-inch cubes
- 2 cups skim milk
- 2 egg whites
- 1 egg
- 4 tbsps. Margarine, sliced
- 5 tsps. Splenda
- 1½ tsp. cinnamon
- ¼ tsp. salt
- 1/8 tsp. ground cloves

Directions:
1. Heat the oven to 350°F.
2. In a medium saucepan, heat milk and margarine to simmering. Remove it from the heat and stir till the margarine is completely melted. Let it cool for 10 minutes.
3. In a large bowl, beat the egg and egg whites until foamy. Add the Splenda, spices, and salt. Beat until combined, then add in the cooled milk and bread.
4. Transfer mixture to a 1½ quart baking dish. Place on rack of roasting pan and add 1 inch of the hot water to the roaster.
5. Bake until the pudding is set and the knife inserted in the center comes out clean, about 40-45 minutes.

Coconut Cream Pie

Preparation Time: 5 minutes
Cooking Time: 10 minutes
Servings: 8
Ingredients:

- 2 cups raw coconut, grated and divided
- 2 cans coconut milk, full fat, and refrigerated for 24 hours
- ½ cup raw coconut, grated and toasted
- 2 tbsps. Margarine, melted
- 1 cup Splenda
- ½ cup macadamia nuts
- ¼ cup almond flour

Directions:
1. Heat the oven to 350°F.
2. Add the nuts to a food processor and pulse until finely ground. Add the flour, ½ cup Splenda, and 1 cup grated

coconut. Pulse until the Ingredients: are finely ground and resemble cracker crumbs.

3. Add the margarine and pulse until the mixture starts to stick together. Press on the bottom and sides of a 9-inch pie pan. Bake for 10 minutes or until golden brown. Cool.

4. Turn the canned coconut upside down and open. Pour off the water and scoop the cream into a large bowl. Add the remaining ½ cup of Splenda and beat on high until stiff peaks form. Fold in the remaining 1 cup of coconut and pour it into the crust. Cover and chill at least for 2 hours. Sprinkle with toasted coconut, slice, and serve.

Coconut Milk Shakes

Preparation Time: 5 minutes
Cooking Time: 5 minutes
Servings: 2
Ingredients:
- 1½ cup vanilla ice cream
- ½ cup coconut milk, unsweetened
- 2 ½ tbsp. coconut flakes
- 1 tsp. unsweetened cocoa

Directions:
- Heat the oven to 350°F.
- Place the coconut on a baking sheet and bake for 2-3 minutes, stirring often, until the coconut is toasted.
- Place ice cream, milk, 2 tbsps. Of coconut, and cocoa in a blender and process them until smooth.
- Pour it into glasses and garnish it with the remaining toasted coconut. Serve immediately.

Peach Custard Tart

Preparation Time: 5 minutes
Cooking Time: 40 minutes
Servings: 8
Ingredients:
- 12 oz. frozen unsweetened peach slices, thaw, and drain
- 2 eggs, separated
- 1 cup skim milk
- 4 tbsps. Cold margarine, cut into pieces
- 1 cup flour
- 3 tbsps. Splenda
- 2-3 tbsps. Cold water
- 1 tsp. vanilla
- ¼ tsp. + 1/8 tsp. salt, divided
- ¼ tsp. nutmeg

Directions:
1. Heat the oven to 400°F.
2. In a medium bowl, stir together the flour and ¼ tsp. of salt. With a pastry blender, cut in the margarine until the mixture resembles coarse crumbs. Stir in the cold water, a tablespoon at a time, just until moistened. Shape into a disc.
3. On a lightly floured surface, roll out the dough to an 11-inch circle. Place in the bottom of a 9-inch tart pan with a removable bottom. Turn the edge under and pierce the sides and bottom with a fork.
4. In a small bowl, beat 1 egg white with a fork, discard the other or save for another use. Lightly brush crust with egg.

Place the tart pan on a baking sheet and bake for 10 minutes. Cool.

5. In a large bowl, whisk together the egg yolks, Splenda, vanilla, nutmeg, and 1/8 tsp. of salt until combined.
6. Pour the milk into a glass measuring cup and microwave on high for 1 minute. Do not boil. Whisk the milk into the egg mixture until blended.
7. Arrange the peaches on the bottom of the crust and pour the egg mixture over the top. Bake for 25-30 minutes, or until set. Cool to room temperature. Cover and chill at least for 2 hours before serving.

Peach Ice Cream

Preparation Time: 15 minutes
Cooking Time: 4 Hours
Servings: 32
Ingredients:
- 4 peaches, peel, and chop
- 8 oz. fat-free whipped topping
- 2 cups skim milk
- ¼ cup fresh lemon juice
- 2-12 oz. cans fat-free evaporated milk
- 14 oz. can sweeten condensed milk
- 1 oz. pkg. sugar-free instant vanilla pudding mix
- ½ cup Splenda - 1 tsp. vanilla
- ½ tsp. almond extract
- 1/8 tsp. salt

Directions:
1. In a large bowl, beat the milk and pudding mix on low speed for 2 minutes. Beat in the remaining Ingredients, except whipped topping until thoroughly combined. Fold in whipped topping.
2. Freeze in the ice cream maker according to the manufacturer's directions, this may take 2 batches. Transfer it to freezer containers and freeze for 4 hours before serving.

Peanut Butter Pie

Preparation Time: 10 minutes
Cooking Time: 4 Hours
Servings: 8
Ingredients:
- 1½ cup skim milk
- 1½ cup frozen fat-free whipped topping, thawed and divided
- 1 small pkg. sugar-free instant vanilla pudding mix
- 1 (1½ oz.) pkg. sugar-free peanut butter cups, chopped
- 1 (9-inch) reduced-fat graham cracker pie crust
- 1/3 cup reduced-fat peanut butter
- ½ tsp. vanilla

Directions:
1. In a large bowl, whisk together the milk and pudding mix until it thickens. Whisk in the peanut butter, vanilla, and 1 cup of whip cream. Fold in the peanut butter cups.
2. Pour it into the pie crust and spread the remaining whip cream over top. Cover and chill at least 4 hours before serving.

Raspberry Peach Cobbler

Preparation Time: 15 minutes

Cooking Time: 40 minutes
Servings: 8
Ingredients:

- 1¼ pounds peaches, peeled and sliced
- 2 cups fresh raspberries
- ½ cup low-fat buttermilk
- 2 tbsps. Cold margarine, cut into pieces
- 1 tsp. lemon zest
- ¾ cup + 2 tbsps. Flour, divided
- 4 tbsps. + 2 tsps. Splenda, divided
- ½ tsp. baking powder
- ½ tsp. baking soda
- 1/8 tsp. salt
- Nonstick cooking spray

Directions:

1. Heat the oven to 425°F. Spray an 11×7-inch baking dish with cooking spray.
2. In a large bowl, stir together 2 tbsps. Of Splenda and 2 tbsps. Of flour. Add the fruit and zest and toss to coat. Pour into the prepared baking dish. Bake for 15 minutes, or until the fruit is bubbling around the edges.
3. In a medium bowl, combine the remaining flour, 2 tbsps. Of Splenda, baking powder, baking soda, and salt. Cut in the margarine with the pastry cutter until it resembles coarse crumbs. Stir in the buttermilk just until moistened.
4. Remove the fruit from the oven and top with dollops of the buttermilk mixture. Sprinkle the remaining 2 tsps. Of Splenda over the top and bake for 18-20 minutes or the top is lightly browned. Serve warm.

Sangria Jello Cups

Preparation Time: 10 minutes
Cooking Time: 4 Hours
Servings: 6
Ingredients:

- 1 cup raspberries
- 1 cup green grapes, halved
- 1 pkg. lemon gelatin, sugar-free
- 1 pkg. raspberry gelatin, sugar-free
- 11 oz. mandarin oranges, drain
- 1½ cup boiling water
- 1 cup cold water
- 1 cup white wine

Directions:
1. Place both gelatins in a large bowl and add boiling water. Stir to dissolve. Let rest 10 minutes.
2. Stir in cold water and wine, cover, and refrigerate for 45 minutes, or until partially set.
3. Fold in oranges, raspberries, and grapes. Spoon evenly into 6 wine glasses. Cover and refrigerate for 4 hours or until set.

Strawberry Cheesecake

Preparation Time: 15 minutes
Cooking Time: 15 minutes
Servings: 12
Ingredients:

- 3 cups medium-size fresh strawberries, halved
- 2 ½ packages fat-free cream cheese, soft
- 1 cup skim milk
- 1/3 cup margarine, melted
- 2 cups graham cracker crumbs
- ¾ cup + 2 tbsps. Sugar substitute
- ¼ cup low-sugar strawberry spread
- 1 envelope unflavored gelatin
- 1 tbsp. lemon juice
- 2 tsps. Vanilla extract
- Nonstick cooking spray

Directions:
1. Heat the oven to 350°F. Spray a 9-inch springform pan with cooking spray.
2. In a medium bowl, combine the cracker crumbs and margarine, stirring to combine. Press on the bottom and up the sides of a prepared pan. Bake for 8 minutes, let cool.
3. Add the milk to a small saucepan and sprinkle gelatin over top, let it stand for 1 minute. Cook over low heat, stirring constantly until gelatin dissolves, about 2 minutes. Let it cool slightly.
4. In a large bowl, beat the cream cheese until smooth and creamy. Slowly add lemon juice and vanilla, beat well.
5. Slowly beat in the gelatin mixture, beating until smooth. Add ¾ cup of sugar and beat just until blended. Pour it into the crust, cover, and chill for 3 hours.
6. In a medium saucepan, combine the berries, 2 tbsps. Of sugar, and strawberry spread. Cook over med-low heat, stirring constantly until the spread melts and berries are coated. Spoon over cheesecake.
7. To serve, loosen cheesecake from the side of the pan and remove. Cut into wedges.

Chapter 16

Sauces Dips and Dressing

Tangy Mexican Salad Dressing

Preparation time: 15 minutes
Cooking time: 5 minutes
Servings: 8
Ingredients:
- ½ cup cilantro, diced fine
- 3 tbsp. fresh lime juice

What you'll need from store cupboard:
- ½ cup sunflower oil
- 2 tbsp. water
- 1 tbsp. apple cider vinegar
- 2 tsp honey
- 1 tsp garlic salt
- ½ teaspoon Mexican oregano
- Freshly ground black pepper, to taste

Directions:
1. Add all Ingredients: to a food processor or blender. Pulse until well blended and emulsified. Taste and adjust seasonings as desired.
2. Store in an air-tight container in the refrigerator. To serve, bring to room temperature and shake well.

Sriracha Dipping Sauce

Preparation time: 1 minute
Cooking time: 2 minutes
Servings: 6
Ingredients:
- 2 tsp fresh lime juice

What you'll need from store cupboard:
- ½ cup lite mayonnaise
- 2 tbsp. Sriracha sauce
- 1 tbsp. Splenda
- 1 tsp Worcestershire sauce

Directions:
1. In a small bowl, stir all the Ingredients: together until smooth.
2. Use right away, or cover and refrigerate until ready to use. Serving size is 1 ½ tablespoons.

Spaghetti Sauce

Preparation time: 20 minutes
Cooking time: 30 minutes
Servings: 6
Ingredients:
- 1 onion, diced
- 1 carrot, grated

- 1 stalk celery, diced
- 1 zucchini, grated
- What you'll need from store cupboard:
- 1 (28 oz.) Italian-style tomatoes, in puree
- 1 (14 ½ oz.) diced tomatoes, with juice
- ½ cup water
- 2 cloves garlic, diced fine
- ½ tbsp. oregano
- 1 tsp olive oil
- 1 tsp basil
- 1 tsp thyme
- 1 tsp salt
- ¼ tsp red pepper flakes

Directions:
1. Heat oil in a large saucepan over medium heat. Add vegetables and garlic. Cook, stirring frequently, until vegetables get soft, about 5 minutes.
2. Add remaining Ingredients, use the back of a spoon to break up tomatoes. Bring to a simmer and cook, partially covered, over med-low heat 30 minutes, stirring frequently.
3. Store sauce in an air-tight container in the refrigerator up to 3 days, or in the freezer up to 3 months.

Pineapple Mango Hot Sauce

Preparation time: 10 minutes
Cooking time: 20 minutes
Servings: 16
Ingredients:
- 2 cherry peppers, diced
- 1 ghost pepper, diced
- 1 cup pineapple, diced
- ½ cup mango, diced
- 2 tbsp. cilantro, diced

What you'll need from store cupboard:
- 1 cup water
- ½ cup vinegar
- 1 tsp olive oil
- 1 tsp Splenda
- 1 tsp paprika
- Salt, to taste

Directions:
1. Heat oil in a large saucepan over medium heat. Add peppers and fruit and cook 8 minutes to soften.
2. Add remaining Ingredients: and bring to a boil. Reduce heat and simmer 20 minutes. Remove from heat and let cool.

3. Add mixture to a food processor and pulse until smooth. Pour into sterilized bottles, secure lids and refrigerate until ready to use.

Pizza Sauce

Preparation time: 5 minutes
Cooking time: 5 minutes
Servings: 8
Ingredients:
- ½ cup yellow onion, diced

What you'll need from store cupboard:
- 15 oz. tomatoes, crushed, no sugar added
- 1/3 cup + 1 tbsp. olive oil
- 3 cloves garlic, diced
- 2 tsp parsley
- 1 tsp rosemary
- 1 tsp thyme
- 1 tsp smoked paprika
- Salt, to taste

Directions:
1. Heat 1 tablespoon oil in a small skillet over medium heat. Add onion and garlic and cook until onions are translucent.
2. In a medium saucepan, over medium heat, stir all Ingredients: together, along with onions. Bring to a simmer and cook 2-3 minutes, stirring constantly.
3. Remove from heat and let cool completely. Store in a jar with an air tight lid in the refrigerator up to 2 weeks. Or in the freezer up to 6 months.

Queso Verde

Preparation time: 10 minutes
Cooking time: 30 minutes
Servings: 10
Ingredients:
- ½ package cream cheese, soft
- ½ cup white American cheese, cubed
- ½ cup white cheddar cheese, cubed
- ½ cup pepper Jack cheese, cubed
- ¼ cup skim milk

What you'll need from store cupboard
- ½ cup salsa verde
- ½ cup green chilies, diced
- Nonstick cooking spray

Directions:
1. Heat oven to 325. Spray a small baking dish with cooking spray.
2. In a medium mixing bowl, combine all Ingredients. Add to prepared baking dish.
3. Bake 30 minutes, stirring every 8-10 minutes, until cheese is melted and dip is hot and bubbly. Serve warm.

Cinnamon Blueberry Sauce

Preparation time: 5 minutes
Cooking time: 10 minutes
Servings: 16
Ingredients:
- 2 cup blueberries

- 2 tbsp. fresh lemon juice

What you'll need from store cupboard:
- ¼ cup Splenda
- ¼ cup water
- 2 tsp corn starch
- ½ tsp cinnamon

Directions:
1. In a small saucepan, over medium heat, Splenda and cornstarch. Stir in remaining Ingredients: and bring to a boil, stirring frequently.
2. Reduce heat and simmer 5 minutes, until thickened. Let cool completely.
3. Pour into a jar with an airtight lid and refrigerate until ready to use. Serving size is 1 tablespoon.

Citrus Vinaigrette

Preparation time: 5 minutes
Cooking time: 10 minutes
Servings: 6
Ingredients:
- 1 orange, zested and juiced
- 1 lemon, zested and juiced

What you'll need from store cupboard:
- ¼ cup extra virgin olive oil
- 1 tsp Dijon mustard
- 1 tsp honey
- 1 clove garlic, crushed
- Salt & pepper, to taste

Directions:
1. Place the zest and juices, mustard, honey, garlic, salt and pepper in a food processor. Pulse to combine.
2. With the machine running, slowly pour in the olive oil and process until combined.
3. Use right away, or store in a jar with an airtight lid in the refrigerator.

Cranberry Orange Compote

Preparation time: 5 minutes
Cooking time: 10 minutes
Servings: 8
Ingredients:
- 1 lb. fresh cranberries, rinsed and drained
- 1 large orange, halved

What you'll need from store cupboard:
- 1 tsp vanilla
- 1 tsp cinnamon

Directions:
1. Add cranberries to a medium saucepan and place over medium heat. Squeeze both halves of the orange, with pulp, into the berries. Stir in vanilla and cinnamon.
2. Cook, stirring frequently, until berries start to open. Reduce heat and continue cooking for 10 minutes, or until mixture starts to thicken.
3. Let cool 15 minutes, then spoon into a jar with an airtight lid. Refrigerate until ready to use.

Creamy Poppy Seed Dressing

Preparation time: 10 minutes
Cooking time: 5 minutes

Servings: 6
Ingredients:
- 1/3 cup light mayonnaise
- ¼ cup skim milk

What you'll need from store cupboard:
- 3 tbsp. Splenda
- 4 tsp cider vinegar
- 2 tsp poppy seeds

Directions:
1. In a small bowl, whisk all Ingredients: together until thoroughly combined. Store in an airtight jar in the refrigerator.

Dry Rub for Pork

Preparation time: 5 minutes
Cooking time: 5 minutes
Servings: 16
Ingredients:
What you'll need from store cupboard:
- 2 tbsp. ground coffee, extra fine ground
- 2 tbsp. chipotle powder
- 1 tbsp. smoked paprika
- 1 tbsp. Splenda brown sugar
- 1 tbsp. salt
- 1 tsp ginger
- 1 tsp mustard powder
- 1 tsp coriander

Directions:
1. Mix all Ingredients: together.
2. Store in airtight container in cool, dry place for up to 1 month.

Easy Cheesy Dipping Sauce

Preparation time: 2 minutes
Cooking time: 5 minutes
Servings: 2
Ingredients:
- ¾ cup skim milk
- ¾ cup reduced-fat cheddar cheese
- 1 tbsp. margarine

What you'll need from store cupboard:
- 1 tbsp. flour
- Pinch of cayenne
- Salt and pepper

Directions:
1. Melt margarine in a small saucepan over medium heat. Whisk in flour and cook, whisking constantly, until golden brown, about 1 minutes.
2. Slowly add milk and continue whisking until no lumps remain. Cook, whisking constantly, until mixture thickens and starts to bubble, 3-4 minutes.
3. Stir in cheese until smooth. Season with cayenne, salt and pepper to taste.

Raspberry & Basil Jam

Preparation time: 5 minutes
Cooking time: 20 minutes
Servings: 24
Ingredients:

- 2 lbs. fresh raspberries
- 1/3 cup fresh basil, diced fine
- 2 tbsp. lemon juice

What you'll need from store cupboard
- ½ cup Splenda

Directions:
1. Add berries and lemon juice to a large saucepan and place over medium heat. Use a wooden spoon to break up the berries. Bring to a low boil and simmer 5-6 minutes, or until mixture starts to bubble.
2. Stir in Splenda and cook, stirring frequently, until Splenda is dissolved and mixture resembles syrup, about 15 minutes.
3. Remove from heat and stir in the basil. Spoon into glass jars with air tight lids. Let cool completely then add lids and refrigerate. Serving size is 1 tablespoon.

Garlic Dipping Sauce

Preparation time: 5 minutes
Cooking time: 5 minutes
Servings: 4
Ingredients:
- 1 cup Greek yogurt
- 1 tbsp. fresh dill, diced fine

What you'll need from store cupboard:
- 2 cloves garlic, diced fine

Directions:
1. In a small bowl, whisk all Ingredients: together.
2. Serve warm or cover and chill until ready to use.

Herb Vinaigrette

Preparation time: 5 minutes
Cooking time: 0 minute
Mix time: 5 minutes
Servings: 12
Ingredients:
- 2 tbsp. shallot, diced fine
- 1 tbsp. fresh basil, diced
- 1 tbsp. fresh oregano, diced
- 1 tbsp. fresh tarragon, diced

What you'll need from store cupboard:
- ¼ cup extra virgin olive oil
- ¼ cup low sodium chicken broth
- ¼ cup red-wine vinegar - ¼ teaspoon salt
- ¼ teaspoon freshly ground pepper

Directions:
1. Place all Ingredients: in a jar with an air tight lid. Secure lid and shake vigorously to combine.
2. Refrigerate until ready to use. Will keep up to 2 days. Serving size is 1 tablespoon.

Horseradish Mustard Sauce

Preparation time: 5 minutes
Cooking time: 5 minutes
Servings: 8
Ingredients:
- ¼ cup fat free sour cream

What you'll need from store cupboard:
- ¼ cup lite mayonnaise

- 1 ½ tsp lemon juice
- 1 tsp Splenda
- ½ tsp ground mustard
- ½ tsp Dijon mustard
- ½ tsp horseradish

Directions:
1. In a small bowl, combine all Ingredients: until thoroughly combined.
2. Store in an air tight jar in the refrigerator until ready to use. Serving size is 1 tablespoon.

Berry Dessert Sauce
Preparation time: 5 minutes
Cooking time: 3 hours
Servings: 12
Ingredients:
- 8 oz. strawberries, hulled and halved
- 6 oz. blackberries - 4 oz. blueberries
- What you'll need from store cupboard:
- ¼ cup Splenda

Directions:
1. Add the berries and Splenda to the crock pot. Stir to mix.
2. Cover and cook for 3 hours on a low heat.
3. Ladle the sauce into a jar with an air tight lid, and let cool completely before screwing on the lid and storing in the refrigerator. Serving size is 1 tablespoon.

Blackberry Spread
Preparation time: 5 minutes
Cooking time: 30 minutes
Servings: 16
Ingredients:
- 1 lb. blackberries
- 1 lemon, juiced

What you'll need from store cupboard:
- ¼ cup Splenda

Directions:
1. Place blackberries, Splenda and lemon juice in a medium sauce pan over med-high heat. Cook berries down, stirring occasionally, about 30 minutes, or mixture resembles a thick syrup.
2. Scoop 1/2 cup of the mixture out and place it in a bowl.
3. Place a fine mesh sieve over the bowl and strain the rest of the mixture through, pressing and scraping to get as much of the moisture out that you can.
4. Discard solids. Stir jam in bowl and place in a jar with an air-tight lid.

Blueberry Orange Dessert Sauce
Preparation time: 5 minutes
Cooking time: 10 minutes
Servings: 16
Ingredients:
- 1 ½ cup orange segments
- 1 cup blueberries
- ¼ cup orange juice

What you'll need from store cupboard:
- ¼ cup water
- 1/3 cup almonds, sliced
- 3 tbsp. Splenda
- 1 tbsp. cornstarch
- 1/8 tsp salt

Directions:
1. In a small saucepan, combine Splenda, cornstarch, and salt. Whisk in orange juice and water until smooth.
2. Bring to a boil over med-high heat, cook, stirring frequently, 1-2 minutes or until thickened.
3. Reduce heat and stir in fruit. Cook 5 minutes. Remove from heat and let cool completely.
4. Store in an airtight jar in the refrigerator until ready to use. Serving size is 1 tablespoon.

Nutrition: Calories 46 Total Carbs 8g Protein 1g Fat 1g Sugar 6g Fiber 0g

Caramel Sauce
Preparation time: 5 minutes
Cooking time: 10 minutes
Servings: 12
Ingredients:
- 2/3 cup heavy cream - 1/3 cup margarine

What you'll need from store cupboard:
- 3 tbsp. Splenda - 1 tsp vanilla

Directions:
1. Add the margarine and Splenda to a medium saucepan and place over low heat. Once the margarine melts, cook 3-4 minutes, stirring occasionally, until golden brown.
2. Stir in the cream and bring to a low boil. Reduce heat and simmer 7-10 minutes, stirring occasionally, until mixture is a caramel color and coats the back of a spoon.
3. Remove from heat and whisk in the vanilla. Cool completely and pour into a jar with an air tight lid. Store in the refrigerator. Serving size is 1 tablespoon.

Cheesy Jalapeno Dip
Preparation time: 5 minutes
Cooking time: 3 hours
Servings: 10
Ingredients:
- 4 pkgs. cream cheese, soft
- 1 ½ cups low fat cheddar cheese, grated
- 1 cup bacon, cooked and crumbled
- 1 cup fat free sour cream
- 1 fresh jalapeño, sliced

What you'll need from store cupboard
- 2 cans jalapenos, diced
- 1 packet ranch dressing mix

Directions:
1. In a large bowl, mix cream cheese, 2/3 cup bacon, diced jalapenos, 1 cup cheddar cheese, sour cream and dressing.
2. Spread in crock pot. Top with remaining bacon and cheese. Arrange sliced jalapeno across the top.

3. Cover and cook on low 3 hours. Serve warm.

Chinese Hot Mustard

Preparation time: 15 mins,
Cooking time: 15 minutes
Servings: 4
What you'll need from store cupboard:
- 1 tbsp. mustard powder
- 1½ tsp hot water
- ½ tsp vegetable oil
- ½ tsp rice vinegar
- 1/8 tsp salt
- 1/8 tsp white pepper

Directions:
1. In a small bowl, mix together the dry Ingredients. Add water and stir until mixture resembles liquid paste and dry Ingredients: are absorbed.
2. Stir in oil and vinegar until thoroughly combined. Cover and let rest 10 minutes.
3. Stir again. Taste and adjust any seasonings if desired. Cover and refrigerate until ready to use.

Italian Salad Dressing

Preparation time: 5 minutes
Cooking time: 5 minutes
Servings: 8
Ingredients:
- 2 tbsp. lemon juice
What you'll need from store cupboard:
- ¾ cup olive oil
- ¼ cup red wine vinegar
- 2 cloves of garlic, diced
- 2 tsp Italian seasoning
- 1 tsp oregano
- ½ tsp honey
- ½ tsp salt
- ¼ tsp black pepper
- ¼ tsp red pepper flakes

Directions:
1. Combine all Ingredients: in a measuring cup or jar. Whisk well.
2. Store in jar or bottle with an air tight lid for up to 1 week. Serving size is 1 tablespoon.

Italian Salsa

Preparation time: 10 minutes
Cooking time: 0 minute
Chill time: 1 hour
Servings: 16
Ingredients:
- 4 plum tomatoes, diced
- ½ red onion, diced fine
- 2 tbsp. fresh parsley, diced
What you'll need from store cupboard:
- 12 Kalamata olives, pitted and chopped
- 2 cloves garlic, diced fine
- 1 tbsp. balsamic vinegar
- 1 tbsp. olive oil

- 2 tsp capers, drained
- ¼ tsp salt
- ¼ tsp pepper

Directions:
1. In a medium bowl, combine all Ingredients: and stir to mix. Cover and chill 1 hour before using.
2. Store in a jar with an airtight lid in the refrigerator up to 7 days. Stir before using.

Alfredo Sauce

Preparation time: 5 minutes
Cooking time: 10 minutes
Servings: 6
Ingredients:
- 1 ½ cup heavy cream
- 1 tbsp. margarine
What you'll need from store cupboard:
- ½ cup reduced fat parmesan cheese
- 4 cloves garlic, diced fine
- Black pepper
- Salt
- Nutmeg

Directions:
1. Melt butter in a medium saucepan over medium heat. Add garlic and sauté for about 30 seconds, until fragrant.
2. Add the heavy cream. Bring to a gentle simmer, then continue to simmer for about 5 minutes, until it begins to thicken and sauce is reduced by about 1/3.
3. Reduce heat to low. Gradually whisk in the Parmesan cheese. Keep whisking over low heat, until smooth. Add salt, pepper, and nutmeg to taste. (If sauce is thicker than you like, thin it out with more cream.)

All Purpose Beef Marinade

Preparation time: 10 minutes
Cooking time: 10 minutes
Servings: 8
Ingredients:
- 6 limes zested
- 1 bunch cilantro, diced
What you'll need from store cupboard:
- ¼ c olive oil
- 6 cloves garlic, diced fine

Directions:
1. Mix all Ingredients: in an airtight container.
2. Keep refrigerated for up to 3 months or frozen up to 6 months. Serving size is 1 tablespoon.

All Purpose Chicken Marinade

Preparation time: 5 minutes
Cooking time: 5 minutes
Servings: 24
Ingredients:
- 1 onion, quartered - ½ lemon, with skin
- ½ orange, with skin
- 3 tbsp. rosemary, diced
- 2 tbsp. thyme, diced
What you'll need from store cupboard

- ½ cup olive oil
- 6 cloves garlic, diced fine

Directions:
1. Place all Ingredients: in a food processor and pulse until combined.
2. Store in an air tight container in the refrigerator up to 3 months. Serving size is 1 tablespoon.

Almond Vanilla Fruit Dip

Preparation time: 5 minutes
Cooking time: 10 minutes
Servings: 10
Ingredients:

- 2 ½ cup fat free half-n-half

What you'll need from store cupboard:

- 4-serving size fat-free sugar-free vanilla instant pudding mix
- 1 tbsp. Splenda
- 1 tsp vanilla
- 1 tsp almond extract

Directions:
1. Place all Ingredients: in a medium bowl, and beat on medium speed 2 minutes. Cover and chill until ready to serve. Serve with fruit for dipping. Serving size is ¼ cup.

Roasted Tomato Salsa

Preparation time: 10 minutes
Cooking time: 30 minutes
Servings: 8
Ingredients:

- 6 plum tomatoes
- 1 ¼ cup cilantro

What you'll need from store cupboard:

- 2 tsp olive oil
- 1 tsp adobo sauce
- ½ tsp salt, divided
- Nonstick cooking spray

Directions:
1. Heat oven to 425 degrees. Spray a broiler pan with cooking spray.
2. Cut tomatoes in half and remove seeds. Place, cut side up, on broiler pan. Brush with oil and sprinkle with ¼ teaspoon salt. Turn tomatoes cut side down and bake 30-40 minutes or until edges are browned.
3. Place cilantro in food processor and pulse until coarsely chopped. Add tomatoes, adobo, and remaining salt. Process until chunky. Store in jar with air tight lid and refrigerate until ready to use. Serving size is 2 tablespoons.

Spicy Asian Vinaigrette

Preparation time: 5 minutes
Cooking time: 10 minutes
Servings: 4
Ingredients:

- 1-inch piece fresh ginger, peel & quarter
- 1 tbsp. fresh lemon juice

What you'll need from store cupboard:

- ¼ cup sesame oil
- 2 cloves garlic, peeled
- 2 tbsp. rice vinegar
- 1 tbsp. Chinese hot mustard
- 1 tsp light soy sauce
- 1/8 tsp red pepper flakes

Directions:
1. Place all Ingredients: in a food processor or blender and process until smooth.
2. Store in a jar with an airtight lid. Serving size is 2 tablespoons

Maple Mustard Salad Dressing

Preparation time: 10 minutes
Cooking time: 5 minutes
Servings: 6
What you'll need from store cupboard:

- 2 tbsp. balsamic vinegar - 2 tbsp. olive oil
- 1 tbsp. sugar free maple syrup
- 1 tsp Dijon mustard
- 1/8 tsp sea salt

Directions:
1. Place all the Ingredients: in a jar with a tight-fitting lid. Screw on lid and shake to combine. Store in refrigerator until ready to use.

Maple Shallot Vinaigrette

Preparation time: 3 minutes
Cooking time: 5 minutes
Servings: 4
Ingredients:

- 1 tbsp. shallot, diced fine

What you'll need from store cupboard:

- 2 tbsp. apple cider vinegar
- 1 tbsp. spicy brown mustard
- 1 tbsp. olive oil
- 2 tsp sugar free maple syrup

Directions:
1. Place all Ingredients: in a small jar with an airtight lid. Shake well to mix. Refrigerate until ready to use. Serving size is 1 tablespoon.

Apple Cider Vinaigrette

Preparation time: 10 minutes
Cooking time: 5 minutes
Servings: 8
What you'll need from store cupboard:

- ½ cup sunflower oil
- ¼ cup apple cider vinegar
- ¼ cup apple juice, unsweetened
- 2 tbsp. honey
- 1 tbsp. lemon juice
- ½ tsp salt
- Freshly ground black pepper, to taste

Directions:
1. Place all Ingredients: in a mason jar. Screw on lid and shake until everything is thoroughly combined. Store

in refrigerator until ready to use. Shake well before using.

Bacon Cheeseburger Dip

Preparation time: 5 minutes
Cooking time: 30 minutes
Servings: 8
Ingredients:
- 1 lb. lean ground beef
- 1 pkg. cream cheese, soft
- 2 cups low fat cheddar cheese, grated
- 1 cup fat free sour cream
- 2/3 cup bacon, cooked crisp and crumbled

What you'll need from store cupboard:
- 10 oz. can tomato with green chilies

Directions:
1. Heat oven to 350 degrees.
2. Place a large skillet over med-high heat and cook beef, breaking it up with a wooden spoon, until no longer pink. Drain off the fat.
3. In a large bowl, combine remaining Ingredients: until mixed well. Stir in beef.
4. Pour into a small baking dish. Bake 20-25 minutes or until mixture is hot and bubbly. Serve warm.

Basic Salsa

Preparation time: 15 minutes
Cooking time: 0 minute
Chill time: 1 hour
Servings: 8
Ingredients:
- 8 tomatoes
- 2-3 jalapeno peppers, depending on how spicy you like it
- 2 limes, juiced

What you'll need from store cupboard:
- 4 cloves garlic
- 1 tbsp. salt
- Nonstick cooking spray

Directions:
1. Heat oven to broil. Spray a baking sheet with cooking spray.
2. Place tomatoes, peppers, and garlic on prepared pan and broil 8-10 minutes, turning occasionally, until skin on the vegetables begins to char and peel way.
3. Let cool. Remove skins.
4. Place vegetables in a food processor and pulse. Add salt and lime juice and pulse until salsa reaches desired consistency.
5. Store in a jar with an airtight lid in the refrigerator up to 7 days. Serving size is ¼ cup.

BBQ Sauce

Preparation time: 5 minutes
Cooking time: 20 minutes
Servings: 20
What you'll need from store cupboard:
- 2 1/2 6 oz. cans tomato paste
- 1 ½ cup water

- ½ cup apple cider vinegar
- 1/3 cup swerve confectioners
- 2 tbsp. Worcestershire sauce
- 1 tbsp. liquid hickory smoke
- 2 tsp smoked paprika
- 1 tsp garlic powder
- ½ tsp onion powder
- ½ tsp salt
- ¼ tsp chili powder
- ¼ tsp cayenne pepper

Directions:
1. Whisk all Ingredients, but water, together in a saucepan. Add water, starting with 1 cup, whisking it in, until mixture resembles a thin barbecue sauce.
2. Bring to a low boil over med-high heat. Reduce heat to med-low and simmer, stirring frequently, 20 minutes, or sauce has thickened slightly.
3. Taste and adjust seasoning until you like it. Cool completely. Store in a jar with an airtight lid in the refrigerator. Serving size is 2 tablespoons of sauce.

Marinara Sauce

Preparation time: 10 minutes
Cooking time: 30 minutes
Servings: 6
Ingredients:
- 28 oz. can dice tomatoes, undrained
- 4–6 cloves garlic, diced fine
- 4 tbsp. extra virgin olive oil
- 2 tbsp. tomato paste
- 1 tbsp. basil,
- 1 tsp Splenda
- 1 tsp salt

Directions:
1. Heat oil in saucepan over medium heat. Add the garlic and cook 1 minute.
2. Stir in the tomato paste and cook 1 minute more. Add the tomatoes and basil and simmer 10-15 minutes, breaking up the tomatoes as they cook.
3. Stir in Splenda and salt. Use an immersion blender and process to desired consistency.
4. Let cool and store in a jar with an airtight lid in the refrigerator up to 7 days. Or use right away.

Orange Marmalade

Preparation time: 30 minutes
Cooking time: 30 minutes
Servings: 48
Ingredients:
- 4 navel oranges
- 1 lemon
- What you'll need from store cupboard:
- 2 ½ cup water
- ¼ cup warm water
- 4 tbsp. Splenda
- 1 oz. gelatin

Directions:

1. Quarter the oranges and remove all the pulp. Scrap the white part off the rind and cut it into thin 2-inch strips. Remove as much of the membrane between orange segments as you can and place the seeds in a small piece of cheesecloth, pull up the sides to make a "bag" and tie closed.
2. Repeat with the lemon but discard the seeds. Cut the lemon rind into smaller strips than the orange rind.
3. Chop the orange and lemon pulp and add it to a medium saucepan along with 2 ½ cups water. Bring to a rapid boil over med-high heat.
4. Reduce heat to med-low and add the bag of seeds. Boil gently for 30 minutes, or until the citrus fruit is soft. Remove and discard the seed bag.
5. Dissolve the gelatin in the warm water. Add it to the orange mixture with ½ the Splenda. Being careful not to burn yourself, taste the marmalade and adjust sweetener as desired.
6. Spoon the marmalade into 3 ½-pint jars with air-tight lids. Seal and chill.

Peach Pepper Relish

Preparation time: 10 minutes
Cooking time: 0 minute
Chill time: 2 hours
Servings: 16
Ingredients:
- 2 peaches, peeled and diced
- 1 green onion, diced fine
- 1/3 cup bell pepper, diced
- 1/3 cup red pepper, diced
- 2 tbsp. fresh mint, diced

What you'll need from store cupboard:
- 1 tbsp. lemon juice
- 1 tbsp. sugar free peach preserves

Directions:
1. In a medium bowl, stir together peaches, onion, peppers, and mint.
2. In a small bowl, combine lemon juice and preserves. Pour over peach mixture and toss to coat.
3. Place in an airtight container and refrigerate up to 2 hours or overnight. Serving size is 2 tablespoons.

Pear & Poppy Jam

Preparation time: 2 hours
Cooking time: 30 minutes
Servings: 32
Ingredients:

- 3 pears, peeled, seeded and chopped
- ½ lemon

What you'll need from store cupboard:
- ¾ cup Splenda
- 1 tbsp. poppy seeds

Directions:
1. Place pears in a large bowl. Sprinkle with Splenda and toss to coat. Squeeze the lemon over the pears and toss again. Let sit for 2 hours so the fruit will release its juice.
2. Place poppy seeds in a medium saucepan over medium heat. Cook, stirring, 1-2 minutes to lightly toast the. Transfer them to a bowl.
3. Add the pears, with the juice, to the saucepan and bring to a boil, stirring frequently. Reduce the heat and let boil 10 minutes or until thickened.
4. Spoon ½ the pears into a blender and process until smooth. Add the puree back to the saucepan along with the poppy seeds. Continue cooking 5-10 minutes or the jam is thick.
5. Spoon into 2-pint sized jars with air tight lids. Let cool completely, screw on the lids and store in the refrigerator. Serving size is 1 tablespoon.

Spicy Peanut Sauce

Preparation time: 5 minutes
Cooking time: 5 minutes
Servings: 20
Ingredients:
- ¼ cup fresh lime juice
- 2 tbsp. fresh ginger, peeled and grated

What you'll need from store cupboard:
- 1 ½ cups reduced-sodium, low-fat chicken broth
- 1 cup reduced-fat peanut butter
- 3 tbsp. Splenda brown sugar
- 2 tbsp. low-sodium soy sauce
- ½ tsp crushed red pepper flakes

Directions:
1. In a small saucepan, over medium heat, heat peanut butter until melted. Add broth and stir until combined.
2. Add remaining Ingredients, and cook over med-low heat 5 minutes, stirring frequently, until thickened.
3. Use over shrimp, scallops, chicken, turkey or beef. Serving size is 2 tablespoons.
4. Store in air-tight container in the refrigerator up to 3 days.

28 Days Meal Plan

Day	Breakfast	Lunch	Dinner	Dessert
1	Walnut and Oat Granola	Warm Chicken and Spinach Salad	Cauliflower Mash	Sticky Ginger Cake
2	Coconut and Berry Smoothie	Stuffed Chicken	French Toast in Sticks	Tiramisu
3	Crispy Pita with Canadian Bacon	Chicken Sandwich	Misto Quente	Toffee Apple Mini Pies
4	Coconut-Berry Sunrise Smoothie	Buttermilk Fried Chicken	Seared Tuna Steak	Pineapple Frozen Yogurt
5	Greek Yogurt Sundae	Zaatar Lamb Loin Chops	Vegetable Soup	Pomegranate Panna Cotta
6	Avocado and Goat Cheese Toast	Pork on a Blanket	Pork Chop Diane	Coconutty Pudding Clouds
7	Oat and Walnut Granola	Vietnamese Grilled Pork	Autumn Pork Chops with Red Cabbage and Apples	Cream Cheese Pound Cake
8	Zucchini Noodles with Creamy Avocado Pesto	Provencal Ribs	Chipotle Chili Pork Chops	Dark Chocolate Coffee Cupcakes
9	Avocado Chicken Salad	Steak	Orange-Marinated Pork Tenderloin	German Chocolate Cake Bars
10	Pancakes with Berries	Marinated Loin Potatoes	Homestyle Herb Meatballs	Gingerbread Soufflés
11	Omelette à la Margherita	Beef with Mushrooms	Lime-Parsley Lamb Cutlets	Lemon Meringue Ice Cream
12	Spanakopita Frittata	Cheesy and Crunchy Russian Steaks	Beef Chili	Mini Bread Puddings
13	Ratatouille Egg Bake	Chicken Wings	Greek Broccoli Salad	Pumpkin Ice Cream with Candied Pecans
14	Cottage Pancakes	Chicken Nuggets	Mediterranean Steak Sandwiches	Raspberry Almond Clafoutis
15	Greek Yogurt and Oat Pancakes	Pork Chops	Roasted Beef with Peppercorn Sauce	Blackberry Soufflés
16	Savory Breakfast Egg Bites	Buffalo Chicken Hot Wings	Coffee-and-Herb-Marinated Steak	Blueberry Lemon "Cup" Cakes
17	Simple Grain-Free Biscuits	Herb Chicken Thighs	Traditional Beef Stroganoff	Blueberry No-Bake Cheesecake
18	Brussels Sprout with Fried Eggs	Air Fryer Beef Steak Kabobs with Vegetables	Chicken and Roasted Vegetable Wraps	Broiled Stone Fruit
19	Vanilla Coconut Pancakes	Fried Pork Chops	Spicy Chicken Cacciatore	Café Mocha Torte

20	Cheesy Spinach and Egg Casserole	Pork Liver	Scallion Sandwich	Cappuccino Mousse
21	Chocolate-Zucchini Muffins	Air Fried Meatloaf	Cheesy Cauliflower Gratin	Caramel Pecan Pie
22	Gluten-Free Carrot and Oat Pancakes	Pork Tenderloin	Strawberry Spinach Salad	Carrot Cupcakes
23	Breakfast Egg Bites	Pork Bondiola Chop	Garlic Bread	Raspberry and Dark Chocolate Mini Soufflés
24	Tacos with Pico De Gallo	Air Fry Rib-Eye Steak	Bruschetta	Tropical Fruit Tart
25	Coconut and Chia Pudding	Lemon Pepper Chicken	Cream Buns with Strawberries	Sweet Potato Crème Brule
26	Tomato Waffles	Caribbean Spiced Chicken	Blueberry Buns	Raspberry Lemon Cheesecake Squares
27	Breakfast Homemade Poultry Sausage	Chicken Tenders	Lean Lamb and Turkey Meatballs with Yogurt	Mini Key Lime Tarts
28	Sausage and Pepper Burrito	Chicken in Tomato Juice	Air Fried Section and Tomato	Moist Butter Cake